THE FINAL ARGUMENT

The Imprint of Violence on Society
in Medieval and Early Modern Europe

If "civilization consists of the attempt to reduce violence to the *ultima ratio*, the final argument" (as the great Spanish political philosopher José Ortega y Gasset once declared), then this volume succeeds in exploring the mechanisms of violence and their symbiotic relationships with medieval and early modern European societies, ranging from England to Spain, from Portugal to Iran. The twelve essays of this volume deal with the place of medieval clergy in war and peace; the institutionalization of clan violence in medieval Iberia which eventually gave rise to the law of modern duelling, the *code duello*; the emergence of norms of punishment for violence which pointed the way to modern criminal law and penology; and a piece of historical detective work with a "definitive" solution for one of the crucial murder mysteries of the early Middle Ages – the wreck of the *White Ship* in 1120.

THE FINAL ARGUMENT

The Imprint of Violence on Society in Medieval and Early Modern Europe

Edited by

Donald J. Kagay
L. J. Andrew Villalon

THE BOYDELL PRESS

First published 1998
The Boydell Press, Woodbridge

ISBN 0 85115 710 6

The Boydell Press is an imprint of Boydell & Brewer Ltd
PO Box 9, Woodbridge, Suffolk IP12 3DF, UK
and of Boydell & Brewer Inc.
PO Box 41026, Rochester, NY 14604–4126, USA

A catalogue record for this book is available
from the British Library

Library of Congress Cataloging-in-Publication Data
The final argument : the imprint of violence on society in medieval
 and early modern Europe / edited by Donald J. Kagay, L. J. Andrew
 Villalon.
     p.   cm.
   Includes bibliographical references.
   ISBN 0–85115–710–6 (hc : alk. paper)
   1. Violence – Europe – History. 2. Violent crimes – Europe – History.
 3. Political violence – Europe – History. 4. Civilization, Medieval.
 5. Europe – Social life and customs. I. Kagay, Donald J.
 II. Villalon, L. J. Andrew.
 HN380.Z9V53   1998
 303.6'094–dc21   97–42176

This publication is printed on acid-free paper

Printed in Great Britain by
St Edmundsbury Press Ltd, Bury St Edmunds, Suffolk

CONTENTS

PART ONE
VIOLENCE AND THE MEDIEVAL CLERGY

PART TWO
MEDIEVAL FAMILIES AND FEUDS

PART THREE
PUBLIC CONTROL AND PRIVATE VIOLENCE
IN EARLY MODERN TIMES

ILLUSTRATIONS

CONTRIBUTORS

John K. Brackett, *University of Cincinnati*
Victoria Chandler *Georgia College*
Timothy J. Coates *College of Charleston*
Michael Frassetto *LeGrange College*
Kent G. Hare *Louisiana State University*
Donald J. Kagay *Albany State University*
James R. King *Midwestern State University*
Cynthia J. Neville *Dalhousie University*
Patricia R. Orr *University of Houston*
John R. Perry *University of Chicago*
Theresa M. Vann *St. John's University*
L. J. Andrew Villalon *University of Cincinnati*

ACKNOWLEDGEMENTS

The editors would like to thank the contributors of this volume for their immense professionalism and patience. A very special thanks must be extended to Ms. Susan Dykstra-Poel and Ms. Caroline Palmer of Boydell & Brewer, without whose help this volume could not have come into being.

ABBREVIATIONS

1235 SE	*The 1235 Surrey Eyre*, ed. C. A. F. Meekings. Castle Arch, Guildford, 1979.
ACA	Archivo de la Corona de Aragón, Barcelona.
ACC	Archivo Catedral de Cuenca.
ACTS	Archivio Storico de Castrocaro, Terra del Sole.
AHDE	*Anuario de Historia del Derecho Español.*
AHN	Archivo Histórico Nacional, Madrid.
AHR	*American Historical Review*
AP	*Placitorum in Domo Capitulari Westmonasteriensi Asservatorum Abbreviatio Temporibus Regum Ricardi, Johannis, Henrici III, Edwardi I, Edwardi II.* London, 1831.
ASC	*Anglo-Saxon Chronicle*, ed. Dorothy Whitelock, with David C. Douglas and Susie I. Tucker. London, 1961.
ASE	Frank M. Stenton, *Anglo-Saxon England*. Oxford, 1971.
ASI	*Archivo Storico Italiano.*
ASP	*Anglo-Saxon Poetry*, trans. Robert K. Gordon. 1927. Repr. London, 1982.
BAE	*Biblioteca de Autores Españoles*, 141 vols. Madrid, 1961–.
BIHR	*Bulletin of the Institute of Historical Research.*
BN	Bibliothèque Nationale, Paris.
BNB	*Bracton's Note Book*, ed. Frederick William Maitland. London, 1887.
BRABLB	*Boletín del Real Academia de Buenas Letras de Barcelona*
Bracton	*Bracton on the Laws and Customs of England*, ed. and trans. Samuel E. Thorne, 4 vols. Cambridge MA and London, 1968–77.
BRAH	*Boletín de Real Academia de Historia.*
Britton	*Britton: The French Text Carefully Revised with an English Translation, Introduction and Notes*, ed. Francis Morgan Nichols. Oxford, 1845.
CAVC	*Colección de los cortes de los antiguos reinos de Aragón y de Valencia y del principado de Cataluña*, ed. Fidel Fita y Colomé and Bienvenido Oliver y Estreller, 27 vols. Madrid, 1896–1922.
CCLP	*Collecção Chronologica da Legislação Portuguesa*, ed. José Justino de Andrade e Silva, 10 vols. Lisbon, 1854–57.
CIMC	*Calendar of Inquisitions, Miscellaneous (Chancery)*, 2 vols. London, 1916.
CP	*The Complete Peerage of England, Scotland, Ireland, Great*

	Britain and the United Kingdom, ed. Vicary Gibbs et al., 13 vols. London, 1910–59.
CPR	*Calendar of Patent Rolls, 1258–1266.*
CPWE	*Crown Pleas of the Wiltshire Eyre, 1249*, ed. C. A. F. Meekings, Wiltshire Archaeological and Natural History Society, Records Branch. Gateshead-on-Tyne, 1961.
CRC	*Cronicas de Reyes de los Castilla* in *BAE* 66–68.
CRR	*Curia Regis Rolls . . . Preserved in the Public Record Office*, 17 vols. London, 1922–1991.
CRWC	*Columbia Records of Western Civilization*, 12 vols. 1927. Reprint, New York, 1991.
CSIC	Consejo Superior de Investigaciones Científicas.
DCD	Muniments of the Dean and Chapter, Durham Cathedral
DCR	*Documentos das Chancelarias Reais . . . Vol. I and Vol. II (1450–1456)*, ed. Pedro de Azevedo. Lisbon, 1915–34.
DHP	*Dicionário de História de Portugal*, ed. Joel Serrao, 7 vols. Oporto, 1992.
DJ	*Documentos de Jaime I de Aragón*, ed. Ambrosio Huici Miranda and Maria Desamparados Cabames Pecourt, 4 vols. (Valencia, 1976–82).
DNB	*The Dictionary of National Biography*, ed. Leslie Stephen and Sidney Lee, 22 vols. London, 1908–1909.
DP	*Descobrimentos e Expansão Portugues*, ed. João Martins da Silva Marques. Lisbon, 1988.
DS	Deutsche Staats Bibliothek, Berlin.
EETS	Early English Text Society.
EH	Bede, *Ecclesiastical History of the English People*, ed. and trans. Bertram Colgrave and R. A. B. Mynors. Oxford, 1969.
EHD	*English Historical Documents, 1042–1189*, ed. David C. Douglas and George W. Greenaway, 13 vols. New York, 1981.
EHR	*English Historical Review.*
ELAR	*The Earliest Lincolnshire Assize Rolls, A.D. 1202–1209*, ed. Doris M. Stenton. Lincoln, 1926.
Elementos	*Elementos para a história do município de Lisboa*, 17 vols. (Lisbon, 1882–1911).
ENAR	*The Earliest Northamptonshire Assize Rolls, A.D. 1202 and 1203*, ed. Doris Mary Stenton. London and Lincoln, 1930.
ES	*España Sagrada. Teatro geographico-historico de la Iglesia de España: origen, divisiones, y terminos de todas sus provincias antigüedades traslaciónes y estado en todos los dominios de España y Portugal*, ed. Enrique Florez de Setien y Huidobro et al., 41 vols. Madrid, 1754–1879.
F	*Fuero de . . .*
Fleta	*Fleta*, ed. and trans. H. G. Richardson and G. O. Sayles, 2

	vols. Selden Society, 72, 79. London, 1955–72.
FLT	*El fuero latino de Teruel*, ed. Jaime Caruana Gómez de Barreda. Teruel, 1974.
GCB	*Gesta comitum barchinonensium. Textos llatí i català*, ed. Louis Barrau-Dihigo and Jaume Massó Torrents. Crònique catalanes, 2. Barcelona, 1925.
Institutes	*The Second Part of the Institutes of the Lawes of England*, Sir Edward Coke, 2 vols. New York, 1979.
Glanvill	*The Treatise on the Laws and Customs of England Commonly Called Glanvill*, ed. and trans. G. D. G. Hall. Oxford, 1993.
HCCA	Victor Balaguer, *Historia de Cataluña y de la Corona de Aragón, escrita para dar la a conocer al pueblo, recordandole los grandes hechos de sus ascendientes en virtud, patriotismo y armas y para difundir entre todas las classes el amor al pais y la memoria de sus glorias pasadas*, 5 vols. Barcelona, 1861.
HRRH	*Historical Reflections / Reflexions Historiques*
LFM	*Liber Feudorum Maior*, ed. Francisco Miguel Rosell, 2 vols. Barcelona, 1945–47.
Marca	*Marca hispanica sive limes hispanicus, hoc est, geographica et historica Cataloniae, Ruscinonis, et circumiacentium populorum*, comp. Pierre de Marca, ed. Etienne Baluze F. Maguet. 1688. Repr. Barcelona, 1972.
Memorial	*Memorial del Pleyto que sobre la propiedad del Valle de Liebana y Campo de Suso sostuvieron Luis Fernandez Manrique, II Marques de Aguilar de Campoo y Diego Hurtado de Mendoza, III Duque del Infantado* in RAH, Salazar M–67, and AHN, Osuna 4252, n. 4.
MGH	*Monumenta Germaniae Historica inde ab a.c. 500 ad a. 1500*, ed. G. H. Pertz et al. Berlin, 1826.
MHV	Monumentae Historiae Vaticanae.
Mirror	*The Mirror of Justices*, ed. and trans. Andrew Horne. William Hughes, 1642. Repr. Washington DC, 1903.
MMA	*Monumenta Missionaria Africana: Africa Occidental*, 15 vols. Lisbon, 1952–1988.
MS	Manuscript.
Osuna	Osuna Collection.
OV	Orderic Vitalis, *The Ecclesiastical History*, ed. and trans. Marjorie Chibnall, 6 vols. Oxford, 1969–80.
PC	*Placita Corone or La Corone Pledee Devant Justices*, ed. and trans. J. M. Kaye. Selden Society Supplementary Series, 4. London, 1966.
PCCG	*Pleas of the Crown for the County of Gloucestershire . . . 1221*, ed. F. W. Maitland. London, 1884.

PKJ	*Pleas before the King and his Justices*, ed. and trans. Doris Mary Stenton, 4 vols. Selden Society, 67, 68, 83, 84. London, 1953–54, 1967.
PL	*Patrologia Latina*, ed. J. P. Migne, 217 vols. Paris, 1841–64.
Pleito	*Pleito sobre el valle de Liébana*, in RAH, Salazar M–14, ff. 141–73.
PRO	Public Record Office, London.
JI	Justices Itinerate
JUST 1/613, 799, 800	Plea rolls, records of pleas heard by itinerant justices in the course of visitations of the general eyre.
KB	King's Bench (Modern Public Record Office designation for what were once known as the *Curia Regis Rolls*).
Pruebas	*Pruebas de la Historia de la Casa de Lara*, ed. Luis Salazar y Castro, vol. 4 of *Historia Genealógica de la Casa de Lara*, 4 vols. Madrid, 1694–97.
R	Registro.
RAH	Real Academia de la Historia, Madrid.
RCR	*Rotuli Curiae Regis: Rolls and Records of the Court Held before the King's Justiciars or Justices*, ed. Sir Francis Palgrave, 2 vols. London, 1835.
RJEGWS	*Rolls of the Justices in Eyre . . . for Gloucestershire, Warwickshire, and Staffordshire, 1221, 1222*, ed. Doris Mary Stenton. Selden Society, 53. London, 1940.
RJEYH3	*Rolls of the Justices in Eyre . . . for Yorkshire in 3 Henry III (1218–19)*, ed. Doris Mary Stenton. Selden Society, 56. London, 1934.
RRAN	*Regesta Regum Anglo-Normannorum, 1100–1135*, ed. Charles Johnson and H. A. Cronne, 4 vols. Oxford, 1956.
RS	*Rerum Brittanicarum Medii Aevi Scriptores*, 99 vols., Rolls Series. London, 1858–1911.
RSE	*The Roll of the Shropshire Eyre of 1256*, ed. and trans. Alan Harding. Selden Society, 96. London, 1981.
RWB	*Register of Walter Bronescombe, 1257–80, Episcopal Registers of Exeter: Bronescombe, Quivil, Bytton (1257–1307)*, ed. F. C. Hingeston-Randolph. London, 1889.
RWFBE	*The Roll and Writ File of the Berkshire Eyre of 1248*, ed. M. T. Clanchy. Selden Society, 90. London, 1973.
Salazar	Salazar Collection, Real Academia de la Historia, Madrid.
SCP	*Select Cases of Procedure without Writ under Henry III*, ed. H. G. Richardson and G. O. Sayles. Selden Society, 60. London, 1941.
SPC	*Select Pleas of the Crown, A.D. 1200–1225*, ed. Frederick William Maitland. Selden Society, 1. London, 1888. Repr. London, 1955.
TRHS	*Transactions of the Royal Historical Society.*

INTRODUCTION

"Civilization consists of the attempt to reduce violence to the *ultima ratio*, the final argument."[1] This characterization by the great Spanish political philosopher José Ortega y Gasset of modern society as an over-arching order which was ultimately held in place by the threat of violence can also stand as a sad epitaph for the whole of the twentieth century. Governments, though very often the cause of violent action, seem unable to control it on a group or individual level. The bequest of Cain, which leads humankind routinely to place members of its own species outside the pale of humanity, is simply too ingrained for law or religion to overcome. Before this backdrop of man's darker side, the following essays will focus on a number of medieval and early modern societies ranging from England to Portugal, from Spain to Iran. Despite the differences in locale and era, they all deal with vehement human action and the reaction of human society to it. In essence, all of these papers deal with the patterns of human group life as it is affected by the occasional savagery of individuals or groups.

The volume is divided into five sections according to chronological or topical criteria. In the first section, a number of papers deal with violence and the clergy in the early medieval period. Though medieval society ideally saw itself as a set of watertight compartments determined by the rank and role of its members, the real world of the Middle Ages was not a palette of blacks and whites but rather innumerable shades of gray caused by the overlapping activities of many different social groups. One of the most pervasive examples of this confusion of roles was the place of the Church in the violent world of war. In the first paper of this section, Kent Hare examines the military activities of the clergy in the Anglo-Saxon host or *fyrd*. By assessing the *Anglo-Saxon Chronicle* and other contemporary documents, especially those dealing with the heriot (a list of weapons given to vassals for battle-use by a lord), Hare draws a picture of tenth-century English clergy who acted as army chaplains as well as true members of the royal host who often brought their own vassals to the battlefield and occasionally fell in battle. Despite their experience in war, none of the Anglo-Saxon churchmen reached the same political power as the great warrior bishops of the Carolingian world. Though their religious and magical role in the *fyrd* seemed paramount, military victory or defeat had far-flung repercussions on the loss or extension of church lands. Hare thus

---

[1]   José Ortega y Gasset, *The Revolt of the Masses* (New York, 1960), chap. 8.

concludes that the Anglo-Saxon clergy were a valuable adjunct to the military efforts of the leaders of Britain's seven kingdoms, despite growing papal and conciliar attempts across Europe to limit such violent undertakings of the clergy.

With the breakdown of Carolingian structures of power and what has been called the "militarization" of western Europe, individual churchmen, like the rest of the societies they served, adapted to the realities of localized power by taking up the norms of feudal dominance, allegiance and service. To the Church as an institution, however, fell the lot of preserving at least the bare outlines of civil government. It is the most important of these "regnal" structures, the peace of God, which stands as the focus of the second paper of this section. Using conciliar, chronicle and sermon evidence of the eleventh century, Michael Frassetto attempts to rebut recent scholarship which has discounted the damping effect of the peace on commoner, nobility and clergy alike. Taking Aquitaine as a focus, Frassetto demonstrates with great clarity that the peace movement of the region, far from having no effect on baronial malefactors, was able to marshall the formidable weapons of excommunication and popular involvement for the control of violence. The founders of the peace movement were not so puritanical or unrealistic to think they could do away with violent behavior altogether, but had to allow bellicose activities under certain conditions and at certain times. Neither were the peacemakers above the use of war in the form of the "peace army" in the defense of the *pax*. Far from having only theoretical effects on the violent world of the eleventh century, the peace, in Frassetto's view, was extremely important in political terms with the delineation of the theory of the tripartite division of society and in military terms with the emergence of the idea and practice of military action for a religious end: the crusade.

Despite its attempt to deal with the nagging question of societal violence through the development of the *pax et treuga*, the Church had to face the continuing problem that clerics could be some of the most flagrant violators of the peace in the lay world. James King reviews and measures the level of clerical violence in thirteenth-century England through a close investigation of juridical records during the Baronial War (1259–1265). King concludes that the rebellion of Simon de Montfort, besides challenging the English Crown to the very core, encouraged violence among all classes, but especially among the clergy. The *eyre* records of this era repeatedly deal with clerics who looted in conjunction with military campaigns but also went into business for themselves as bandits and highwaymen. Though most of these miscreants were from the ranks of the lesser and seriously impoverished clergy, a good number of the greater churchmen were also involved in such violent and illegal activity. Both regular and secular clergy figure in the crimes recorded in the juridical documentation of the mid-thirteenth century and King concludes that on one level, at least, the English clergy, like Friar Tuck, were not mere victims of a land marred by civil war but were often the cause of it.

In the second section of the book, which investigates the violent exchanges of medieval families, we pass from the violence of clergy to that of lay society. Like members of clerical institutions, clan and family groups attempted to establish means for the control of or muting of the vehement actions of their members. This control process was accomplished in both a legal and extralegal manner. One of the most pervasive methods of such control was the influence exercised by kinship. In the first paper of this section, Andrew Villalon, by a close analysis of chronicle and documentary evidence, reconsiders the theory of Helen Nader that kinship indeed damped violent exchanges within families and between clans. He explores the Castilian concept of "kinship" (*deudo*) as it directed the political and social relationship of the premier Castilian families, most especially the Mendoza/Manrique clan. Though Villalon agrees that *deudo* could solve disputes between clansmen by tying rivals through marriage or arbitrated settlement, he emphasizes that the selfsame kin connection could engender and deepen frustrations which would fester and finally erupt in violent action between individuals and encourage blood feuds between branches of the clan. Such rivalries were also intensified with the emerging significance of the *mayorazgo*, the entailed estate, which settled all of a family's lands on the oldest son, thus largely dispossessing the younger siblings and causing great resentment in the process. In real terms, then, the lesson of the Mafia in the twentieth century could easily apply to the later Middle Ages; that is, the drive for power by persons could far outweigh the benefits of group solidarity.

The other papers of this section deal with feudal and royal control of violence in the major Iberian societies of the Middle Ages. In the second, Donald Kagay focuses on the mechanism of the *diffidamentum*, the formal rupture of ties between lord and vassal. Tracing this procedure from its Merovingian roots, Kagay demonstrates that it passed from individual feudal contract to public law in the Crown of Aragon. Though the "defiance" attempted to deflect violence, it was ultimately unsuccessful in both feudal and royal settings. So, too, were the principal outcomes of the *diffidamentum*, the wager by battle and the duel. While the former was barely used after the thirteenth century, the latter produced a body of custom which eventually emerged as the *code duello*. The duel eventually ran foul of the royal authority of the new Spanish state as laws from the Catholic kings down to Felipe V first restricted and then outlawed the practice. The defiance, however, lingered on to influence both a citizen's right of resistance against an unjust government and the procedure by which one nation declares war on another.

In the last paper of the section, Theresa Vann revisits the theory which claims that the frontier with Islam served as a means of manipulating and sublimating the violent members of society by settling them in the "no man's land" which bordered on the Islamic *taifa* states. Analyzing the Turner thesis, as adapted to Spain by Sánchez Albornoz and Lacarra, that the frontier of medieval Castile acted as a "safety valve" for the poor and criminal elements of the settled society, Vann tests this "criminal exportation" model by assessing the single Castilian *fuero* on which the theory is based. Calling into question earlier interpretations of this critical evidence by comparing it with later royal law, she concludes that the frontier thesis as a single persuasive explanation of reconquest and settlement can be safely rejected for Castile as it largely has been for America.

The third section, which deals with the mechanisms by which violence erupted and was controlled in the early modern era, consists of two papers. In the first John Brackett discusses the "language of violence" as it developed in the bellicose world of the sixteenth-century Romagna. The focus of his study is the region's "moral imagination" by which men of all classes initiated violence through the expert use of the insult. Utilising a number of Florentine and Ramagnoli court record collections, he compiles a vocabulary of jibes and expletives by which one ridiculed another concerning appearance, parentage or lack of intelligence. This glossary of insulting words very often led to violent exchanges, most often initiated by the party who felt himself or his family maligned by this purposefully destructive language. Such behavior, according to Brackett, established a "debt" of outrage which the victim had to pay back in kind or lose face. Certain words could thus not be said unless the speaker intended to back them up with violent action.

In the second paper of this section, the self-policing of groups over their violent individuals is discussed by John Perry who investigates certain population groupings of Safavid Iranian cities known as *Haydari* and *Ne'mati*. While such communal groups have a long history in all Islamic states, the two groups which Perry discusses began to emerge as important features of Iranian life in the seventeenth century. These factions, which Perry compares to modern gangs or "soccer hooligans," established their dominance over certain neighborhoods of Iranian cities or villages and protected "turf" with intermittent bloody clashes with their rivals. Such battles, which were described by more than one foreign observer from the seventeenth century onward, were regular features of Iranian life until well into the twentieth century. Despite the potentialities for bloodletting bred from this situation, the faction fights were conducted according to well-worn, unspoken rules which attempted to halt violence at the threshold of vendetta.

In the fourth section, we pass to a prime function of government – the punishment of the violent offender. In the first paper, Timothy Coates focuses on the Portuguese penal system of the early modern era. Discussing generally the adjudicative norms of medieval Portugal, Coates then proceeds to explore more fully the history of exile in the realm. This punishment was reserved for only the most serious of crimes. It is interesting that in Portugal these included heresy, sodomy and counterfeiting. In the Middle Ages, Portuguese courts exiled criminals to towns along the Castilian and Islamic borders. As Da Gama, Cabral and many other explorers planted the Portuguese flag of commercial and political exploitation in lands as scattered as India, Brazil and North Africa, the judicial system adapted, sending "exiles" (*desgredados*) first to the galleys and then to the administrative and military centers scattered across the globe. Many of the exiles remained in the colonies after they had served their sentences, thus constituting an important source for the undermanned Portuguese colonial efforts.

The last two papers of this section take as their subject the legal position of women before the burgeoning judicial machinery of later medieval England. In the first, Patricia Orr deals with female litigation in the English court system of the thirteenth century. Beginning with Glanvill and Bracton, the great judicial authorities of the era, Orr proceeds to assess the dictum that a woman was not allowed to appeal cases in royal courts except to gain redress for her husband's murder or for any personal injury done to her. Orr then follows this "limiting rule" through a number of jurisprudential works down to the Elizabethan jurist Edward Coke and concludes that there were certain legal exceptions and loopholes which might allow women to present their cases before the law. Even when the appeal was not allowed by the letter of the law, certain female cases, such as the homicide of a woman's relatives, were heard and a number of complicated tactics might be used to springboard civil suits into the arena of criminal law. Despite such possibilities or tactics, it is clear from Orr's work that few real avenues to the English court system lay open to those women whom the law was supposed to serve.

In the last paper of this section, Cynthia Neville explores the involvement of women in criminal activities and their treatment before the law of later medieval England. Following the lead of Barbara Hanawalt for the first half of the fourteenth century, Neville centers her investigation on the northern counties of England in the period 1300–1460. Examining some four thousand cases in the volatile north country which bordered on Scotland, she found the judicial records of over eight hundred women. Theft, larceny, robbery and even murder were among the grievous crimes many of which many of these women were accused. She shows, however, that many of these indictments sprang as much from the actions of the accused as from the state of constant war which raged across the English–Scottish frontier for much of the period under consideration. The tumult caused by periodic Scottish raids gave ample opportunity for women and men to engage in looting and other crimes. Such a continual state of unrest also caused English judges to accuse, sometimes with very little evidence, northern villagers of spying for the Scots. Unfortunately for the people of the north country, who turned to crime often merely to feed themselves and their families, foreign invasion was not considered a mitigating circumstance by the English law.

In the last section of the book, the reader is treated to a detective story of sorts concerning one of the great unsolved quandaries of English medieval studies, the wreck of the *White Ship* (25 November 1120). The investigator of these long-dead events, Victoria Chandler, analyzes Orderic Vitalis's account of the catastrophe and determines who gained and who lost from the wreck. Taking such factors as tenurial and dynastic advancement into account, she points an accusing finger at some of the Norman nobles who gained many of the fiefs of those who had died in "the terrible sea." Chandler's prime suspect, however, is Stephen of Mortain, who acceded to the English throne in 1135 – a fact which was aided by the death of his cousin William Clito in the 1120 accident. Whether the wreck of the *White Ship* was the result of natural causes or human agency, Chandler very skillfully demonstrates that an event long past often retains enough factual texture to support a wide range of theories – all of them plausible but each based on different arrangements of the evidence.

PART ONE

Violence and the Medieval Clergy

Clerics, War and Weapons in Anglo-Saxon England

KENT G. HARE

In its entry for 1056, the *Anglo-Saxon Chronicle* says of Leofgar, bishop of Hereford in the reign of Edward the Confessor (1042–1066):

> He gave up his chrism and his cross, his spiritual weapons, and took his spear and his sword after his consecration as bishop, and so went campaigning against Griffith the Welsh king, and they [the Welsh] killed him there and his priests with him, and Aelfnoth the sheriff and many good men with them.[1]

The tone of this annal indicates that the chronicler recognized a tension and inherent contradiction between the functions of warrior and priest. As stated earlier in the eleventh century by the Anglo-Saxon homilist, Wulfstan of York, in his *Institutes of Polity*, "neither a wife nor the warfare of this world in any way befits a priest."[2] Nevertheless, among the many problems confronting Anglo-Saxon bishops and clerics, military obligation to what passed for "the state" in this period was one of the most vexing. As administrators of the vast land holdings of the Anglo-Saxon Church, it fell to the prelates, bishops and abbots, to organize the fulfillment of military duties incumbent upon those estates.[3] But whereas secular landholders were expected to fulfill military obligation by themselves leading contingents of warriors from their lands to fight in the king's *fyrd* or army, how were those clerics to meet their obligations when it was the official doctrinal position of the Church in the early Middle Ages was that there could be no compatibility between the vocations of religion and war?

---

1 [*ASC*], s.a. 1056; David C. Douglas and George W. Greenaway, eds., *English Historical Documents, 1042–1189* [*EHD*], 13 vols. (New York, 1953), 2:134–35, doc. 1.

2 Wulfstan, *The Institutes of Polity*, sec. 12, "Concerning Men in Orders," *Anglo-Saxon Prose*, trans. Michael Swanton (London, 1975), p. 133.

3 At the beginning of 1066, the total income from the Church's landholdings in England was greater than the combined incomes of the king and the House of Godwine. See David Hill, *An Atlas of Anglo-Saxon England* (Toronto, 1981), p. 100. The proportion of land held by the Church is not likely to have changed much in the eleventh century (Hill, p. 105, fig. 186). If anything, the Anglo-Saxon Church had held *more* land in the ninth century than in the tenth or eleventh, particularly in the northern areas overrun by the Vikings. See Robin Fleming, "Monastic Lands and England's Defence in the Viking Age," *EHR* 100(1985): 249–65.

The problem of fielding the required number of warriors to the *fyrd* according to the hidage or assessed value of the estate was addressed by using a method in common with other landholders. Church land was leased out to subtenants who became the prelate's commended men and served as his warriors. Who then led the forces of tenant-warriors drawn from ecclesiastical estates? The secular lord fulfilled this duty of command in person, fighting with his warriors in the *fyrd*, as part of the duty upon his land as a whole. But in light of the ban on clerics participating in war, other arrangements would seem necessary for ecclesiastical lords. In Anglo-Saxon England, tenants could fulfill the duties of military command incumbent upon churchmen as landlords. For instance, the bishop of Worcester in 1066 had a tenant named Eadric, described as "the pilot of the bishop's ship and the leader of the same bishop's military forces owed to the king's service."[4]

Tenant-commanders like Eadric notwithstanding, the historical records for Anglo-Saxon England tantalize with the possibility that clerics did at times lead troops into battle. Besides the description of Bishop Leofgar's ill-fated sortie against the Welsh, the *Anglo-Saxon Chronicle* mentions in passing Ealhstan, ninth-century bishop of Sherbourne, as one of the commanders sent by King Egbert of Wessex (802–839) against Kent in a somewhat more successful campaign.[5]

The presence of bishops and abbots on other battlefields is usually evidenced by their obituaries. The entry in the *Anglo-Saxon Chronicle* for 871 is explicit. In recounting the battle at Meretun between the West Saxons and the Danes it states bluntly that "Bishop Heahmund [of Sherbourne] was killed there."[6] When in 1016 Cnut the Dane (c.992–1035) won the bloody battle of Ashingdon, among "all the nobility of England there destroyed" were Bishop Eadnoth of Dorchester and Abbot Wulfsige of Ramsey.[7]

Most evidence placing clerics at battle sites is, however, too vague to reveal the role they played. For instance, in 940, Archbishop Wulfstan I of York (not to be confused with his sermonizing successor of the eleventh century, properly

---

4 Thomas Hearne, ed., *Hemmingi Chartularium Ecclesiae Wigoriensis*, 2 vols. (Oxford, 1723), 1:81, cited and trans. in Richard P. Abels, *Lordship and Military Obligation in Anglo-Saxon England* (Berkeley, 1988), p. 123.

5 "Then [Egbert] sent from the army his son Aethelwulf and his bishop Ealhstan and his ealdorman Wulfheard to Kent, with a large force, and they drove King Bealdred north across the Thames." *ASC* s.a. 825 (823) in *EHD*, *c.500–1042* (New York, 1955) 1:171, doc. 1. Abels' (pp. 49, 225) inference that this is an example of a churchman bearing arms goes beyond the source.

6 *ASC* s.a. 871 in *EHD* 1:178, doc. 1.

7 *ASC* s.a. 1016; *EHD* 1:227, doc. 1. I cannot, however, agree with Foot's interpretation of annal 836 that bishops Herefrith and Wigthegn died in battle. See Sarah Foot, "Violence against Christians? The Vikings and the Church in Ninth-Century England," *Medieval History* 1(1991): 12. The fact that the annal lists the two bishops, along with two ealdormen, among the fallen, might seem to support Foot's reading. However, Whitelock's annotation to the annal reveals that the bishops appear in the lists of

designated as Wulfstan II) accompanied the Norwegian-Irish king Olaf Guthfrithson of Northumbria on a raid south into the midlands. He and Olaf ended
up besieged in Leicester by the West Saxon king, Edmund the Elder
(899–924).[8] Although the *Chronicle* specifies no role for the archbishop, the
twelfth- century writer Simeon of Durham, drawing on Northumbrian material, reported that Wulfstan and his southern counterpart, Archbishop Oda of
Canterbury, negotiated a truce between the kings – thereby attesting to the
presence of the southern prelate as well.[9] The West Saxon kings would later
consider the northern archbishop a serious political threat. In 947, after
Northumbria had submitted to the house of Wessex, Wulfstan, with the rest of
the Northumbrian councilors, foreswore the pledges they had made to
Edmund's brother and successor, King Eadred (946–955), and for a time
accepted Eric Blood-Axe (–954) as their king.[10]

In 952, Eadred imprisoned the archbishop, "because accusations had often
been made to the king against him."[11] In general, the sources record only the
clerics' presence and fate on the field of battle, not their specific actions, except
when mention is made of kings hearing Mass immediately before entering
battle.[12] It must be admitted in fact that the most obvious function of these
clerics was that of providing spiritual support to participants on campaign, aid
entirely within the tradition of Western Christendom. Some of the same
ecclesiastical canons prohibiting clerical participation in war expressly permitted chaplains to accompany armies and to minister to the troops, and even
permitted the clerics to carry with them what Friedrich Prinz calls "victory
bringing relics."[13] Wulfstan of York can at least be assumed to have been
providing spiritual support to Olaf Guthfrithson in 940.

Such spiritual assistance rendered by clergy was considered a necessary
element in a medieval commander's arsenal. The Venerable Bede considered
the cause of West Saxon military misfortunes under the seventh-century king
Cenwalh to have been the expulsion of his bishops; in Bede's own words, "a
kingdom which was without a bishop was, at the same time, justly deprived of

Winchester, holding the episcopal office one after the other. See *ASC* s.a. 836 in *EHD*
1:172, doc. 1, n. 3.

8   *ASC* s.a. 940–943 in *EHD* 1:202, doc. 1.
9   Simeon of Durham, *Historia Regum*, s.a. 939, in Thomas Arnold, ed., *Symeonis Monachi
Opera Omnia*, 2 vols., Rolls Series [RS], 75 (London, 1882–1885), 1:94. See also Frank
M. Stenton, *Anglo-Saxon England [ASE]* (Oxford, 1971), p. 257.
10 *ASC* s.a. 947–948 in *EHD* 1:203–4, doc. 1.
11 *ASC* s.a. 952 in *EHD* 1:204, doc. 1.
12 Asser, *Life of Alfred*, chap. 38, in *Alfred the Great: Asser's Life of King Alfred and Other
Contemporary Sources*, ed. and trans. Simon Keynes and Michael Lapidge (London,
1983), p. 79.
13 Friedrich Prinz, "King, Clergy and War," in *Saints, Scholars and Heroes: Studies in
Medieval Culture in Honour of Charles W. Jones*, ed. Margot H. King and Wesley M.
Stephens, 2 vols. (Collegeville MN, 1979), 2:305. Despite the fame of the later Anglo-
Saxon kings, particularly Athelstan, as relic-collectors, see David W. Rollason, *Saints
and Relics in Anglo-Saxon England* [Oxford, 1989], pp. 159–62; *ASE*, p. 356, I have

divine protection."[14] In granting land to the Church under terms of perpetual tenure, kings not only hoped for the eternal gift of salvation from God, but also expected the Almighty would intervene through the Church. One of the purposes of a bequest to the Church by King Oswiu of Northumbria (655–670), in thanksgiving for victory over the pagan king Penda of Mercia (632–655), was that "a site and means might be provided for the monks to wage heavenly warfare and to pray with unceasing devotion that the race might win eternal peace."[15] The first declarations in the laws of King Wihtred of Kent (690–725) were that "the Church [is to be] free from taxation," and that "the king is to be prayed for, and they are to honour him of their own free-will, without compulsion."[16] The connection is reiterated by Wihtred in a subsequent charter: "From this day and moment, [Church lands] are to be free from all exaction and tribute as well as all expenses and attacks," but the king in return demanded the prayers, "honor and obedience" of the beneficiary churchmen.[17]

Striking examples of clergy invoking supernatural aid for success in battle appear throughout the Anglo-Saxon historical record. A step along Edwin of Northumbria's (617–633) road to conversion was his victory in 625 over Cwichelm of Wessex, gained through the prayers of Bishop Paulinus in exchange for Edwin's own promises to consecrate his newborn daughter to Christ and himself to abandon idolatry and to serve the Christian God.[18] The death of King Ecgfrith of Northumbria (670–685) at the battle of Nechtanesmere in 685 came as a result of his earlier, unprovoked raid on the Irish, who called down God's vengeance upon him.[19] In his *Life* of the seventh-century bishop Wilfrid of Ripon, Eddius Stephanus observed that "the Lord fought for the few" in response to clerical intercession. Left beached on the coast of Sussex by a sudden storm, Wilfrid and his companions were threatened by the still-pagan locals. The heathen chief priest began to attack the party "by means of his magical arts" – whereupon one of Wilfrid's companions slew the wizard by means of a stone "blessed by all the people of God and hurled from his sling after the manner of David." The prayers of Wilfrid with his fellow Christian priests enabled his companions to repel the South Saxons, not once but three times before the tide rolled in and floated their ship safely away just ahead of a fourth assault.[20]

found no reference to such relics actually carried into battle in Anglo-Saxon England.

14 Bede, *Ecclesiastical History of the English People* [*EH*], ed. and trans. Bertram Colgrave and R. A. B. Mynors (Oxford, 1969), pp. 236–37, bk. 3, chap. 7.

15 *EH*, pp. 292–93, bk. 3, chap. 24.

16 *Laws of Wihtred, king of Kent (695)* in *EHD* 1:362, doc. 31, arts. 1, 1.1.

17 *Grant by Wihtred, King of Kent, of privileges to the churches and monasteries in Kent, 8 April A.D. 699*, in *Cartularium Saxonicum: A Collection of Charters Relating to Anglo-Saxon History*, ed. Walter de Gray Birch, 3 vols. (1887; repr., New York, 1964), 1:143–44, doc. 99; Abels, p. 50.

18 *EH*, pp. 164–67, bk. 2, chap 9; *ASC* s.a. 626 in *EHD* 1:149, doc. 1.

19 *EH*, pp. 426–29, bk. 4, chap. 26.

20 Eddius Stephanus, *The Life of Bishop Wilfrid*, ed. and trans. Bertram Colgrave (1927; repr., Cambridge, 1985), pp. 28–29, chap. 13.

As Richard Abels notes, the success of such efforts was not assured – a fact the unlucky Welsh monks at the battle of Chester (c.613) discovered in their last moments. The staunch partisan of Roman orthodoxy, Bede, recorded that the prayers for victory offered up by these schismatics, obstinately resistant to the efforts of Augustine of Canterbury to set them straight on the dating of Easter, availed little when the still-pagan Aethelfrith of Northumbria (–617) perceived the supernatural threat they posed and ordered them slaughtered. As Aethelfrith asserted, "If they are praying to their God against us, then, even if they do not bear arms, they are fighting against us, assailing us as they do with prayers for our defeat."[21]

The tendency of the authors of our clerical sources both to interpret events according to their theological views and to exaggerate the efficacy of the Church's support must not be overlooked for they testify to attitudes current in their time.[22] Evidence from the early eleventh century indicates that even the liturgy included formal invocations of divine aid against the Vikings in an age of invasion. The Latin version of the 1009 edict of Ethelred II "the Unready" (979–1014) mandates for each minster a daily Mass entitled "Against the heathen." This edict also mandates that similarly titled prayers, as well as the third psalm, "Why, O Lord, are they multiplied," were to be sung by the whole community while prostrate before the altar.[23] The spiritual warfare which formed part of the calling of Christianity in general and of monasticism in particular[24] could be turned outward against enemies in this world. Undoubtedly contingents of priests and monks offered up prayers and supplications on many an English battlefield, perhaps led by the bishops and abbots whose names were recorded in the sources primarily when they fell in battle.

But there are hints that clerics in Anglo-Saxon England might in practice have had a closer association with "harder" weapons than ecclesiastical canons allowed. Prohibitions and denunciations of arms-bearing by English clerics come from a seventh-century council on the affairs of the English Church as well as from the pen of the eighth-century Anglo-Saxon missionary in Francia, St. Boniface, in a letter to Archbishop Cuthbert of Canterbury.[25] Early in the eleventh century, the *Law of the Northumbrian Priests* contains an arresting injunction: "If a priest comes with weapons into the church he is to compensate for it."[26] No mention is made of a blanket prohibition against the cleric bearing

---

21 *EH*, pp. 240–41, bk. 2, chap. 2; Abels, pp. 50–51.
22 Abels, p. 51.
23 *Edict when the "Great Army" came to England (VII Ethelred, probably 1009)* in *EHD* 1:410, doc. 45, arts. 6.2, 6.3, nn. 7–9.
24 Adolf Harnack, *Militia Christi: The Christian Religion and the Military in the First Three Centuries*, trans. David McInnes Gracie (Philadelphia, 1981), pp. 27–64, esp. 37, 49–51.
25 Patrick Wormald, "Bede, 'Beowulf' and the Conversion of the Anglo-Saxon Aristocracy," in *Bede and Anglo-Saxon England*, ed. Robert T. Farrell, *British Archaeological Reports* 46(1978): 51.
26 *Law of the Northumbrian priests (probably 1020–1023)* in *EHD* 1:437, doc. 53, art. 37.

weapons – only that he must not carry them into the church, a consecrated place. One may infer from this statute that armed priests were otherwise accepted as a matter of course. This attempt at clerical arms-regulation is only slightly less ambiguous than an entire series of documents linking clerics with weapons.

From the late tenth century, when English wills first appeared in any number, those of bishops specified a heriot to be left to the king. Heriot was in origin the return to a lord of equipment provided by the lord to his commended man so that the latter could carry out the duties required of him by the former.[27] The duties were, of course, military in nature, and the equipment took the form of weapons and armor. Although the king is not specified as such in these wills, it is unlikely that such highly placed prelates were commended to any lord other than the king. In her commentary on one of these wills, Dorothy Whitelock so identifies Bishop Aelfwold's lord as the king.[28] These heriots are evidence for the commendation relationship existing between ecclesiastical landlords and the king. They are also important because the heriots returned to the king by these clerics are similar to those returned by any other figure – when specified, they almost always include weapons and armor. From the mid-tenth century, the will of Bishop Theodred of London itemizes the heriot due to his lord as including a pair of swords, four shields, and four spears, in addition to four horses.[29] From the late tenth century, the will of Bishop Aelfwold of Crediton specifies a heriot to be granted to his lord including coats of mail, helmets, spears, shields, and horses.[30] And in the early years of the eleventh century Archbishop Aelfric of Canterbury bequeathed to his lord a total of sixty helmets and coats of mail.[31] Only the will of Aelfric of Elmham among those of bishops is unusual in specifying just two marks of gold, with no mention of weapons or armor, as heriot to his "royal lord Harald [Harefoot (1035–1040)]."[32]

The wills clearly associate bishops with weapons – but how closely? From the sheer volume of the heriot left by Archbishop Aelfric (sixty helmets and coats of mail), it seems likely that the heriot was for the lands which the bishops administered, its magnitude tied to the number of fighting men required of the land under its hidage assessment. The heriot list contained in the laws of Cnut does not specify clerics,[33] a fact commented on by Whitelock which led her to

---

The Old English original of this statute is in F. Liebermann, ed., *Die Gesetze der Angelsächsen*, 3 vols. (Halle, 1903), 1:382: *Gif preost mid wæpnum innan circan cume, gebete þæt*, with a German trans., *Wenn ein Priester mit Waffen in die Kirche kommt, büsse er das* ("he is to do penance for it").

27 Of the more than fifty Anglo-Saxon wills which survive, mostly in later copies, less than a dozen date from before the middle of the tenth century. See Dorothy Whitelock, *Anglo-Saxon Wills* (Cambridge, 1930), p. xli.

28 *Will of Bishop Aelfwold of Crediton (997–1012)* in *EHD* 1:536, doc. 122.

29 *Will of Theodred, bishop of London (942–951)* in *EHD* 1:510, doc. 106.

30 *Will of Bishop Aelfwold* in *EHD* 1:536, doc. 122.

31 *Will of Aelfric, archbishop of Canterbury (1002–1005)* in *EHD* 1:544, doc. 126.

32 *Will of Bishop Aelfric* in *Anglo-Saxon Wills*, pp. 70–73, doc. 26.

33 *Laws of Cnut (1020–1023)* in *EHD* 1:429, doc. 50, arts. 71–71.5.

suppose that episcopal heriot was "voluntary," an effort on the part of the bishops to obtain from the king respect for the provisions of their wills.[34] Considering the central fact that bishops exercised temporal lordship as well as spiritual authority, it is more likely that heriot derived not from the bishop's status in the Church, but rather from his relationship to the king as a holder or administrator of land incurring military service. The weapons served as a pool from which the prelate supplied his commended men. There is no indication that the prelate himself carried or used tools of war beyond armor even if he accompanied troops into battle. That churchmen did wear armor is supported by iconographic evidence from the eleventh century. In the famous scene in the Bayeux Tapestry where Bishop Odo brandishes his *baculus*, the bishop appears to be clad in some kind of over-garment covering a suit of mail comparable to that of the other Normans pictured in the tapestry. This mail is exposed around his neck, on the back of his head and perhaps at his sleeves. He very clearly wears a conical helm.[35]

Weapons included in heriot bequests need not have been used personally by the grantor. Women also returned to their lords heriot which included weapons and armor. For example, a tenth-century woman named Aelfgyfu made the following request in her will: "I grant to my royal lord the estates and two armlets and six horses and as many shields and spears."[36] Unless one is willing to argue that weapons in a woman's heriot imply that she actually used them, such heriot evidence as there is for the bishops in the end tells nothing about whether they carried and used weapons.[37]

Prinz's studies of eighth- and ninth-century Francia show how the prohibition against clerical participation in warfare was modified in practice if not explicitly in canon law to "decriminalize" warrior prelates.[38] Hammered by not only the Vikings from the north but the Saracens from the south and the Magyars from the east, Charles Martel and his successors who became the Carolingian kings of Francia rendered such prohibitions moot.

Two circumstances drove the shift toward active clerical participation in Frankish wars against heathens on all sides. One was a tradition of "princely bishops" which grew out of their involvement in politics and city defense

---

34 Whitelock, *Anglo-Saxon Wills*, p. 100.
35 See David M. Wilson, ed., *The Bayeux Tapestry: The Complete Tapestry in Colour* (London, 1985), plate 67.
36 *Will of Aelfgyfu* in *Anglo-Saxon Wills*, pp. 20–21, doc. 8.
37 It must be noted as well that one of the executors of the will of Archbishop Aelfric of Canterbury was Archbishop Wulfstan II of York, the homilist. Recalling Wulfstan's stated view that a priest had no more business participating in secular war than in marriage, it seems unlikely that this archbishop would have countenanced warrior clerics. But note also that Archbishop Aelfric's will specified only armor, not swords or spears. See *Will of Aelfric, Archbishop of Canterbury* in *EHD* 1:544, doc. 126, including Whitelock's introductory commentary.
38 Prinz, pp. 301–29; idem, *Klerus und Krieg im früheren Mittelalter* (Stuttgart, 1971).

during the fifth century when Gaul was literally "going to pieces." The other was an increasing number of Frankish nobles in the episcopacy. These Germanic bishops were not just nobly-born clerics raised to episcopal dignity. Charles Martel awarded the rich bishoprics of the old, wealthy, and powerful Gallo-Roman *civitates* to his loyal military supporters. For example, the bishopric of Trier passed from Liutwin to his son, Milo. Both father and son were firm partisans of Charles. Milo also held in plurality the see of Reims. His episcopal rule was indistinguishable from that of a secular lord. St. Boniface, attempting a general reform of the Frankish church in the mid-eighth century, numbered him among the "drinkers and slackers and hunters." Even more reprehensible in Boniface's estimation was Milo's contemporary, Bishop Gewilib of Mainz, another crony of Charles Martel. Like Milo, Gewilib succeeded his father in the episcopacy. Nevertheless, when his father fell in battle, Gewilib pursued a blood feud against the slayers.[39]

By the middle of the eighth century, Frankish clergy were, according to Prinz, "nothing other than the imperial aristocracy in ecclesiastical vestments and part of the Carolingian ruling structure both by birth and by function."[40] Personal military service by these "imperial bishops" became not only the norm but was required. A solution to the tension between the canonical impossibility of such episcopal military service on the one hand and its political unavoidability on the other was effected by the Synod of Soissons in 744, followed by decrees in the same spirit throughout the ninth century. While the absolute prohibition against participation in war by the lesser clergy was maintained, special rights were conceded *de facto* to the prelates. Only *clerici*, *presbyteri*, and *diaconi* are specifically forbidden to fight; *episcopi* and *abbates* are conspicuously not included in the prohibition. Prinz argues not simply from silence. The accompanying prohibitions maintained against clerical participation in hunting continued to include the prelates along with the lesser clergy. The distinction between bishops arming for war, which was implicitly allowed because not forbidden, and their arming for the hunt, which was explicitly prohibited, seems to have been made on the grounds of *necessitas* – war provided defense to the realm and therefore benefited society; hunting was a private affair, conducted for personal amusement.[41] The canons codified the social stratification of the Frankish clergy. The offices of the prelates drawn from the traditionally warlike Germanic nobility were exalted even more than had been the Gallo-Roman episcopacy.

In a study of how heroic poetry can shed light on the early Anglo-Saxon Church and the conversion of the nobility, Patrick Wormald points out the similarity between the situations in the English and Frankish Churches.[42] As

---

39 J. M. Wallace-Hadrill, *The Frankish Church* (Oxford, 1983), pp. 137, 178.
40 Prinz, "King, Clergy and War," p. 315.
41 Ibid., pp. 303–18.
42 Wormald, pp. 32–95.

he observes, the Anglo-Saxon Church was from the beginning as aristocratic as the society itself. Monasticism and royalty were integrated; many monastic foundations were established to be presided over by princess-abbesses; kings repeatedly "opted out" (in the words of Clare Stancliffe) to the religious life – a phenomenon unique to the Anglo-Saxons among all the Germanic peoples of the barbarian west.[43] The connections between aristocracy and episcopacy were just as close. Archbishop Egbert of York, the recipient of Bede's famous letter,[44] was the brother and uncle of Northumbrian kings. A striking example of the Anglo-Saxon episcopacy was Wilfrid, a friend to kings and a rich landholder, a lord both of fighting-men and of clerics.[45] The fusion of aristocratic cultural values and Christianity which drove the Northumbrian Renaissance in the seventh and early eighth centuries also infused into the Anglo-Saxon Church hierarchy the values of the Germanic warrior nobility, as would happen as well in Francia in the next century. In such a milieu, not only would the composition by a Christian cleric of the poem *Beowulf*, permeated by the heroic ethos of his pagan ancestors, seem unsurprising,[46] but the involvement of clerics in war would seem less unexpected. Prinz's comment regarding the Frankish aristocratic episcopacy would appear appropriate for Anglo-Saxon England as well:

> By observing that the origins of the bishops were to be found in a traditionally warlike nobility we touch an important element, namely a sort of hereditary psychological blocking mechanism which simply prevented those prelates of aristocratic origin from being able to observe Christianity's clear prohibitions against fighting and war.[47]

Leofgar of Hereford would seem to be such a bishop with a "mental block." The chronicler is, in fact, explicit when he states that, even as a priest before his appointment as bishop, Leofgar maintained the trappings of the warrior nobility: "He wore his moustaches during his priesthood until he became bishop."[48] Leofgar is the only Anglo-Saxon cleric explicitly stated to have

---

[43] Clare Stancliffe, "Kings Who Opted Out," in *Ideal and Reality in Frankish and Anglo-Saxon Society: Studies presented to J. M. Wallace-Hadrill*, ed. Patrick Wormald et al. (Oxford, 1983), pp. 154–76.

[44] Bede, *Letter to Egbert, archbishop of York (5 November 734)*, in *EHD* 1:735–45, doc. 170.

[45] Wilfrid's companions when washed up in Sussex were a force of men provided him so he could "enter Gaul in great estate" to obtain episcopal consecration from an indisputably "catholic" bishop. In thrice fighting off the heathens, even with the prayers of Wilfrid and his clergy, it is "with no little slaughter" – of the South Saxons. "Marvelous to relate, only five of the Christians were slain." Eddius, *Life of Wilfrid*, ed. and trans. Colgrave, pp. 26–27, 28–29, chaps. 12 and 13. The West Saxon scholar Aldhelm, in his *Letter to the clergy of Bishop Wilfrid*, in *EHD* 1:730–31, doc. 165 urged Wilfrid's clergy to follow their lord into exile as faithful thegns.

[46] Wormald, p. 58.

[47] Prinz, "King, Clergy and War," pp. 304–5.

[48] *ASC* s.a. 1056, in *EHD* 2:134, doc. 1. The magnificent whiskers of his lord, Earl Harold Godwineson of Wessex, may be seen in the Bayeux Tapestry.

taken up "his spear and his sword." He might well have been influenced by the Frankish warrior bishops who, by the 1050s, were already an old phenomenon. Interestingly, the short episcopate of Leofgar came within a few years of the pontificate of Leo IX (1049–1054), who planned and led a military campaign against the Normans of southern Italy.[49] Leofgar's bellicose nature as bishop, however, is unlikely to have resulted from direct imitation of the martial activities of the highest prelate in the Church. His refusal to shave his moustache, the symbol of a warrior noble, indicates Leofgar's determination to maintain a martial appearance, even in the priestly order. More likely the activities of both Leo and Leofgar should be considered symptomatic of the mid-eleventh-century shift toward acceptance of holy war which paved the way for the First Crusade.[50]

In conclusion, Anglo-Saxon bishops had some association with the tools of war, if only as heriot granted to their lord. As landlords themselves, bishops had to provide weapons to their tenant-warriors. The ambiguous Northumbrian prohibition on priests carrying weapons into a church seems to indicate that clerics might carry them elsewhere. But the sources do not support the conclusion that Anglo-Saxon bishops normally fulfilled either the warrior function of their social class or the military obligation on their lands by personally taking up arms. That they sometimes did lead warriors from their lands is illustrated by the example of Bishop Ealhstan in the ninth century. Episcopal commanders may be best considered as an extension of the functions of organizing and directing civic defense which had fallen to bishops of threatened cities during the age of the *Völkerwanderung*. Such a tributary flowed into the development of Frankish warrior-bishops, and although there were no such examples of bishops directing civic defense on English soil, Gregory the Great, the very pope who initiated the conversion of the Anglo-Saxons, had found it necessary to take such actions to prevent his own city from falling to the Lombards. For all the social and political pressure on aristocratic prelates to provide military service, official Church doctrine against clerical participation in war and the lack of clear evidence to the contrary make the Worcester arrangement seem a more likely way for an Anglo-Saxon ecclesiastical lord to fulfill his military obligation. With the exception of Leofgar in the eleventh century, no documented Anglo-Saxon figure approaches the famous eighth-century warrior-bishops of Francia who so scandalized St. Boniface. There was no English Milo of Trier nor a Gewilib of Mainz.

---

[49] Carl Erdmann, *The Origin of the Idea of Crusade*, trans. Marshall W. Baldwin and Walter Goffart (Princeton, 1977), pp. 118–25.
[50] Ibid.

Violence, Knightly Piety and the Peace of God Movement in Aquitaine

MICHAEL FRASSETTO

The Peace of God Movement has received much attention recently from scholars who have sought to identify its immediate impact and subsequent influence on medieval society.[1] Although there is no uniform opinion, consensus has emerged recognizing the importance of the Peace as part of a broad movement which would redefine the structure of society and reform the Church.[2] Marcus Bull, however, has challenged many of the assumptions concerning the Peace of God, including the notion of its assumed role in the

---

[1] The most important recent contribution is Thomas Head and Richard Landes, eds., *The Peace of God: Social Violence and Religious Response in France around the Year 1000* (Ithaca NY, 1992). See also Bernard Bachrach, "The Northern Origins of the Peace Movement at Le Puy," *Historical Reflections / Reflexions Historiques* [*HRRH*] 14(1987): 405–22; Thomas N. Bisson, "The Organized Peace in Southern France and Catalonia, c.1140–c.1233," *American Historical Review* [*AHR*] 82(1977): 290–311; Roger Bonnaud-Delamare, "Les institutions de paix en Aquitaine au XIe siècle," *Recueils de la société Jean Bodin* 4(1961): 415–87; Daniel F. Callahan, "Ademar de Chabannes et la Paix de Dieu," *Annales du Midi* 89(1977): 21–43; H. E. J. Cowdrey, "The Peace and Truce of God in the Eleventh Century," *Past and Present* 46(1970): 42–67; Georges Duby, "Laity and the Peace of God," in *The Chivalrous Society*, trans. Cynthia Postan (Berkeley, 1977), pp. 123–33; idem, *The Three Orders: Feudal Society Imagined*, trans. Arthur Goldhammer (Chicago, 1978), pp. 21–43, 134–39; Hartmut Hoffmann, *Göttesfriede und Treuga Dei, Schriften der Monumenta Germaniae Historica* (Stuttgart, 1964); Richard Landes, "The Dynamics of Heresy and Reform in Limoges: A Study of Popular Participation in the 'Peace of God' (994–1033)," *HRRH* 14(1987): 219–40; E. Magnou-Nortier, "La place du concile de Puy (vers 994) dans l'évolution de l'idée de la paix," in *Mélanges offerts à Jean Dauvillier* (Toulouse, 1979), pp. 489–506; and Steven D. Sargent, "Religious Responses to Social Violence in Eleventh-Century Aquitaine," *HRRH* 12(1985): 219–40. A useful historiographic survey is Frederick S. Paxton, "History, Historians, and the Peace of God," in Head and Landes, *The Peace of God*, pp. 21–40.

[2] Paxton, pp. 21–40; Duby, "Laity and the Peace of God," pp. 128–33 and Amy G. Remensnyder, "Pollution, Purity, and Peace: An Aspect of the Social Reform between the Late Tenth Century and 1076," in Head and Landes, *The Peace of God*, pp. 280–307. For a dissenting opinion, see E. Magnou-Nortier, "The Enemies of the Peace: Reflections on a Vocabulary, 500–1100," in *The Peace of God*, pp. 58–79.

formation of the idea of the crusade.[3] Bull argues that because scholars have failed to consider the knights' attitudes, they have overstated the contemporary appeal of the Peace and its influence on later developments. He argues further that despite some participation by the military and religious aristocracies, the Peace did not appeal to the common soldier and failed to create a new ethos for knighthood.[4] For Bull, the Peace was not a phenomenon of long-term significance nor did it exert much influence beyond the limited circle of the secular and religious elite of Aquitaine.

Although Bull's work offers a valuable corrective in its emphasis on the attitudes of the knights themselves, it does not provide an accurate characterization of the ideals of and the participants in the Peace of God Movement. His interpretation fails to appreciate fully the resonance that the religious sanctions and cultic rituals of the Peace had with all members of lay society. Although he correctly notes that the Peace was not an unqualified success, Bull unnecessarily diminishes the importance of the movement in the development of eleventh-century reform and the idea of the crusade because of his failure to recognize the impact that religious sanctions had on the knightly class. Indeed, the Peace of God employed religious sanctions and popular participation to alleviate social dislocation at the millennium. Consequently, the Peace helped redefine the organization of feudal society.

Emerging at a time of far-reaching and violent social and political transformation,[5] the Peace was designed originally to secure the protection of the Church and the peasants from the predatory activities of the castellans.[6] The

---

3 Marcus Bull, *Knightly Piety and the Lay Response to the First Crusade: The Limousin and Gascony c.970–c.1130* (Oxford, 1993), pp. 21–69. The classic statement of the influence of the Peace of God on crusader ideals is Carl Erdmann, *The Origin of the Idea of Crusade*, trans. Marshall W. Baldwin and Walter Goffart (Princeton, 1977), pp. 57–94.

4 Bull, p. 50, where he notes, "It would, therefore, be mistaken to imagine that the Peace in northern and western Aquitaine was intended to stimulate a code of conduct applicable equally to all arms-bearers."

5 The extent of this transformation has been demonstrated by a number of scholars including Guy Bois, *The Transformation of the Year One Thousand*, trans. Jean Birrell (New York, 1992); Pierre Bonnassie, *La Catalogne du milieu du Xe siècle à la fin du XIe siècle: Croissance et mutations d'une société* (Toulouse, 1975); idem, *From Slavery to Feudalism in South-Western Europe*, trans. Jean Birrell (Cambridge, 1991); Guy Devailly, *Le Berry du Xe au milieu du XIIIe siècle: Étude politique, religieuse, sociale et économique* (Paris, 1973); George Duby, *La société aux XIe et XIIe siècles dans la région mâconnaise* (1953; repr., Paris, 1971); Jean-François Lemarignier, "La dislocation du *pagus* et le problème des *consuetudines*," in *Mélanges d'histoire du Moyen Âge dédiés a la mémoire de Louis Halphen* (Paris, 1951), pp. 401–10; Elizabeth Magnou-Nortier, *La société laïque et l'Église dans la province ecclésiastique de Narbonne de la fin du VIIIe siècle à la fin du XIIe siècle* (Toulouse, 1974); and Jean Pierre Poly and Eric Bournazel, *The Feudal Transformation, 900–1200*, trans. Caroline Higgitt (New York, 1991).

6 On the nature of the violence and exploitation by the castellans see Bull, pp. 23–33; André Debord, "The Castellan Revolution and the Peace of God in Aquitaine," in Head

first councils stated the desire to restrict all violence against the Church, the poor and weak. The canons approved at Charroux in 989 pronounced anathema on those who harmed churches or attacked unarmed clergy.[7] These decrees also sought to protect the peasants and their livestock from unlawful seizure.[8] At Le Puy in 994, Bishop Guy and the clergy and nobles agreed that peasants, clergy and livestock had to be protected from violence and that no evil custom should be implemented against any religious community.[9] In the face of growing feudal warfare, religious leaders took action to limit the activities of the warrior class and to redefine their social function.

The first steps taken in the late tenth century were continued in the opening decades of the eleventh. Under the combined leadership of the duke and bishops of Aquitaine, the canons of the first Peace assemblies were repeated at the councils of Limoges in 994,[10] Poitiers in 1000/1014,[11] Charroux in 1028,[12] Poitiers in 1030/1032[13] and Bourges and Limoges in 1031.[14] These councils

---

and Landes, *The Peace of God*, pp. 135–64; Georges Duby, "The Evolution of Judicial Institutions in Burgundy in the Tenth and Eleventh Centuries," in *The Chivalrous Society*, pp. 15–58; and Christian Lauranson-Rosaz, "Les mauvais coutumes d'Auvergne (fin Xe–XIe siècle)," *Annales du Midi* 102(1990): 557–86.

[7] J. D. Mansi, ed., *Sacrorum conciliorum nova et amplissima collectio*, 53 vols. (Leipzig: H. Walter, 1902–27), 19:89–90. Charroux has traditionally been recognized as the first of the peace councils but Bachrach (pp. 405–21), and Christian Lauranson-Rosaz, "Peace from the Mountains: The Auvergnat Origins of the Peace of God," in Head and Landes, *The Peace of God*, pp. 104–34, have identified forerunners to this council.

[8] Mansi, 19:90.

[9] Magnou-Nortier, "La place du concile du Puy," pp. 499–500.

[10] Ademar, *Chronique*, p. 158, bk. 3, c. 35.

[11] Mansi, 19:265–68.

[12] Ademar, *Chronique*, p. 194, bk. 3, c. 69.

[13] Alfred Richard, ed., *Chartes et documents pour servir à l'histoire de l'abbaye de Saint-Maixent*, 1:108–11.

[14] Mansi, 19:501–8 and 507–48 respectively. I am assisting Daniel Callahan in the preparation of an edition of the sermons and account of the councils of Bourges and Limoges by Ademar of Chabannes located in Paris (Bibliothèque Nationale [BN], MS Lat. 2469, ff. 1r–112v) and Berlin (Deutsche Staats Bibliothek, Berlin [DS], MS Lat. Phillipps 1664, ff. 58v–116r). It must be noted that the accounts of these two councils come only from the manuscripts of Ademar, a noted forger, and must be treated with some caution. It has been suggested that the councils never actually took place, but instead occurred only in the mind of Ademar. This view is too critical and, although it is unlikely that the councils took the precise shape Ademar gave them, it is likely that meetings were held at Bourges and Limoges in 1031. Given Ademar's desire to demonstrate conciliar sanction for the apostolicity of St. Martial, it is probable that he included both authentic and false canons in the conciliar account. On the other hand, the similarity of the Peace decrees at Bourges and Limoges with those of other Peace councils provides support for the belief that Ademar's version of events contains elements of truth about the Peace of God. See also Daniel Callahan, "Ademar of Chabannes and the Peace Council of Limoges of 1031," *Revue Bénédictine* 101(1991): 32–49, and idem, "Ademar de Chabannes et la Paix," pp. 21–43; Louis Saltet, "Les faux d'Ademar de Chabannes: décisions prétendues sur Saint Martial au concile de Bourges du 1er novembre 1031,"

restated the need to protect the defenseless members of society from the destructive activities of the castellans. The Peace sought to restrict the legitimate focus of knightly violence while establishing a more ordered society. In the process of limiting the range of knightly military activities, the advocates of the Peace further redefined the role of the knight in society. Indeed these later councils expanded the terms of the Peace and implemented a broad reform program. Thus, beginning as a means of protecting society from the violence of the warrior class, the movement came to advocate the reformation of Church and society.[15]

The Peace councils sought not only to curtail acts of violence but also to redefine the organization of society.[16] The canons of all councils from Le Puy to Limoges reveal the attempt to create distinct social orders. At the Council of Le Puy and the first Council of Poitiers, the canons defined the special status and obligations of the clerical order. Regular and secular clergy were classified as members of a separate social class with specific spiritual duties – a class whose members were prohibited from acting as knights. At Le Puy, the clergy were ordered not to carry "secular arms."[17] The clergy were also separated from the other orders of society by strict regulations against clerical marriage or concubinage.[18] Moreover, the concern to purify the clergy and provide them with a distinct identity led to prohibitions of simony at Le Puy and Poitiers.[19] Thus these councils came to restructure social organization by distinguishing the functions of the clerical and the military orders.

The identification of the ecclesiastical estate as a distinct order was continued at the councils of Bourges and Limoges in 1031. The canons of Bourges

Bulletin de littérature ecclésiastique 27(1926): 145–60, and idem, "Un cas de mythomanie historique bien documenté: Ademar de Chabannes (988–1034)," *Bulletin de littérature ecclésiastique* 32(1931): 149–65; Michael Frassetto, "The Art of Forgery: The Sermons of Ademar of Chabannes and the Cult of St. Martial of Limoges," *Comitatus* 26(1995): 11–26, and Robert Lee Wolff, "How the News was brought from Byzantium to Angoulême; or, The Pursuit of a Hare in an Ox Cart," *Byzantine and Modern Greek Studies* 4(1978): 139–89.

15 On the Peace and the reform currents of the eleventh century, see Remensnyder, pp. 280–307.

16 This is one aspect of the movement that Bull fails to appreciate fully. For a more sympathetic discussion of this change see Duby, "Laity and the Peace of God," pp. 123–33 and idem, *The Three Orders*, pp. 129–46 and 156–58; Hans-Werner Goetz, "Protection of the Church, Defense of the Law, and Reform: On the Purposes and Character of the Peace of God, 989–1038," in Head and Landes, *The Peace of God*, pp. 259–79; R. I. Moore, "The Peace of God and the Social Revolution," in *The Peace of God*, pp. 317–26; and Poly and Bournazel, pp. 151–62.

17 Magnou-Nortier, "La place du concile du Puy," p. 499: *Clerici non portent secularia arma.* The canon from the council of Charroux forbidding attacks on unarmed clergy may have been a tentative step toward restricting the use of arms by churchmen and toward defining the clergy as a distinct social order.

18 Magnou-Nortier, "La place du concile du Puy," p. 499, and Mansi, 19:260.

19 See Remensnyder, pp. 285–90.

reveal a concern for separating the clergy from all other orders.[20] These canons legislate on matters ranging from the tonsure to the issue of the status of those seeking ordination. They also offer very clear denunciations of simony and nicolaism. Indeed, the abolition of clerical marriage was of great importance because its rejection was the clearest indication of the clergy's separate status from the laity. Moreover, according to Ademar, the leaders of the Council of Limoges included in their official proceedings the decrees of their predecessors at Bourges.[21] To supplement the decrees of Bourges, those assembled at the Council of Limoges, also approved decrees against simony and nicolaism.[22]

The effort to restrict knightly violence and to establish the clergy as a distinct order had the cumulative effect of providing a clearer definition of the responsibilities of the knights themselves. The Peace Movement, therefore, was the first phase of a broader social transformation that would lead to the creation of clearly distinguished clerical and military orders each with specific functions in society. A new understanding of the priesthood and knighthood began to crystallize at the Peace councils, an understanding that would communicated itself to the knightly class through the use of excommunication, oaths and the cult of the saints.

Excommunication was one of the most effective tools available to the Peace councils. All conciliar accounts bear witness to the threatened use of this weapon against those who violated the peace. At the Council of Charroux and the first Council of Poitiers, the bishops promised excommunication to anyone who failed to obey the Peace. The canons of Charroux declared that anyone who harmed churches or violated the property of the peasants would be anathema.[23] At both councils of Poitiers, the assembled princes exchanged hostages and acknowledged excommunication as the legitimate penalty for any violation of their vow to preserve the peace.[24] Bishop Guy at the Council of Le Puy also proclaimed the ban of excommunication against enemies of the peace. The bishop explained the terms of the ban and revealed how powerful a weapon it was. He declared that the clergy should not pray for excommunicates nor celebrate the mass for them nor offer them communion. If anyone should die while excommunicate, that person could not be buried in sacred ground.[25] The use of the ban was proposed again at the Council of Elne-Touloges in 1027. At this council the ban was defined in terms similar to those utilized at Le Puy with the addition that anyone who died while under this sentence could not have his

20 Mansi, 19:503–6.
21 Ibid., pp. 535–36.
22 Ibid., pp. 544–46.
23 Ibid., pp. 89–90, and Letaldus of Micy, *Delatio corporis s. Juniani ad synodem Karoffensem, Patrologia Latina* [*PL*], ed. J.P. Migne, 217 vols. (Paris, 1841–64), 13:823–26.
24 Mansi, 19:267–68, and *Chartes et documents*, 1:108.
25 Magnou-Nortier, "La place du concile du Puy," p. 499.

name recited in the prayers for the dead and would be automatically condemned to damnation.[26]

The most extensive discussion of excommunication, however, is to be found in the corpus of Ademar of Chabannes. His commentary demonstrates the seriousness with which contemporaries approached this threat and the power it possessed to bind souls to damnation. In several of his sermons, Ademar discusses the use of excommunication by the bishops of the Peace councils. In one sermon referring to the Council of Limoges of 994, Ademar reveals the importance of spiritual sanctions for these synods by demonstrating the association of the cult of the saints and the use of the ban. The events of this assembly included the translation of the relics of St. Martial and the display of miracles by the saint.[27] Having displayed the relics of St. Martial, the bishops warned the people of Aquitaine to cease their sinful ways, obey the peace, reject violence and respect the safety of the poor. They declared that peace breakers would be cast from the Church, refused communion, deprived of association with others and marked by perpetual infamy until they sought reconciliation and were received by the bishop.[28] Ademar notes that those who violated the peace would be cursed by the Church just as those who obeyed the Peace would be blessed. Moreover, the association of Martial with the council and its sanctions suggested that the violators of the Peace of God would suffer the malediction of the Church on earth and the saints in heaven. Clearly, these spiritual sanctions were employed to coerce the knights into accepting the council's decrees by otherwise depriving them of the comfort of the Church and the protection of the saints.

Ademar's corpus holds further attraction on this matter because it provides an example of the conciliar leaders' willingness to use the interdict and extend the penalty of excommunication from individuals to the entire community.[29] After discussing the Council of Limoges of 994, Ademar records the use of the interdict by Bishop Alduin to punish "the sins of the people, the rapine of the

---

26 Mansi, 19:484; Karen Kennelly, C.S.J., "Catalan Peace and Truce Assemblies," *Studies in Culture* 5(1975): 42.
27 BN, MS Lat. 2469, ff. 87r–88v, edited in Delisle, pp. 293–96. The association of the Peace with the cult of the saints appears in another sermon in this manuscript on ff. 96r–97r. This sermon also demonstrates the use of simple excommunication and general interdict.
28 BN, MS Lat. 2469, f. 88r.
29 Bull, pp. 48–50, notes that this was the more serious penalty imposed by the Peace councils and was aimed at the great powers of Aquitaine. Although recognizing the seriousness of excommunication, he argues that the use of the interdict further proves the elite focus of the Peace Movement because this tool was used to coerce the powerful. He fails to consider the impact that the interdict would have had on the *milites*, the vassals of the powerful, and the frequent reference to excommunication of individuals in the sources. The use of both weapons, it may be argued, demonstrates the concern of the Church to persuade the high and low members of the warrior class to support the Peace or suffer eternal damnation.

knights and the devastation of the poor."[30] A more detailed conversation on the use of the interdict appears in the Council of Limoges in 1031. Following their discussion of excommunication, the bishops, according to Ademar, turned their attention to the interdict and agreed to impose it if the *principes militiae* refused to uphold the Peace. Once imposed, the interdict would prohibit the public performance of the mass, baptism, marriage, burial and other sacramental offices.[31] Churches would be closed and altars and all holy objects would be removed from public view.[32] The bishops eased the burden by agreeing to lift the interdict as each prince returned to the fold rather than waiting to lift it once all had returned.[33] However it was to be applied, the fathers of the Council of Limoges, according to Ademar, signaled their readiness to use the interdict, as well as simple excommunication, against peace breakers.

The evidence from the councils demonstrates that excommunication was thought to be a powerful instrument of coercion by the clergy who imposed it. Evidence suggests that the laity too understood the penalties excommunication carried and that, therefore, they would follow the dictates of the Peace councils. Fulk Nerra, perhaps the most ferocious warrior of this violent age, understood the danger of excommunication to his soul and undertook pilgrimage to avoid this penalty.[34] Ademar, moreover, notes the numerous pilgrimages undertaken by the warriors of Aquitaine. Viscount Guy of Limoges went as a pilgrim to the Holy Land and Duke William traveled to Rome, Compostella and Jerusalem.[35] William, count of Angoulême, undertook pilgrimage to Jerusalem in 1026 with a great crowd of lay and ecclesiastical nobles (*magna caterva nobilium*).[36] Although Ademar does not indicate that these pilgrims had been anathematized by the Church, it may be that they, like Fulk Nerra, were motivated by more than purely pious impulses and were concerned also with avoiding the penalty of excommunication.

Descriptions of burial practices provide more evidence that excommunication was an effective weapon because of the knights' concerns for their own salvation. The knights recognized that proper Christian burial was essential to the well-being of their souls. Ademar offers several examples in his *Chronicon* of warriors who sought burial in consecrated ground. Arnold, count of Angoulême, and William Iron-Arm, duke of Aquitaine, adopted the monastic habit late in life to secure the blessings of dying while in orders and to obtain

---

[30] Ademar, *Chronique*, p. 158, bk. 3, c. 35.
[31] Mansi, 19:541–42.
[32] Ibid., p. 542.
[33] Ibid.
[34] Bernard Bachrach, *Fulk Nerra, the Neo-Roman Consul, 987–1040* (Berkeley, 1993), p. 114.
[35] Ademar, *Chronique*, pp. 156–57, bk. 3, c. 40–41.
[36] Ibid., p. 189, bk. 3, c. 65.

burial in the monastery's cemetery.[37] Aldebert, count of Perigord, whose martial activities led to his death, was buried in holy ground at Charroux.[38]

In the *procès-verbal* of the Council of Limoges, Ademar furnishes several examples of the knightly desire for Christian burial. He tells of a viscount who was killed while excommunicated and who was then refused burial in a cemetery despite the pleas of his knights.[39] He also repeated the legend first told by the bishop of Cahors of a knight who was excommunicated by the Council of Bourges, died, and was then buried by his own knights at the church of St. Peter. After the knights several times reburied the corpse which had each time been flung from holy ground by divine intervention, they accepted the judgement of God; as a result, they interred the body far from the church.[40] Thus, despite Bull's arguments, it is clear that the bishops used excommunication to force the knights to accept the Peace and that the knights did so because of their own religious convictions.

The Peace councils employed another spiritual instrument to obtain the obedience of the knightly class: the sacred oath.[41] The oath was a traditional means to secure order and an intrinsic part of feudal society as it developed in the eleventh century. It was a ritual of great religious power because it invoked divine intervention.[42] Violators of the oath were guilty of the grave sins of sacrilege and perjury and were promised terrible punishments for those sins.[43] The knights, well aware of the awesome power of the sacred oath, swore fidelity to their lords and obedience at the councils. Indeed, because the oath was a common means of establishing ties within the warrior elite, it became an important tool of the Peace Movement.

Examples of bishops obtaining oaths from knights and nobles can be found in many conciliar records. Ademar tells us that the first meeting at Limoges concluded with the duke and his princes swearing an oath of peace and justice.[44] In the decades to follow, oaths would be taken by the princes at a number of councils. At Poitiers, "the duke and other princes swore this restoration of peace and justice and gave hostages and accepted the threat of excommunication."[45] Around 1025, William of Angoulême obtained oaths of

---

37 Ibid., pp. 156–57, bk. 3, c. 40–41.
38 Ibid., p. 156, bk. 3, c. 34.
39 Mansi, 19:540–41.
40 Ibid., p. 541.
41 Interestingly, Bull fails to consider the use and significance of the oath in his discussion of the Peace Movement.
42 Callahan, "The Peace of God and the Cult of the Saints," pp. 172, 176–77, and François Louis Ganshof, *Frankish Institutions under Charlemagne*, trans. Bryce Lyon (Providence RI, 1968), pp. 86–90.
43 Duby, *The Three Orders*, p. 28, and Heinrich Fichtenau, *Living in the Tenth Century: Mentalities and Social Orders*, trans. Patrick J. Geary (Chicago, 1991), pp. 412–15.
44 Ademar, *Chronique*, p. 158, bk. 3, c. 35.
45 Mansi, 19:267.

peace from two of his vassals and, in 1028, all the princes of Aquitaine swore to uphold the peace at the Council of Charroux.[46] In the 1030s, Rodulfus Glaber observed, "the great, middling and poor" vowed to preserve the Peace at councils throughout Aquitaine.[47] Much like excommunication, the oath became a tool of the Peace Movement, used to guarantee the obedience of the knights.

The importance of swearing an oath at the councils is further established by Ademar in his sermons. In two homilies celebrating the events of 994, Ademar asserted that the laity, including the nobles and high born, had sworn to uphold the peace.[48] He argued that not only at the assembly of 994 but at all the sessions of the Peace in Limoges, such oaths and pacts of peace had been taken. In one sermon purportedly written for a council in 1031, he asserts that the bishops, common people, princes and nobles of Aquitaine joined to confirm a pact of peace.[49] In another sermon, Ademar describes the activities of an assembly which closed with the bishop's order that all present at the council swear an oath to preserve peace and justice.[50] Furthermore, in Ademar's version of the events of 1031, Bishop Jordan is said to have recalled an earlier council held in 1028 to celebrate the dedication of the church of the Holy Savior. At this assembly, the bishops, princes and nobles had confirmed a pact of peace.[51] According to Ademar, the "knights, princes and captains of the people" attending the later Council of Limoges repeated this earlier oath to preserve the Peace of God.[52]

Swearing of oaths became a prominent feature of the Peace councils precisely because it could secure the fundamental goal of curtailing the violence of the knights. Indeed, as Geoffrey Koziol notes, the oaths "targeted those who violated the sanctuary of churches or seized the livestock of other lords' peasants or burned houses or destroyed mills."[53] Although the nobles took the oath of peace, it was clear that it was designed to restrict the violence of castellans and knights. And it is equally clear that the knights themselves took the oath at the Peace councils. The accounts of the various assemblies record the involvement of nobles in the ritual of the oath of peace. There are further observations that all members of the laity of Aquitaine attended the councils and swore the oath. Ademar, in his *procès-verbal* of the Council of Limoges, portrayed Jordan addressing the *milites* directly, encouraging them to act like

---

[46] Ademar, *Chronique*, pp. 186, 194, bk. 3, c. 60, 69.

[47] *Rodulfi Glabri Historiarum Libri Quinque*, ed. and trans. John France (Oxford, 1989), pp. 194–97, bk. 4, c. 15–16.

[48] BN, MS Lat. 2469, ff. 86v–88r.

[49] Ibid., f. 89r.

[50] Ibid., ff. 91v–92r.

[51] Mansi, 19:526–28.

[52] Ibid., pp. 529–30.

[53] Geoffrey Koziol, *Begging Pardon and Favor Ritual and Political Order in Early Medieval France* (Ithaca NY, 1992), pp. 134–37.

Zaccheus by returning all they had seized to the rightful owners. The bishop then praised the peace and exhorted the "princes and captains of the people" to swear the oath.[54] Thus, at Limoges and the other Peace assemblies, all the laity, including the dukes, the counts and, especially, the knights, took a vow to preserve the peace.

The religious sanction of excommunication and the oath were reinforced by an even greater spiritual power: the cult of the saints.[55] Saintly relics were the centerpiece of the assemblies and their physical presence inspired awe among those in attendance, including the knights. The importance of saints and their relics in early medieval spirituality cannot be overstated.[56] As the focus of regional devotion, the saint's cult provided a sense of community to its adherents in an often tumultuous age. The saint's shrine was a center of pilgrimage at which prodigies, miracles and healings frequently occurred. Because the cult of the saints was the object of intense devotion and religious enthusiasm, the inclusion of saints' relics at the Peace assemblies drew all orders of clergy and laity together at these meetings and provided heavenly sanction for the movement.

Elements of the "sanctified peace" appeared at the earliest councils and became increasingly prominent at the later councils.[57] As Letaldus of Micy explains in his account of the translation of St. Junianus, relics were an important element at the Council of Charroux. The relics of numerous saints were translated to the meeting in 989 where they performed great miracles and several cures to show their support for the Peace.[58] Throughout the early decades of the eleventh century, the association of saints' relics and Peace assemblies continued, reaching its culmination in the great councils of the

---

54 Mansi, 19:529.
55 The importance of the cult of the saints for the movement is most effectively demonstrated by Bernard Töpfer, "The Cult of Relics and Pilgrimage in Burgundy and Aquitaine at the Time of the Monastic Reform," in Head and Landes, *The Peace of God*, pp. 41–57. See also Callahan, "The Peace of God and the Cult of the Saints," pp. 168–79; Landes, "Between Aristocracy and Heresy," pp. 184–218; Bull (pp. 39–42) also recognizes the importance of saints' cults for the Peace Movement but fails to recognize the cult's impact on the knights and the general population.
56 There has been much useful work on the cult of the saints in the Middle Ages. See Peter Brown, *The Cult of the Saints: Its Rise and Function in Latin Christianity* (Chicago, 1981); Heinrich Ficthenau, "Zum Reliquienwesen im früheren Mittelalter," *Mitteilungen des Institutes für Osterreichische Geschichtsforschung* 60(1952): 60–89; Patrick Geary, *Furta Sacra: Thefts of Relics in the Central Middle Ages* (Princeton, 1990); Thomas Head, *Hagiography and the Cult of the Saints* (Cambridge, 1990); Nicole Herrmann-Mascard, *Les Reliques des saints: Formation coutumière d'un droit*, Collection d'histoire institutionnelle et sociale, 6 (Paris, 1975) and Raymond Van Dam, *Saints and their Miracles in Late Antique Gaul* (Princeton NJ, 1993).
57 Bisson, p. 293.
58 *Delatio, PL,* 137:823–26.

1030s.[59] In Aquitaine at the millennium of the Passion, Rodulfus Glaber reports, great councils occurred "to which were borne the bodies of many saints and innumerable caskets of relics."[60] The saints performed miracles at these councils, healing many sick people and restoring abundance to the fields.[61] In this way, the popularity of the cult of the saints attracted the laity to the councils and encouraged the co-operation of the clergy and the warrior class.

The most important evidence concerning the presence of relics and the operation of saintly power at the councils comes from the corpus of Ademar. His account of the Council of Limoges shows the interconnection between the cult of the saints and the Peace Movement.[62] At this meeting, the bishops, the duke and his retainers came together before the people of Aquitaine to petition the aid of the saints in ending a plague of the "fire sickness" and in affirming the peace. Only after the procession of the relics of St. Martial and other saints was the sickness cured and the peace concluded. Thus Ademar reveals the growing awareness in his day that only under the patronage of a great saint could the peace be effectively instituted.

Ademar's sermons provide the most dramatic proof for the importance of saints' relics in the Peace councils. In several sermons commemorating councils held in Limoges, Ademar describes the miraculous intervention of the saints.[63] He reports that great prodigies and supernatural events took place as relics were being translated to the meeting or at a saint's tomb while the Peace council was taking place. The sermons also reveal the exalted status St. Martial had achieved because of his position as the patron of the Peace Movement.[64] Although the attempt to declare Martial an apostle failed, it is unlikely that such a radical step would have been taken had the people of Limoges not recognized the special place Martial had assumed in their movement. He guaranteed the peace in 994 and would continue to secure it as the appeal of his cult grew in the first decades of the eleventh century. Indeed, Ademar's obsession with the cult of St. Martial and the association of his patron with the Peace Movement is only an extreme expression of the attitude that his contemporaries, secular and religious, held in regard to Martial and the cult of saints.

The dramatic growth in the cult of St. Martial and the general popularity of the cult of saints further illustrate the importance of relics for the Peace Movement. The inclusion of relics at the assemblies attracted the attention and support of the people of Aquitaine. Clearly, the cult of saints did not appeal only

---

59 For further discussion see Töpfer, pp. 44–52; Landes, "Between Aristocracy and Heresy," pp. 191–205.
60 *Rodulfi Glabri Historiarum*, pp. 194–95, bks. 4, 5, c. 14.
61 Ibid., pp. 196–97, bks. 4, 5, c. 16.
62 Ademar, *Chronique*, p. 158, bk. 3, c. 35.
63 BN, MS Lat. 2469, ff. 77v–78v, 87r–88v and 90v–92v.
64 For discussion of Martial's role as peace-bearer and further references from Ademar's sermons see Callahan, "Ademar de Chabannes et la Paix," pp. 38–42.

to the clergy and nobility, but to all members of society. At all levels of society, people understood the awesome might of the saints and feared their vengeance. Indeed, the incorporation of the saints' relics into the Peace Movement was one of the most effective ways its leaders had to enforce the goals of the Peace on all members of society, including the knights.

The cult of saints offered the leaders of the movement one further powerful weapon: popular participation in the councils.[65] Indeed, contemporary accounts reveal the attendance of great crowds at council meetings. Attracted by the saints' relics and a desire for order, the *populus* made a significant contribution to the success of the Peace. Here again, Bull fails to consider the full implications of the role of the *populus* in the Peace Movement.

Chronicles of the movement testify to the presence of large crowds of people at the councils of Charroux, Le Puy, Elne-Toulouges, and Poitiers.[66] It is Rodulfus Glaber who provides one of the most dramatic accounts of the active involvement of the people at the councils of Aquitaine.[67] Upon hearing of these assemblies, the people, "great, middling and poor, came rejoicing and ready, one and all, to obey the commands of the clergy."[68] So great was the popular enthusiasm that, when the bishop raised his crozier in celebration, the crowd proclaimed in one voice "Peace! Peace! Peace!"[69] This clearly prefigured popular activity at the crusader councils.

In his *Chronicon* and his sermons, Ademar discussed the active role taken by throngs of laity of all ranks at the councils. Indeed, as he showed in his account of the terrible trampling of fifty people at a church in Limoges in 1018, crowds were a common feature of religious ceremonies during the first decades of the eleventh century.[70] Evidence of popular participation also appeared in Ademar's account of the discovery of the relics of John the Baptist in 1010, which were displayed at a great assembly held by the duke and the bishops and attended by "numerous princes and an innumerable amount of people."[71] The translation of John and the other saints very clearly recalls the sanctified Peace councils themselves. Although Ademar mentions no oath associated with the event, he describes this celebration in terms very similar to those of the Peace assemblies and identifies the participation of lay and religious leaders, saints'

---

65 Landes, "Between Aristocracy and Heresy," pp. 194–205; Loren C. MacKinney, "The People and Public Opinion in the Eleventh-Century Peace Movement," *Speculum* 5(1930): 181–206; Sargent, pp. 222–28; and Töpfer, pp. 41–57.
66 For Charroux, see Mansi, 19:89 and *PL*, 137:823–26; for Le Puy, Magnou-Nortier, "Place du Concile du Puy," p. 499; for Elne-Toulouges, Mansi, 19:483; and for Poitiers, Mansi, 19:265 and *Chartes et documents*, 1:108.
67 *Rodulphi Glabri Historiarum*, pp. 194–97, bks. 4, 5, c. 14–16.
68 Ibid., pp. 194–95, bks. 4, 5, c. 14.
69 Ibid., pp. 196–97, bks. 4, 5, c. 16.
70 Ademar, *Chronique*, p. 173, bk. 3, c. 49. See also Landes, "Between Aristocracy and Heresy," pp. 202–13.
71 Ademar, *Chronique*, pp. 179–82, bk. 3, c. 56. See also Sargent, pp. 225–28.

relics and, especially, the *populus*. However we should define the translation of John's relics, this event and the trampling of 1018 reveal the religious enthusiasm of the laity and their involvement in religious ceremonies.

Ademar provides further evidence for the activities of the laity in his sermons and account of the Council of Limoges. The crowd assumes an important role in his discussion of the life of St. Martial. He often cites the great numbers of pagans converted by St. Martial when he preached in Aquitaine. There are several incidents in which St. Martial supposedly converted and baptized large numbers of people including twenty-two thousand followers of Duke Stephen.[72] In several sermons, Ademar recounts the attendance of the people at the Peace councils.[73] He identified all lay groups and the *vulgaris plebs* which attended the councils.[74] In one sermon, he noted that he could not continue his discourse on the mysteries of the faith because of the presence of people who might misunderstand his teaching and fall into error.[75] Finally, there are several references in Ademar's *procès-verbal* to the attendance of the people at the Council of Limoges in 1031. He notes that "all the people of Limoges came together at this assembly to celebrate the dedication of the cathedral church and to declare the peace."[76]

The appearance of the *populus* in the accounts of the Peace councils has two important consequences. First, the crowd was another tool used by the leaders of the movement to accomplish their goals. The great crowds of the laity could act as a counterweight to backsliding knights and nobles who failed to uphold their vow to protect the Peace. The active participation of the lower orders of society provided the leaders with a powerful group of supporters who could be organized into an army to make war on war.[77] Although no match militarily for the knights, the multitude of peasants could be a great psychological weapon to enforce the goals of the Peace and curtail knightly violence. Furthermore, the appearance of the *populus* at the councils suggests that it was not only the leaders of the Peace Movement who were attracted by its ideals and by the saintly relics which were brought out to support them. Although directed by the duke and bishops of Aquitaine, the active participation of the crowd indicates that devotion to the cult of the saints was practiced by society as a whole. Acceptance of the spiritual rewards and punishments meted out by the saints was a fundamental component of the ideology of the Peace Movement

---

72 BN, MS Lat. 2469, ff. 53v–55v, 57r, 58r, 62r–63r, 81r and 86r. Bull (pp. 40–41) appears to neglect the importance of popular participation in the Peace Movement and to undervalue the role of the knights at the councils.

73 BN, MS Lat. 2469, ff. 87r–94r.

74 Ibid., f. 89r.

75 DS, MS Lat. Phillipps 1664, f. 123v.

76 Mansi, 19:508.

77 Thomas Head, "The Judgment of God: Andrew of Fleury's Account of the Peace League of Bourges," in Head and Landes, *The Peace of God*, pp. 219–38.

and any success it had was due to the general recognition of the saints' support
for the movement. The enthusiastic involvement of the crowd at the councils
is evidence that all members of the laity, including the knights, embraced the
ideals of the movement.

Although the Peace League of Bourges may have brought to an end one
phase of the Peace of God, the ideals of the movement continued in the Truce
of God and in smaller manifestations during the decades after 1038.[78] Of
greatest significance is a continuing concern for the ideals voiced at these early
councils. Those ideals represented the beginnings of a broad movement that
would realize their most dramatic manifestations in the Gregorian Reform and
the Crusades. Indeed, the Peace itself helped to shape the idea of knighthood
by restricting the legitimate focus of feudal violence. To accomplish this end,
the leaders of society forged an alliance at the Peace councils drawing on the
support of the *populus* and employing the spiritual sanctions of excommunication, the oath and the cult of saints. These very methods influenced the behavior
of the knights themselves who, with the great nobles and common people, must
surely have participated in the councils where they encountered a code of
conduct which would redefine knighthood itself and lay the foundation for the
idea of crusade.

[78] For the continued influence of the ideals of the Peace see Cowdrey, 56–67; Geoffrey
Koziol, "Monks, Feuds, and the Making of the Peace in Eleventh-Century Flanders,"
in Head and Landes, *The Peace of God*, pp. 239–58; and Remensnyder, pp. 280–307.

The Friar Tuck Syndrome:
Clerical Violence and the Barons' War

JAMES R. KING

The very question of clerical involvement with violence in medieval Europe should be something of an anomaly, since the essence of the vocation of the cleric was spiritual and therefore, non-violent in nature. In all truth, that should have been especially the case for the thirteenth century, since it had witnessed the appearance of one of the most important models of spirituality among the clergy to appear at any time or place in the person of St. Francis of Assisi. By the mid-years of the century, his followers had spread his manner of spiritual devotion to every corner of Europe. In England, they were established in almost every significant town by 1250. On the other hand, the period was also responsible for the origins of that tale of adventurous derring-do involving Robin Hood and his merry men which included the rather enthusiastically violent cleric, Friar Tuck.[1] Although clerical participation in warfare was common enough in the early Middle Ages, from the time of the investiture controversy in the eleventh century, the reform element in the western Church had worked diligently to suppress such activity among the clergy and to make them conform to the spiritual and non-violent mode of behavior which was more appropriate for men of the Church. So how successful were they? Was it St. Francis or Friar Tuck who provided the most attractive model for the thirteenth-century cleric?

In the case of England, a substantial body of evidence exists to suggest that it was Friar Tuck. Furthermore, the evidence demonstrates that it was not only ordinary members of the lesser clergy who were willing to resort to violence to obtain their ends. Perhaps the most amusing and clearest incident involving the potential extent of clerical violence occurred in the case of a dispute between the archbishop of Canterbury, Boniface of Savoy, and the canons of St. Paul's, London. In 1250, the prelate attempted to enforce his metropolitan rights with

---

[1] There is, of course, a great body of scholarship involving the character of Robin Hood. For different interpretations, see R. H. Hilton, "The Origins of Robin Hood," *Past and Present* 17(1959): 22–49; J. C. Holt, "The Origins and Audience of the Ballads of Robin Hood," *Past and Present* 18(1960): 89–107; and Maurice Keen, "Robin Hood – Peasant or Gentleman," *Past and Present* 19(1961): 7–15 and esp. 14.

regard to the canons of the cathedral and, in the process of doing so, Boniface and his entourage became involved in a pushing match with the canons as he tried to force his way into their residence. During the struggle which followed, his clerical robes gaped open to reveal that under them the archbishop was wearing a full suit of body armor.[2] It is apparent that Boniface clearly represented the traditions of the warrior archbishop Turpin of the *Song of Roland* far more than those of the ecclesiastical reformers of his day.

It was the events of the barons' war, or Simon de Montfort's rebellion as it is sometimes called, that truly illustrated the willingness of the English clergy, at least, to engage in violence with all the enthusiasm of their lay counterparts. The barons' war was a conflict which inspired intense support by the clergy as opponents of the king and his party.[3] Five of the seventeen bishops of England were totally identified with the movement and another five generally supported it.[4] Furthermore, nearly all the monastic houses in the realm were willing to identify themselves with the movement. For my part, however, it was the activity of the lesser clergy which inspired my greatest interest and it was the investigation of that support which led directly to evidence of violent behavior on their part which was far too general to ignore.

The pattern of violence and disorder associated with the barons' war spanned the years from 1263 until 1267. It included the major battles of Lewes and Evesham, several significant sieges of the strongholds of partisans of both sides, and a general tendency toward violent attacks on the property of partisans and innocent by-standers alike. After being defeated and captured at the battle of Lewes in the spring of 1264, King Henry III lost control of his government to the rebel leaders until their own total defeat by his son Edward at Evesham

---

2 Mandall Creighton, "Boniface of Savoy," *The Dictionary of National Bibliography* [*DNB*], ed. Leslie Stephen and Sidney Lee (London, 1908–1909), 2:812–14.

3 The barons' war was studied most extensively by R. F. Treharne. His published work on the subject includes: *The Baronial Plan of Reform, 1258–1263* (Manchester, 1932); "The Significance of the Baronial Reform Movement," *Transactions of the Royal Historical Society* [*TRHS*], 4th ser. 25(1943): 35–72; "The Personal Role of Simon de Montfort in the Period of Baronial Reform and Rebellion, 1258–1265," *Proceedings of the British Academy* 40(1955): 75–102; *Simon de Montfort and Baronial Reform* (Rio Grande OH, 1986). It was treated extensively by Sir Maurice Powicke in his volume for *Oxford History of England: The Thirteenth Century* (Oxford, 1962); and idem, *King Henry III and the Lord Edward*, 2 vols., (Oxford, 1947). See volumes in the *Thirteenth Century England* series (Woodbridge, Suffolk, 1985–). The most important contributions which relate to the issues here are the work of D. A. Carpenter and Huw Ridgeway.

4 In late 1265, eight of the seventeen bishops of England were sued by the king's attorneys for their involvement in the rebellion, Public Record Office, London [PRO], King's Bench [KB] 174, m. 2d (49 Henry III). These cases are included in *Placitorum in Domo Capitulari Westmonasteriensi Asservatorum Abbreviatio Temporibus Regum Ricardi, Johannis, Henrici III, Edwardi I, Edwardi II* (London, 1831), p. 159. The eight were the bishops of Durham, Ely, Lincoln, London, Chichester, Winchester, Salisbury, and Worcester. (Technically KB is the modern Public Record Office designation for what were once known as the *Curia Regis Rolls*.)

in early August 1265. Although rebel strongholds held out against his forces for nearly two more years, particularly at Kenilworth and in the Isle of Ely, the king was able to begin the process of identifying and punishing his enemies by the autumn of 1265. In doing so, his government produced the evidence which enables us to get a glimpse of the activity of individuals who usually remain anonymous, that is, the lesser members of society.

The tendency of the historical record to focus almost entirely on the leaders of society presents a maddening problem for social historians of the Middle Ages. Only occasionally do the lesser individuals in society make an appearance in the surviving evidence. In this case, however, there is a substantial group of records which allows us a broader view than is normally possible. They were produced as a result of the king's determination to discover and identify his enemies and friends coupled with the growing efficiency of the English royal government in its ability to do the king's will.

The origin of those records was an almost mad, disorganized pattern of confiscation of property from rebels and supposed rebels with the subsequent wholesale granting of those lands to royal favorites and supporters immediately after the defeat and death of Simon de Montfort at Evesham. The process became so unpredictable that Henry III was quickly forced to order an inquest in order to protect his own interests. The inquest was produced by the appointment of local knights known as *seisitores* who had the responsibility of handling the disposition of rebel lands in their vicinity and of determining the names and holdings of the rebels in the same region.[5] Although a few clerics turn up in that inquest, most were ignored because few members of the clergy held lay fees.

For clerics as well as the great majority of lesser individuals involved in the rising, the most effective source of information is the records of the royal courts, which quickly became active after Evesham because of the royal determination to punish acts of violence which occurred during the struggle. Unfortunately, while the legal records contain an enormous amount of information which goes far beyond the details of the functioning of the law, they are very difficult to interpret clearly. No one has managed to express the problems posed in their use more effectively than S. F. C. Milsom who remarked that "it is the property of legal sources, especially from the Middle Ages, that they will tell the investigator nearly everything except what he wants to know."[6] While it is difficult to judge the validity of his comment for all the Middle Ages, it is

---

5 The returns are included in the first volume of the *Calendar of Inquisition, Miscellaneous (Chancery)* [*CIMC*], 3 vols. (London, 1916). For a careful analysis of the inquest see, E. F. Jacob, *Studies in the Period of Baronial Reform and Rebellion, 1258–1267*, vol. 7 of *Oxford Studies in Social and Legal History*, ed. P. Vinogradoff, 7 vols. (Oxford, 1925), pp. 150–51.

6 In his introduction to the re-issue of the second edition of Frederick Pollock and Frederic William Maitland's *The History of English Law before the Time of Edward I*, 2 vols. (Cambridge, 1968), 1:xxv.

very accurate for the records of 1265–1272. And so we know that during the period from the autumn of 1265 until the end of 1268 when the royal courts involved were full of cases generated by the rebellion, they were almost never able to produce a decision. We know, on the other hand, who it was who brought the suit, who was sued, and what injuries were alleged to have been inflicted. Although that information is essential it would be much more meaningful if we could find a judgment by the court. Moreover, while the record is silent on the crucial issue of guilt or innocence, it is full of information about which we have only a marginal interest. It records in great detail the names of all those men pledged as surety by the parties for their appearance in court. Such information was essential for the court; unfortunately, details about the actual incident involved in the case were not.

In the past two decades, two efforts have been made to use English legal records to study the social phenomenon of crime and violence. James Given has surveyed the nature of homicide in thirteenth-century England, while Barbara Hanawalt focused her study on crime in the early fourteenth century. Their efforts were subsequently intensely assessed by Edward Powell, and his comments also apply to the records of 1265–1272.[7] Powell's primary criticism of both Given and Hanawalt was that they relied far too much on evidence which was inadequately analyzed. Undoubtedly, both would equally dispute that criticism.[8] The issue of the validity of the records, which is the essence of Powell's criticism of Given and Hanawalt's methodology, is particularly troubling because the use of the legal records from the period of the barons' war presents all the problems common to their studies. Powell pointed out that Hanawalt in particular treated even those acquitted as being guilty for the purposes of her study.[9] In truth, criminal records always pose the ever troubling issue of guilt since even the most obtuse defender of the legal process is aware that whenever a verdict of guilty is rendered we are still left with the sure and certain knowledge that sometimes the guilty are found innocent and the innocent guilty. Whether such an injustice occurs as a result of error or because of bias on the part of jurors we can only guess. Because the legal records of the period 1265–1272 are by far the most extensive source we have for the activity of the partisans of both sides, the issue of their validity must be addressed.

The legal records relating to the barons' war were first surveyed many years ago by E. F. Jacob. He pointed out that they fall into two groups. The first group consisted of suits brought before the justices of the King's Bench beginning with the Michaelmas term of 1265 and lasting until after the death of Henry III

---

7   Barbara A. Hannawalt, *Crime and Conflict in English Communities, 1300–1348* (Cambridge MA, 1979); James Buchanan Given, *Society and Homicide in Thirteenth-Century England* (Stanford, 1977); and Edward Powell, "Social Research and the Use of Medieval Criminal Records," *Michigan Law Review* 79(1981): 967–78.
8   Powell, pp. 971–73.
9   Ibid., p. 971.

in 1272.[10] The second group emanated from a special eyre commissioned by the king in September 1267 to deal exclusively with problems concerning the rebellion. This second group of records are known from the terms of the royal commission which established the eyre *de terris datis et occupatis*. The justices of the eyre were charged both to hear cases arising from disputes over the lands of rebels confiscated and regranted after Evesham and to investigate trespasses which had occurred as a result of the uprising.[11] They were provided with a list of questions to put to local jurors, queries of the conventional sort in such circumstances.[12] These queries concern the identification of supporters of the earl of Leicester, of those who had committed robberies, arson, and murder of loyal subjects, of neutrals who had suffered at the hands of rebels, and so on. One is of particular interest with regard to the clergy. The justices were specifically enjoined to determine who among the archbishops, bishops, and all men of religion of any rank whatsoever had aided or abetted Simon de Montfort in any way.[13] There can be little doubt that royal officials knew about extensive clerical support for the rebellion since clerics most certainly fell under the other questions of the inquest. The clergy, moreover, were the only group in the entire realm to be so singled out.

The presentments produced by the *de terris datis* inquests are therefore a major source for the activity of the clergy during the period. There are two other categories of evidence which grew out of the eyre. First, there are records concerning the status of lands regranted after the rebellion, and contested in a series of lawsuits. Such cases rarely involved the clergy since they seldom had lands other than their benefices. The second category of evidence involved records which alleged the commission of some sort of violence during the disturbance. The records detailing violence are almost identical to the property suits brought before the justices of the King's Bench. It is thus the presentments which give the *de terris datis* rolls their special interest. On every roll there are usually as many presentments as suits recorded while at times they are the most frequent sort of entry.

The use of the presentments as historical evidence involves almost all the problems which are characteristic of the legal sources generally. For example, we are at best forced to accept the word of men who might themselves have

---

10 George O. Sayles printed a suit for lands under the terms of the *Dictum of Kenilworth* from the Michaelmas term of 1275, brought by Robert de Ferrars against Roger Lestrange: *Select Cases in the Court of King's Bench* (London, 1936), 1:20–21.

11 Jacob, pp. 162–63.

12 Included in T. Stapleton, ed., *Liber de Antiquiis Legibus, seu Chronica maiorum et Vicecomitum Londoniarum* (London, 1846), p. 96.

13 Ibid., "La in enquerra ausibien des Erveskes, Eveskes, de tute gens de religion, de quel ordre ke il seient, cum de persones et de gens prestres a de clers e de tute autre manere de genz, ki ce sunt, ki apertement procurerent de busenies de Cunte de Leicestre, et cels ke tindrent ad lui en atrent le gent par menconges et par faucetes, par priser le Counte, et blamer la partie le Rei et sun fiz."

been involved in the struggle. Some loyalists may have concocted charges of trespass against old enemies who may or may not have been rebel sympathizers. Others were so sympathetic to the baronial movement that they were not only active in the rebellion, but afterwards refused to respond to the inquest. E. F. Jacob cited a number of these: the townships of Brill, Amersham, and Marlow in Buckinghamshire; the hundreds of Kennetbury and Hungerford in Berkshire; six townships in Norfolk; and Bury St. Edmunds in Suffolk.[14] There were doubtless others who, while responding to the inquest, slanted their answers to protect their friends. A rather more confusing characteristic which the inquests share with the great majority of the trespass suits is the failure of the accused party to appear. In such cases the pledges would be amerced, but there is no sure indication about the validity of the charges.[15] As a result, our knowledge of the matter is limited to the simple fact that suspicion had been raised about the individual cited.

We find men cited for a wide variety of crimes from robbery to receiving or buying stolen goods. If the accused party appeared, the jurors quickly returned their verdict, as in the case of Reginald de Hadel who was found guilty of looting the goods of John Mansel, the king's great clerk.[16] The juries were sometimes expanded to twenty-four members when the verdict was sought. In particular, if the alleged act had taken place outside the township or hundred where the presentment was made, an expanded jury of twenty-four men made up of twelve men from each place was often used to return the verdict. Thus when the jurors of the hundred of Wardon in Northamptonshire charged Gerard, vicar of Sulgrave, of receiving in his home looters from the garrison of Kenilworth, the verdict was given by a panel of twenty-four men of that hundred. They rejected his claim that he had been robbed by the men of Kenilworth. They said, instead, that he had conspired with them in the theft of goods from his own parsonage.[17]

In another Northamptonshire case, the jurors of Andfordisho charged that John de Montgomery had robbed clerks coming from Oxford as well as a merchant from Bowell. The jurors of Spello also charged him with being a principal looter. The verdict was returned by a combined jury of the two hundreds. They declared that he had robbed the clerks of a tabard and books

---

14 Jacob, pp. 291–93.
15 The records of the inquest are categorized as Justices Itinerate [PRO, JI] by the Public Record Office. Those that survived are Assize Rolls, Henry III, ff. 42, 59, 83, 237, 569B, 618, 821, and 1207. On the Berkshire roll (PRO, JI 42) this occurs in approximately 20 percent of the cases although sometimes the accused party later appears. A Reginald de Hadel, for example, defaulted causing his pledges to be amerced, and then in a case on the same membrane appeared to answer a charge that he had taken the goods of the justice Nicholas de Yatingdon who was presiding. He was found guilty (PRO, JI 42, m. 1d).
16 PRO, JI 42 m. 2d.
17 PRO, JI 618b, m. 12d. This practice was discussed by Jacob, pp. 197–98.

worth 10 shillings, and that he and others stole goods worth 50 shillings from the merchant.[18] There were also a number of occasions among the Berkshire cases where the accused simply appeared, acknowledged their guilt, and accepted the judgment of the justices.[19]

Even in cases when the jurors returned a verdict of not guilty, they sometimes affirmed that the alleged act had actually taken place. For example, in a Buckinghamshire case heard by the justice Nicholas de Yatingdon and his colleagues, a certain Richard Groscet was accused of stealing from Richard, a chaplain of Hartwell, two boards for book binding. Groscet denied the charge, saying that he had innocently received the boards from Robert, son of Nigel, an enemy of the king. He said that he had known nothing about the robbery. The jurors accepted his plea, but in their verdict they affirmed that the chaplain had indeed been robbed.[20] In a similar case, John fitz Robert of Bery in Cambridgeshire was charged by the jurors from the hundred of Stowe of looting all the goods found in the church of Caxton. Fitz Robert denied the charge and the jurors of Stowe supported his pleas finding instead that the church of Caxton had been robbed by Richard de Lufton and others.[21] Another such case occurred in Suffolk when the jurors of the hundred of Colne presented John de Seincher and John de Hokevile of Boxted for robbing from Thomas, parson of Hemley, goods worth 20 marks. Again the jurors cleared the defendants while affirming that the parson had indeed been robbed.[22]

The actual suits which point to the incidence of clerical involvement with the rebellion were those which alleged the commission of some sort of violence, theft, imprisonment, and so on. They appear in substantial numbers on the *de terris datis* rolls and in great numbers on the rolls of the justices of the King's Bench. Such suits usually contain variations of the following formula:

> X appeared on the fourth day against Y concerning a plea in which it was alleged that during the disturbance that had existed in the realm he came with force and arms to the manor of the aforesaid and carried off goods and chattels.[23]

In some of these cases, the association with the rebellion is indicated by the phrase "after the peace recently proclaimed," and in a few instances the two phrases were even combined. There were also a few passages in which the phrase "time of war" was used.

---

[18] PRO, JI 618b, m. 9.

[19] Typically, *Elyas Pardon de Blebur et Robertus Godrich de eadem recognoverant quod emerunt de bonis predicti Nicholaii depredatis. Ideo in misericordia* (PRO, JI 42 m. 4d).

[20] PRO, JI 59, m. 15.

[21] PRO, JI 83, m. 23d.

[22] PRO, JI 821, m. 5.

[23] See Jacob, p. 202: "X optulit se quarto die versus Y de placito quare vi et armis occasione turbacionis habite in regno venit ad manerium predicti et bona et catella asportavit."

There are many of these suits. Even with the problems of interpreting their meaning, they provide us with the greatest opportunity we have from any records of the period to identify members of the lesser clergy and so to follow their activities during the rebellion. They do indeed present us with formidable problems of interpretation. On the whole, the suits are quite brief. There are few details of the alleged trespasses enumerated in them, and it is only when an occasional defendant appears and denies the allegation that we learn more. Most commonly, they end with the phrase "and he/they did not come," thus denying us any further knowledge of the case. There were more than 750 cases of that sort brought before the justices of the King's Bench between 1265 and 1268. In each one, accusations were made concerning one or more injuries done to the plaintiff, the place where the alleged injuries had been inflicted was noted, one or more defendants were cited by name, and in most but not all instances damages were claimed in a specific amount.

Despite the fact that these suits were framed in accordance with the common form of action known as trespass, they were not brought under that writ. At Windsor during the autumn of 1265, the king's council granted a judicial writ of attachment which was available without cost to those who had suffered damages during the rebellion.[24] Cases identified with the phrases "on the occasion of the disturbance" and "after the peace . . . recently publicly proclaimed" were obviously the product of that writ. There were over one hundred such cases brought before the justices which involved the clergy in some way. During the same period, however, the rolls contain another 250 cases involving the clergy which were identical to the cases mentioning the disturbance except that the relevant identifying phrases were omitted. Upon first examination of the records that omission seems to provide a clear-cut distinction between cases which were the product of the rebellion and ordinary cases of trespass. After closer examination, however, that seemingly obvious distinction begins to blur. There is much evidence that the identifying phrases were not used with sufficient consistency to warrant excluding cases which lacked them from consideration. Needless to say, if all seeming trespass actions from the period could be treated as products of the rebellion, the volume of available evidence would be greatly increased.

The factors which argue for treating all trespass actions generated immediately following the battle of Evesham as probable products of the rebellion derive from the habits of both the plaintiffs and defendants of the period. Because of the reluctance of the defendants to appear, the legal system of the realm was very hard pressed to give satisfaction to the plaintiffs. On the other hand, the plaintiffs of the era were often very determined individuals and so they brought the same suit in term after term. As a result, almost half of the

---

[24] Ibid. See particularly note 2 in which he discusses the council's decision to provide the writ.

cases on the rolls are duplicates of suits brought originally in an earlier term. In those duplicate cases, the identifying phrases were sometimes used and sometimes not. And so, in a suit brought by Nicholas de Haversham against William, parson of Yardley Hastings in Northamptonshire, and other individuals, Nicholas first charged that the trespass took place during the disturbance.[25] When he renewed his suit during the next term of court (Hilary 1267), he used the usual terms associated with actions of trespass, that is, that the defendants had come "with force and arms."[26] All later renewals of the suit identified it with the disturbance.[27]

The confusion of usages appeared also in a suit brought by William le Mortyn against a group including the abbot of Brome. The suit was first brought during the Michaelmas term of 1265 at which time no mention was made of the disturbance.[28] When William renewed his suit for a second time, however, he charged that the events had occurred during the disturbance.[29] The same pattern appeared in a Herefordshire suit from the Michaelmas term of 1266 brought by Nicholas de Hundeslawe against a number of men including Walter Tope, prior of Llanthony Priory. Nicholas initially charged that the defendants came to his lands with force and arms, and robbed him of goods and chattels valued at 60 shillings.[30] He renewed his suit in the following term (Hilary 1267) and again a year later in the Hilary term of 1268; each time states the charge in the same manner. Then suddenly, in the Trinity term of 1268, he

---

[25] PRO, KB 26/177, m. 17.

[26] PRO, KB 26/178, 11d. In two consecutive cases, Nicholas charged large groups, of eleven people in the first instance and seventeen in the second, with intrusion into his manor of Haversham. In the first case, he charged that "ipsi similiter cum aliis occasione turbacionis habite in regno bona et catalla sua in manerio sui de sui de Haversham inventa ceperunt et asportaverunt et manerium illud combusserunt ad dampnum ipsius Nicholi et ad gravemen ut dicit. Et ipsi non venerunt . . ." In the following case, the charge omits the phrase "during the disturbance," but otherwise is almost identical. Again he charged that "ipsi similiter cum aliis vi et armis venerunt ad manerium ipsius Nicholi de Haversham et domos suas combusserunt et arbores parci sui ibidem inventa ad valencia centum librarum ceperunt et asportaverunt contra pacem etc. Et ipsi non venerunt."

[27] PRO, KB 26/181, m. 2; 181, m. 20; 184A, m. 11d; 185, m. 12d; and 186, m. 5d. After this last suit from the Michaelmas term of 1268 the case disappears from the record.

[28] PRO, KB 26/174, m. 15. There were an exceptionally large number of defendants listed in this suit "de placito quare venerunt ad parcum ipius Willelmi de Moryn de Brunneby et omnes arbores eiusdem parci succiderunt et asportaverunt in grave dampnum ipsius Willelmi de contra pacem."

[29] PRO, KB 26/175, m. 17. This appears to be the same suit. The number of defendants was vastly reduced, but the charge remained virtually the same. "De placito quare occasione turbacionis etc . . . venerunt ad boscum predicti Willelmi in Brunesby et boscum succiderunt consumpserunt et asportaverunt in dampnum ipsius Willelmi sexagenta marcarum. Et ipsi non venerunt."

[30] PRO, KB 26/177, m. 24.

charged that the trespass had occurred during the disturbance.[31] It seems apparent that no great precision of form was maintained in the suits of the period.

There are other indications which lead to the same conclusion. There are a number of trespass suits which were brought against royalists in which the actions of the defendants were not attributed to the disturbance, albeit the identity of the litigants makes it clear that political antagonism was the root cause of the incident. In one, a rebel baron named William Bardolf brought a suit against five men including John, parson of Redham in Norfolk, and his brother Oliver, charging them with an assault. William claimed that the accused were men of the abbot of Langley and that when he had tried to take draft animals in accordance with the service owed him by the abbot, they had resisted and beat up his men.[32] By the mid-years of the thirteenth century, there was a major question about the status of feudal service since the power of lords had been under serious attack by the royal government since the introduction of the writ of *precipe* in the reign of Henry II.[33] The connection between feudal service and the rebellion is very unclear from the records which survive. We do know, however, that a common defense offered by many of the individuals presented by the local jurors to the justices of the *de terris datis* inquest was that they had been ordered to go by their lord. In William Bardolf's case, he would not have had access to the free writ because it was not available to rebels. It does make clear that violent behavior was not limited to one side in the struggle.

Another such case involved an important Suffolk rebel, William de Criketot. William was closely associated with the abbot of Bury St. Edmunds from whom he held lands at Ashfield. In this case, feudal service was not rejected since the abbot was among those English monastic leaders most seriously implicated as supporters of the rebellion. William charged in a suit recorded in the Michaelmas term of 1267 that his manors of Kelsale, Fordley, Middleton, and Westleton had been despoiled of goods worth 100 marks by several men including a cleric, a certain Roger, brother of Augustus of Dunwich.[34] As in the

---

31 PRO, KB 26/185, m. 3d. The other entries for this case are PRO, KB 26/178, m. 20d; 182, m. 10; and 186, m. 9d.
32 PRO, KB 26/174, m. 14; and 175, m. 22d. The charges included the rather strong wording of "verberaverunt, vulneraverunt, et maletractaverunt." The suit was brought again in the Easter term of 1268 (184A, m. 17); in Trinity term 1268 (185, m. 1d); and then in three separate entries from the Trinity term of 1269 (189, m. 1d, m. 23d; and 190, m. 2).
33 J. E. A. Jolliffe, *The Constitutional History of Medieval England: From the English Settlement to 1485* (New York, 1961), p. 255.
34 PRO, KB 26/181, m. 12d. William made two attempts through actions of *levari facias* to the bishop of Norwich to cause the cleric Roger, brother of Augustus of Dunwich, to appear. There is no indication that he succeeded (PRO, KB 26/182, m. 4d; and 184A, m. 5).

previous instance, the suit does not specify direct involvement in the disturbance, but it most certainly had been a product of the disorders of the time.

These are among a broad range of cases where the issue of ordinary trespass
and activity associated with the rebellion are regularly confused. As a result, it
is impossible to know with any certainty about the status of any of the trespass
suits of the period. It is certain, on the other hand, that the impact of the
rebellion on the business of the court was overwhelming. The rolls of the
justices of the King's Bench indicate that trespass cases generally amounted to
about 50 to 60 percent of the total number of cases heard during a given term.
That percentage skyrocketed during the period after the autumn of 1265 when
the number of trespass actions accounted for a low of 74 percent in one term to
a high of nearly 90 percent for the Hilary term of 1267. During the same period,
cases with the phrases which clearly identified the action with the rebellion
ranged from one-third to one-half of all trespass actions in each court term. It
was only late in 1268 that the number of trespass suits dropped to the levels
customary prior to the rebellion.

In addition to the lack of any clear certainty about the association of trespass
actions with the rebellion, there are other problems involved with the use of the
legal records. The most serious of these problems was created by the almost
total failure of individuals charged with crimes to appear and defend themselves. When the defendants failed to appear, the law gave no remedy to
plaintiffs other than ordering the sheriff to bring them into court. Yet there is
little evidence that sheriffs and other authorities had much success in doing so.
That left the plaintiffs with only one option, to renew their suit over and over
again. And so, the same suit appears on the rolls for term after term, sometimes
with minor changes, but with no apparent resolution of the case. Considering
the obvious concern of the king's council in providing the special writ for
individuals harmed by the rebellion, it is most unfortunate that this writ seldom
led to any real remedy for the injured parties. While we can sympathize with
the plaintiffs in their frustrations, it becomes an equal frustration for us, since
in most instances our knowledge of the alleged injuries is reduced to the level
of one man's word against another's.

As a result of the failure of defendants to appear, our evidence of the incident
is reduced to the knowledge that a suit was brought which charged that a certain
cleric or group of clerics were alleged to have committed a trespass against the
plaintiff. Of course, even if every suit on the rolls had ended before a jury which
rendered a verdict, we could not be certain that the charges were valid. Innocent
men are convicted in court and guilty men are cleared. On the other hand, the
major problem here is not the miscarriage of justice but the fact that we have
almost no legal decisions whatsoever.

What meaning can be assigned to the accusation of Geoffrey de Percy that
a group of men including two clerics – Richard Ravenscot, parson of the church
of Lyminge, and Thomas, parson of the church of Halstead – looted his manor
of Horton in Kent during the disturbance? As it almost always happened, none

of the accused appeared to answer the suit. Were they guilty? We do not find any evidence of either guilt or innocence.[35] A similar instance occurred in a Hertfordshire suit brought by John de Arcubus against William, parson of Tewin, and several others. John charged that during the disturbance they plundered his manor of Eckington of goods and chattels worth 100 marks. As usual, the defendants failed to appear.[36] Their pledges were amerced and the sheriff was ordered to have them in court in the next term, but the results were essentially the same. When they did not appear, orders were issued to the bishop of Lincoln to make William come to court and to the bailiff of the bishop of Ely to produce the laymen. At that, the record of the case ends and we know nothing more of John's suit.[37]

The frustration associated with non-appearance in these suits is not limited to cases involving the lesser clergy. Even though one would suppose that they had too much to lose by doing so, higher churchmen also failed to appear. For example, during the Michaelmas term of 1265, Henry de Caldecott sued a total of eighteen men of the liberty of Bury St. Edmunds for illegally carrying off his goods and chattels from Aveley during the disturbance. This group included four clerics identified simply as "John, Peter, Benedict, and Hugh le Clerks." While the others were men of no particular interest to us, the first man named in the suit was the abbot of Bury St. Edmunds himself.[38] One might expect that any person as prominent as the abbot would have appeared to defend himself, but he did not. During the following year, Henry de Caldecott renewed his suit against the abbot and the others on several occasions. The last such instance was in the Michaelmas term of 1266.[39] The abbot still refused to appear. He was as willing to ignore such suits as an ordinary ploughman, or the most impoverished of minor clerics.

This problem of non-appearance involved the issue of mesne process which was the most glaring weakness of the royal judicial system.[40] Except for instances like the *Assize of Novel Disseisin*, non-appearance did not result in judgments by default, and so the court was left with very weak mechanisms for getting defendants into court. Thus, the only hope of plaintiffs was to persevere and renew their suits. In cases from the period, involving clerics of all ranks, almost 48 percent of the suits were duplicates. Usually the plaintiffs renewed their suits three or four times and then dropped them. Over 350 suits which

35 PRO, KB 26/178, 11d.
36 PRO, KB 26/174, m. 13d.
37 PRO, KB 26/175, m. 16.
38 PRO, KB 26/174, m. 18.
39 PRO, KB 26/175, m. 16; and 177, m. 24.
40 The problem of mesne process was discussed by Maitland, *History of English Law*, 2:591–95. See also Charles Johnson, "Notes on Thirteenth-Century Judicial Procedure," *EHR* 67(1947): 508–11. For a detailed discussion of the problem, especially with regard to Bracton, see Donald W. Sutherland, "Mesne Process upon Personal Actions in the Early Common Law," *Law Quarterly Review* 82(1966): 482–90.

involved clerics were brought before the justices of the King's Bench during the years after the battle of Evesham. In these, the defendants appeared for trial in only twenty-five instances. In two of the suits, the cases were resolved when the plaintiffs retracted their writs.[41] In the remaining twenty-three, the parties agreed to "put themselves on the country" and thus submitted their cause to jurors. In seventeen of those cases no verdict of any kind was ever recorded. Of the remaining six cases, the jurors acquitted three defendants and convicted three.[42] Needless to say, it is impossible to make any real judgments about the great volume of cases which never were brought to a decision other than to note that the courts could seldom manage to assemble a jury even when the defendants were willing to appear.

There are two additional questions to be considered about the evidence in the legal records. First, since the trespasses involved in the suits were mostly acts of violence and theft, we need to satisfy ourselves that they were political acts, and not just the unprincipled behavior of unscrupulous men using the rebellion as an excuse to even old scores and to enrich themselves. And second, we must somehow satisfy ourselves about the guilt or innocence of those who were charged but refused to appear and defend themselves. In other words, did failure to appear imply guilt?

The question of the meaning of the violence was thoroughly considered by E. F. Jacob who concluded that, while there was an element of paying off old grudges, most of the acts of violence were clearly political acts. As he put it, "to see political significance of some kind in every act of robbery and violence would, of course, be absurd," but, having said that, it was still true that the estates of prominent royalists were plundered in a thorough and systematic

---

41 One was a suit brought by Peter of Savoy against Gilbert Hanetyn, prior of Holy Trinity, Edelinton. The suit was dismissed when the prior finally appeared in the Easter term of 1268, when the the suit was retracted. The prior may well have been taking advantage of Peter of Savoy's death, which had occurred just before and which would have forced the end of his suit (PRO, KB 26/184A, m. 14d). The other instance which is equally unclear was William de Say v. John de Say (PRO, KB 26/181, m. 14d).

42 A variety of cases were involved. In a Cornwall case a certain Julius le Clerk was amerced for false claim in a suit against Philip de Bodigan (PRO, KB 26/177, m. 5). In a second case, Richard de Braham sued a certain Ralph le Clerk on a charge of robbery of his goods at Ravensden, Bedfordshire. He was freed on a technicality because he was mis-called Ranulf in the writ (PRO, KB 26/175, m. 6). The third suit involved a suit by Robert de Capella against the abbot of Peterborough. He claimed he was robbed "after the peace" of goods worth 40 shillings at Tychmersh. The abbot pleaded that he took them to collect a debt and was upheld by the jurors (PRO, KB 26/178, m. 13). In the three suits in which the defendants were convicted only one was obviously a rebellion case. It was a Lincolnshire suit brought by Eudo la Zuche against Master Henry de Wyham (PRO, KB 26/189, m. 10). The other two are less clear. One was a Worcester suit by the prior of Ormesby against Richard de Brewse and Gilbert de Haysaunt (PRO, KB 26/189, m. 10); and the other was a suit from Kent by the abbey of Battle against Adam de Pende and Walward Atteholm (PRO, KB 26/182, m. 6). It is worth noting that Battle Abbey suffered badly from the rebels at the time of the battle of Lewes.

way.[43] Moreover, those estates were ravaged by men of the local district, not by wandering bands of rebel marauders. Jacob cited the cases of royalists' such as Robert de Tattershall, Thomas de Audeham, Eudo la Zuche, and John de Grey. The attacks on their property were all similar, and in every instance clerics were very much involved.[44] The legal records are, in fact, full of suits by prominent royalists including from the king's brother, Richard of Cornwall, his brother-in-law, Peter of Savoy, the Savoyard Imbert de Montferrand, and barons like Thomas Corbet. Another instance involved attacks on the estates of the king's very important clerk, John Mansel. The number of prominent rebels cited in these cases coupled with the return of the royalists, is so striking that we can only conclude that strong overtones of political antagonism prompted the violence.

Jacob argued that the attacks were actively organized by a network of rebel sympathizers who traveled all over England for Simon de Montfort. He took special note of men identified as *procuratores et custodes pacis* for the earl; one such was the cleric presented by the jurors of Polebrook in Northamptonshire for preaching against the king. The chief agents who organized those wide-ranging attacks seem to have been Simon de Montfort's own bailiffs and stewards who were shown little mercy by the justices when charges were brought against them after the death of the earl.[45] It seems clear that the acts of violence and the robberies charged in these suits were largely politically motivated. We can conclude that the clerics and others charged in these suits were acting, for the most part, for reasons which transcended simple revenge and greed.

We are still faced with the problem of deciding why so many clerics appeared on the rolls. Over 500 members of the clergy are named in the records, either as plaintiffs or defendants with the latter outnumbering the former by about four to one. They range in importance from abbots to unbeneficed clerks who appear simply as "John le Clerk," or "William the Chaplain." Included are archdeacons, deans, members of cathedral chapters, abbots, priors, and men from every significant monastic group in England, as well as individuals from every level of the parochial clergy. Even when we cannot discover the final disposition of their cases, considerable evidence exists from other sources, such as the patent and close rolls, to the effect that many of those charged in the suits were indeed rebels.

Among those clearly identifiable, the most important political and social figure was the abbot of Bury St. Edmunds. An entry in the patent rolls for 27 October 1265 noted that the abbot and convent of St. Edmunds were re-admitted to the king's grace and peace since the king had relented in his anger

---

[43] Jacob, p. 224.
[44] Ibid., pp. 224–25.
[45] Ibid.

against them.[46] In addition, their barony, which had been confiscated, was restored to them. It certainly argues that in the previously mentioned suit of Henry de Caldecott the abbot did not appear to defend himself because he had no defense to make. In another instance, John de Surrey, chaplain, was charged before the justices of the *de terris datis* inquest in Cambridgeshire for buying goods stolen from the church of St. Peter, Trimbleton.[47] In the patent rolls for 1268, he was pardoned of the king's anger for trespasses done during the disturbance.[48] And again, we find Alan de Rypinghale, parson of Rypinghale (Rippingale), who along with several others was accused of going to the church of Gosberton in Lincolnshire, where they assaulted John of Rye and took his goods stored there.[49] In 1268, the attackers of John de Rye were prosecuted in the king's court and were then pardoned.[50]

Perhaps the most noteworthy instance of multiple entries in the records involved Walter, parson of Hartfeld. He was included in the special inquest of 1267 as having been taken with the rebels at Tonbridge Castle.[51] Further, he was among many others accused by Peter of Savoy for trespasses before the justices *de terris datis* for Sussex. As was typical, he did not appear.[52] Then in 1267, Walter was among many other men pardoned along with Peter de Montfort.[53] A similar pattern involved Master Henry Sampson who appeared both as accused and accuser in suits before the justices *de terris datis*. In a Berkshire suit, he accused six men of despoiling his property, at the same time as he was being implicated as a rebel in three separate cases from Northamptonshire.[54] His status as rebel was confirmed by entries in the Patent Rolls for 1266, which identified him as a cleric of Simon de Montfort and proceded to receive him back into the king's peace.[55] Cases such as these support the conclusion that those accused of trespasses during the period were guilty.

During the period when so many suits were initiated in the courts, clerics of every rank appeared on the rolls of the justices. They included abbots and priors, an occasional prioress, monks, archdeacons, deans, pastors, vicars, chaplains, and many who were identified only as "clerics" without any note of their origins. Members of the lesser clergy present a serious problem of

---

[46] *Calendar of Patent Rolls, 1258–1266* [*CPR*], p. 525.

[47] PRO, JI 83, m. 26.

[48] *CPR 1258–1266*, p. 267.

[49] PRO, KB 26/181, m. 1d. See also KB 26/182, m. 16d and 185, m. 20.

[50] *CPR 1266–1272*, p. 192.

[51] *CIMC*, p. 231.

[52] PRO, JI 1207, m. 5d.

[53] *CPR 1266–1272*, pp. 148–50.

[54] The Berkshire case is PRO, JI 59, m. 1; and the Northamptonshire cases are JI 618b, m. 18, m. 18d, and m. 25.

[55] *CPR 1266–1272*, pp. 315, 562. The place names of medieval villages and manors which regularly appear in the records are sometimes impossible to identify. Where possible they appear in the modern form in the text. On those occasions in which an accurate modern rendering cannot be found they appear inside quotation marks.

identification in the records since the references to them are so often incomplete. Eighty-five individuals are cited whose precise identity cannot be determined because the records refer to them only as "Adam le Clerk," or "Nicholas le Chapelyn." In such cases it is most likely that the defendant was not known to the plaintiff and so we too are left ignorant about his exact identification. Normally there would have been no way to discover anything more about the William le Clerc who, with many others, was charged by Thomas de Audeham for damages to his manors at Wodeland, Audeham, and Freyedville.[56] In this case, however, the failure of the defendant to appear actually becomes an advantage to us. Thomas renewed his suit several times and, on one of those occasions, William le Clerc appears in the record as William le Clerc *of Wrotham*.[57] This is unusual, however, since we seldom learn more in later suits than in the first.

A further difficulty with the term "cleric" or *clericus* is that there is no way to determine with any great precision what it meant in the thirteenth century. *Clericus* was used rather vaguely to refer to men in minor orders. Frequently, it referred to boys who were attending schools before proceeding to ordination.[58] The term *capellanus* seems to have had a fairly precise meaning in the period. As a general rule, it designated men who served as parish priests. In the fourteenth century, the term tended to disappear from the bishops' registers and was superseded by *sacerdos* or *presbyter*.[59] There is only one instance when a cleric was called a priest in the legal records from the rebellion period: Robert, who was called the priest of the chapel of St. Mary, Southampton. Robert was among a number of men sued by the royal justice, William de St. Omer.[60] As a priest of the chapel, he was probably an assistant to the chaplain. J. R. H. Moorman argued that *capellanus* was used in the registers of thirteenth-century bishops, such as Walter Grey, Hugh of Wells, and Robert Grosseteste, to refer to men who had already served in some parish as an assistant priest, in contrast to the boys and young men who received a benefice while still in school.[61] It seems clear that *clericus* and *capellanus* were used to describe the unbeneficed

---

56 PRO, KB 26/177, m. 9.
57 PRO, KB 26/ 178, m. 19 (Hilary 1267). The original suit was brought in the Michaelmas term a few months earlier. In the meantime, Thomas had renewed his suit twice. KB 177, m. 28d, and m. 31.
58 J. R. H. Moorman, *Church Life in England in the Thirteenth Century* (Cambridge, 1955), pp. 34–35. Since parish clerks needed to be only in minor orders, a good many were married and so Clerk became a surname passed on to their children. The clerk might also be a manorial clerk, sheriff's clerk, or clerk of some prominent layman. In the case of royal clerks, however, the term *clericus regis* almost always referred to an actual cleric in the thirteenth century.
59 Ibid., pp. 35–36.
60 PRO, KB 26/185, m. 9. There was another cleric, Geoffrey, parson of Dungwide, among the defendants. They were charged with cutting off trees worth £200 from the justice's wood at Brembesawe.
61 Moorman, p. 36.

lesser clergy at the time of the disturbance. On the other hand, the truly surprising aspect of the records is the relatively high instance of beneficed clergy among the accused. At a time of violent activity such as the rebellion, it would not have been surprising for the unbeneficed clergy to join in the violence, and yet the number of beneficed clergy cited in the records is essentially equal to the unbeneficed. There were seventy-one rectors of churches and twenty-four vicars among the accused for a total of ninety-five as opposed to only eighty-five individuals who were clearly unbeneficed. The issue of why members of the beneficed clergy and monastics would have engaged in such a general pattern of violence is a central question for the period.

Although the clergy involved represented every region of England, the nature of the struggle and the general pattern of population in the realm had the natural effect of concentrating them more in some areas than in others. The most heavily populated regions of England during the thirteenth century were East Anglia and the southern counties stretching below the Thames valley across from Kent to Somerset and Devonshire. As it happened, those regions were also the sites of some the most serious fighting during the period. A good deal of destruction accompanied the campaign associated with the battle of Lewes. Consequently, Sussex generated a considerable volume of suits involving clerics. Similarly, the focus of the continuing opposition to the king after the battle of Evesham was the administrative unit, the Isle of Ely. Since the Isle of Ely largely divided East Anglia from the neighboring regions of Cambridgeshire and spilled over into Lincolnshire, a great deal of the violence was associated with those areas. As a result, the natural concentration of cases in Norfolk and Suffolk was made even greater by their proximity to the rebels in the Isle. The same was true of the regions around Northampton, where the king originally rallied his forces before Lewes, and around Kenilworth Castle, which held out against the king through most of 1266.

The unpopularity of certain royal supporters also governed the distribution of cases. The two most despised prelates in England during this period were the bishops of Hereford and Norwich. As a result, they drew down on themselves and their lands a considerable degree of violent attention. Peter d'Aigueblanche of Hereford was a Savoyard who had accompanied William de Valence to England at the time of the king's marriage. He became a major irritant to the English clergy during the 1250s because of his efforts to enhance the collection of papal taxes levied on the clergy of the realm to support Rome's attempt to expel the Hohenstaufens from the throne of Sicily.[62] The bishop of Norwich

---

[62] Peter d'Aigueblanche was so disliked by the monastics of England that one of the St. Albans chroniclers wrote of him that "his memory exhales a sulphurous odor": H. T. Riley, ed., *Gesta Abbatum S. Albani*, vol. 4 of *Chronica Monasterii S. Albani*, RS, 1863–1876, p. 379; T. F. Tout wrote his biography for the *DNB*, 15:946–51. See also, Nigel Yates, "Bishop Peter de Aquablanca (1240–1268): A Reconsideration," *Journal of Ecclesiastical History* 22(1971): 303–4.

was Simon Walton, a former chief justice of the King's Bench who was the most determined royalist among the prelates in England. During the period when Simon de Montfort and his supporters controlled the royal government, Simon Walton was a continual thorn in their side.[63] Unlike most of the other royalist bishops, who were abroad with the king or at the papal court, Walton remained in his diocese and did everything he could to frustrate the rebels. Since the rebellion had particularly strong support around Norwich, his activity definitely served to exacerbate the situation there.

In the records from the counties near the Isle of Ely, 290 clerics were accused of violence or some form of trespass. The highest incidence was from east of the Isle where Norfolk had seventy-four, and Suffolk and Essex had thirty-five each. Cambridgeshire, which encompassed most of the Isle proper, and had thirty-seven cases, while Northamptonshire, Lincolnshire and Buckingham-shire had thirty-six, thirty-three and twenty-four respectively. The area with the second highest incidence included Kent, Sussex and Hampshire and their nearby neighbors with a total of 109 accused clergy. Kent had the largest number with thirty-seven. In the remaining counties in the west and south-west, the incidence of clergy involvement was considerably smaller. The cases from these areas generally cited only one or two defendants in contrast with the large number charged in the eastern and south-eastern counties where it is apparent that veritable gangs of clergy preyed on the lands and properties of the region.

The sheer numbers charged in some of the suits from the region touching the Isle of Ely is striking. For example, Reginald de la Wode charged thirty individuals – including two clerics identified as William, vicar of the church of Dunton, and Ralph de Stokes, chaplain – with destroying his crossbow and its equipment, cutting and carrying off his grain at Sandringham, Houghton, Appleton, Ingoldisthorp, Yelverton, and Wolferton, as well as felling his trees at "Grensuth," to the amount of damages of £100.[64] An even more striking instance involved a suit by Ralph fitz Ranulf against fifty-nine individuals, including four clerics: Richard of Durham, parson of Crownthorpe (Cringle-thorp); John, chaplain of Crownthorpe; Roger, chaplain of Manton and Thomas le Trang. All were accused of taking Ralph's goods and chattels from Hether-sett and Pickenham.[65] The suit was renewed several times. Ralph later cited as well a Master Hamo of the Hospital and then Peter de Say, Master of the

---

63 Walton was disliked so much that he was lumped together with Peter d'Aigueblanche in the "Song of the Barons," which praised those who attacked the two bishops in 1263. Of Walton, the author said, "Et ly pastors de Norwis, qui devours ses berbis, assez sout de ce conte; Mout in perdi de ses biens, mal ert que lessa riens, ke trop en saviet de honte." Thomas Wright, ed., *The Political Songs of England: From the Reign of John to that of Edward II* (London, 1849), p. 62.

64 PRO, KB 26/175, m. 2d, and 177, m. 6d. In the latter suit, the clerical state of William, vicar of Dunton, was confirmed when the bishop of Norwich was ordered to produce him in court.

65 PRO, KB 26/175, m. 3.

Hospital of Carbrook.[66] Although the official of the archbishop of Canterbury was ordered to produce the clerics in 1266, there is no record that they ever responded by appearing to defend themselves.

One of the most litigious plaintiffs of the period was Matilda de Neville. Her property appears to have been set upon by a veritable army of clerics, including John, parson of the church of Witchingham; Hugo, chaplain of Witchingham; Geoffrey le Whyte, vicar of Prileston; Robert, chaplain of Hempnall; Robert, parson of the church of Kirkby; Roger de Ponte of Ellingham, prior of Ellingham; Giles, vicar of Bedingham; Ralph, parson of Topcroft; William, parson of the chapel of Topcroft; John Outre, parson of Ilketeshall; Henry, parson of Brome; Morgan de Ilketshall, prioress of Bungay; John, parson of Whitlingham; Adam, chaplain of Whitlingham and John, chaplain of Hedenham. They and many others were charged with cutting down her woods at Hedenham.[67] Although Matilda renewed her suit again and again, there is no record that any of the above appeared to defend themselves. She was still trying as late as 1270.[68] The charge of cutting down woods is worth noting since it was common to a great number of the trespass suits. Forest land represented such a valuable form of property in the Middle Ages that it was a frequent object of attack. Furthermore, forest land afforded a fine opportunity to any enemy wishing to inflict serious damages since trees take so long to be replaced.[69]

Another plaintiff whose lands in Norfolk were plagued by a clerical gang was the royalist baron, Robert de Tattershall. In a suit originating in the Hilary term of 1266, he charged a total of forty-two defendants with attacks on his manors of Topcroft, Denton, Tibenham, Gateford, Fawsley and Babingley. Among the defendants were Reginald Benetod, abbot of Bury St. Edmunds; Richard, parson of Fundenhall; Milo, chaplain of Kirksted; Geoffrey, chaplain of Garboldesham; and John de Carlton, chaplain.[70] This is the second case cited involving the abbot of Bury St. Edmund's and, once again, the abbot refused to appear in court to defend himself. In a Lincolnshire suit, Robert charged forty-six men with attacks on his manors in that county at Tattershall, Maltby, Candlesby, Kirkby, Sturton (by Scawby), Tydd (St. Mary, Witham) and St. Botulphs (Boston). Again a significant number were churchmen: Gilbert, cleric

---

66 PRO, KB 177, m. 8d; 178, m. 6; and 182, m. 9. The hospital of Carbrook was originally under a group of nuns, but had become a house of the Knights Hospitallers. Dom David Knowles and R. Neville Hadcock, *Medieval Religious Houses in England and Wales* (London, 1953), p. 350.

67 PRO, KB 26/177, m. 24d.

68 PRO, KB 26/178, m. 21d and 22; 181, m. 13d; 182, m. 18; 184A, m. 17; 193, m. 11; and 201, m. 1d. The number of defendants gradually diminished in the later renewals of her suit.

69 See Jean Birrell, "Common Rights in Medieval Forests," *Past and Present* 117(1987): 22–49, esp. 26–27.

70 PRO, KB 26/175, m. 9. The suit continued to appear until the Trinity term of 1268. PRO, KB 181, m. 9; 182 m. 14d; and 185 m. 18.

of Weston; Brother Geoffrey of Peterborough; John le Clerk; William, vicar of Croft; Gilbert de Bigby, cleric; Michael the cleric; and Walter, cleric of Skendleby.[71] It is worth noting that members of this group were generally unbeneficed and poorly identified. On the other hand, the group also included a monk of the abbey of Peterborough, one of the monastic houses which clearly supported the rebels.

In the counties well away from the influence of the Isle of Ely, the cases recorded generally involved only a few defendants. Among them are two Devonshire suits which revolved around a very intriguing issue. Among the prelates of the period there were five who can be identified as open and active supporters of the rebellion. At the same time, there were a few whose support for the king was total; among them, for example, Peter d'Aigueblanche of Hereford and Simon Walton of Norwich. There were several, however, who vacillated, occasionally co-operating with the rebel cause while retaining the king's confidence. The Devonshire suits relate to one of these men, Walter Bronescombe of Exeter.[72] During the rebellion, Bronescombe willingly participated in the clerical council of 1264 which voted a substantial aid to the rebel government for the purpose of repelling any attempted invasion by the king's party.[73] Despite this seeming association with the rebel cause, he was included on the commission of twelve leading men who framed the *Dictum of Kenilworth*, the settlement which eventually allowed the rebels to make their peace with the king.[74] Since the bishop was so easily reconciled with the king, what, then, was the true extent of his commitment to the rebellion? The fact that a number of the bishop's diocesan officials were integrally involved in the disturbances of the period lends considerable weight to the argument that Walter Bronescombe was very close to the Montfortian bishops even if it did not undermine his position with the king.

There are many instances of clerics suing other clerics for damages done during the period. For example, in a Suffolk suit, John de Mendlesham, parson of the church of Alpheton, charged fourteen men, including the clerics Master Giles de Bareton, Adam, the chaplain of 'Bradesend', and Master Henry de Fornham. He charged that they seized his goods and chattels.[75] In another Suffolk case, the prior of Lewes accused a number of men, including William de Qureye, chaplain, of coming to his woods at Carlton and Willingham and carrying off trees worth £1,000.[76] There were a series of Norfolk suits involv-

---

71 PRO, KB 26/175, m. 25; 177, m. 25d; 178 m. 20; and 181, m. 9d.

72 Walter Bronescombe was among the minority of thirteenth-century bishops whose register has survived. F. C. Hingeston-Randolph, ed., *Register of Walter Bronescombe, 1257–80 [RWB]* (London, 1889).

73 *A.D. 1205–1313*, vol. 2 of *Councils and Synods: With Other Documents relating to the English Church*, ed. F. M. Powicke and C. R. Cheney (Oxford, 1964), pp. 698–99.

74 *CPR 1258–1266*, pp. 671–72.

75 PRO, KB 26/174, m. 13d; 175, m. 16d; 177, m. 10d; and 178, m. 13d.

76 PRO, KB 26/193, m. 29d; and 197, m. 13.

ing Robert de Wonekote, parson of St. Mary's, Massingham, who seems to have attracted considerable clerical antagonism. In the Hilary term of 1268, he charged that Master Robert de Wyleby and several others broke into his house at Massingham and carried off property worth £20, then burned down the church.[77] Robert also sued John, prior of Shouldham, and two brothers of the house along with a number of others for robbing him of goods worth 100 marks.[78] Finally, he charged William, vicar of "Tysso," and others, including a Walter the clerk, with carrying off his grain and causing him serious damages which amounted to 100 shillings.[79]

Of all the secular clerics involved in the violence, none was more active than Master Henry Sampson, a clerk of Simon de Montfort who was admitted to the king's peace in February 1266.[80] He was prominently involved in the returns from the *de terris datis* inquests in a series of cases which make it clear that the violence of the period was directed as much against the supporters of the rebellion as against the royalists. Master Henry brought suits before the justices in both Buckinghamshire and Northamptonshire. He charged six men in Buckinghamshire with unspecified trespasses against him.[81] In the suit from Northamptonshire, he charged a great number of men with looting manors at Easton, Wittering, Holewell, Creaton, and Buckminster with loss of goods worth £200.[82]

Even more intriguing than the acts of violence by members of the secular clergy were those attributed to monastics. The activity of the abbot of Bury St. Edmunds has already been mentioned and, although his behavior was obviously that of a partisan rebel, he was very definitely not unique. In fact, all the major monastic orders were represented among the opponents of the king. Among those accused of various levels of rebel activity were twenty-four Benedictine houses, seventeen Augustinian, thirteen Cistercian, four Cluniac, three Gilbertine, and three Premonstratensian. Four houses of Benedictine nuns, along with one Augustinian and one Cistercian nunnery, were accused. Among those accused were some of the most important in England. Besides Bury St. Edmunds, the Benedictine houses included Peterborough, St. Albans, Ramsey, the monastic chapter of St. Swithin's, Winchester, and Shrewsbury. Among the Cistercians, those cited included Beaulieu, Sibton, Hulton, Thame, and Newenham. Among the Augustinian canons, the number of communities and priors accused is even more impressive. The list includes the priors of Breamore, Pentney, Letheringham, Great Bricett, Fineshade, Shulbred, Ravenstone, Royston, Llanthony, Taunton, and Kenilworth. The Cluniac houses of

---

77 PRO, KB 26/182, m. 6d; renewed in 184A, m. 8d, and 185, m. 20.
78 PRO, KB 26/205, m. 22; and later 207, m. 8d.
79 PRO, KB 26/205, m. 22.
80 *CPR 1258–1266*, p. 562.
81 PRO, JI 59, m. 1.
82 PRO, JI 618b, m. 25.

Lewes, Castle Acre, Prittlewell, and Daventry were all accused as were the Gilbertine houses of Shouldham in Norfolk, Fordham in Cambridgeshire, St. Katherine's in Lincoln, and Clattercote in Oxfordshire. Finally, charges were lodged against the abbot of the Premonstratensian canons at Leyston and Canon Nicholas of the house at Lavendon.[83] Although less severely implicated, some of the nuns were also accused, among them the previously mentioned Morgan de Ilketelshall, prioress of the Benedictine convent of Bungay in Suffolk;[84] Agnes de Swyndon, prioress of the Benedictine house of Polesloe in Devonshire;[85] and the unnamed prioress of the Benedictine house of Ickleton in Cambridgeshire.[86] In addition, jurors of the *de terris datis* inquest in Berkshire charged the prioress of the Augustinian nuns at Goring with looting the goods of Roger, parson of "Berewefold."[87]

The monastic houses accused were located all over the realm. In the west, the prior and convent of St. Peter and Paul, Shrewsbury, were forced to seek the king's pardon for their trespasses.[88] South of Shrewsbury, in Worcestershire, two Benedictine houses were implicated. One of those was Bishop Walter de Cantilupe's cathedral priory of Worcester, certainly not surprising given his prominence among the Montfortian bishops. The other house was the Benedictine abbey of Pershore, members of which the abbot of Westminster accused of breaking into his park at "Tydesle." The suit named the abbot of Pershore as well as three of his monks: Henry de Wynchecombe, Robert de Worcester, and Geoffrey de Childecott.[89] In the south-west three more Benedictine houses were implicated. Suits were brought against the abbots of Abbotsbury in Dorset, and Athelney and Muchelney in Somerset, all by prominent individuals. The abbot of Abbotsbury was sued along with Walter de la Wyle, bishop of Salisbury, Master Thomas de la Wyle, and a William le Clerk of Tyderlegh with a number of others by the royalist baron, Robert de Aguilon.[90] The abbot of Athelney was sued along with Richard, prior of the Augustinian house of Taunton, by Peter de Champvent, who was a Steward of the Household under Edward I.[91] Among the co-defendants in this suit were four parsons: William

---

83 PRO, JI 59, m. 6. He was charged with buying stolen grain. The canon acknowledged buying the grain, but denied that it was stolen. The jurors disagreed and he was amerced.

84 See above, note 68.

85 PRO, KB 26/175, m. 5d. The prioress was one of nineteen defendants accused by John de Stokes of plundering his property. They failed to appear and the suit was not renewed.

86 PRO, KB 26/174, m. 13. She was among twenty-seven defendants sued by Simon de Wycomb for injury to his goods at Dukesworth.

87 PRO, JI 42, m. 10. She denied the charge, but no verdict was recorded.

88 *CPR 1266–1272*, p. 113.

89 PRO, KB 207, m. 9. This suit from the Trinity term of 1272 is one of the very last recorded cases connected with the disturbance.

90 PRO, KB 26/177, m. 22. He accused them of looting his manor of Holedich. Robert de Aguilon is identified by Jacob, p. 283, n. 2.

91 T. F. Tout, *Chapters in the Administrative History of Medieval England*, 6 vols. (1920, repr., Manchester, 1967), 6:41.

de Sumers, parson of "Ple Abbot"; Robert de Wik, parson of Hacche; Roger, parson of Capland; and Richard de Becton, parson of Ashill.

The *de terris datis* roll for Berkshire includes frequent mention of two of the largest and wealthiest of the Benedictine houses, Abingdon and Reading.[92] The abbot of Reading was charged with harboring the enemies of the king, aiding the rebels with money, sending his men against the king and acting as a representative for the rebel cause. He was also charged with having revealed to Simon de Montfort the fact that Warin de Bassingburn would make an attempt to free Lord Edward from Wallingford Castle. The abbot responded by denying that he was an enemy of the king. He went on to swear that he had rendered service to the rebels in response to orders issued by sheriffs and duly authorized by the king. Although the case was referred to the next parliament, the local jurors supported his story.

While the Berkshire cases are somewhat ambiguous, there is no doubt about that of St. Swithin's, Winchester. There, the prior and convent were assessed a fine of 500 marks in 1266 in order to regain the good will of the king.[93] Another Hampshire house involved was the alien priory of Ellingham whose prior, Roger de Ponte, was among those charged by Matilda de Neville.[94] In Lincolnshire, St. Leonard's, Stamford and Deeping St. James were charged by Eudo la Zuche with cutting off his wood of "Kilpisham," causing damage amounting to 50 marks.[95] The case of Bury St. Edmunds is, of course, special. In addition to the evidence provided by the considerable number of suits against the abbot and his house, we know that shortly after the battle of Evesham the king confiscated the house's lands. We also know that those lands were quickly restored to the monastery, since by late October, 1265 Bury St. Edmunds had been received back into the king's grace and peace.[96] The price for this reconciliation was heavy since the monastery was required to pay a fine of more than £260.[97]

The abbeys of Ramsey and Peterborough in Northamptonshire were also very much involved in the rebellion. There is no doubt that both abbots actively supported the rebel cause. The inquest of 1265 revealed that both had sent military contingents to Kenilworth.[98] The evidence from the inquest is confirmed by a case from the Northamptonshire *de terris datis* roll. Robert de Tyndile was accused of robbing the two abbots during the disturbance. His defense consisted of the claim that he was a follower of Lord Edward at a time

---

[92] PRO, JI 42, m. 10. The case is discussed in detail by Jacob, p. 295.

[93] *CPR 1258–1266*, p. 558. It was finally paid in May 1269. *CPR 1266–1272*, pp. 339–40.

[94] See above, note 68.

[95] PRO, KB 26/186, m. 28.

[96] *CPR 1258–1266*, p. 471. This order restoring the liberty to the abbot was reissued in March 1267, *CPR 1266–1272*, p. 45.

[97] *CPR 1258–1266*, p. 525.

[98] *CIMC*, 1:254. The abbot of Ramsey made fine of nearly £90 to regain the king's favor: *Close Rolls of the Reign of Henry III, 1258–1264*, pp. 195–96.

when the abbots were the king's enemies. He charged that the abbot of Peterborough was at Northampton when it was under rebel control and that the abbot of Ramsey was at Kenilworth. On the basis of this defense, he was acquitted.[99]

In an Essex case, Geoffrey de la Mare, accused of being at Northampton with anti-royal forces, said that the abbot of Peterborough ordered him to go there.[100] The abbot of Peterborough and several others were also accused by Robert de Capella with committing trespasses against him at Titchmarch.[101] Two other important Benedictine houses played a major role in the rebellion. In a Yorkshire case, the abbot of Whitby and nine others were charged by Walter le Granur with stealing his goods and chattels.[102] The abbot of St. Albans was implicated to the point where he had to seek the king's peace.[103] When the justices *de terris datis* were sitting in Buckinghamshire, the later abbot appeared and brought a writ from the king which forgave him all the trespasses committed during the time of the disturbance.[104]

The Cistercian houses involved were also scattered throughout England. The abbot of "Newenham" in Devonshire was fined just over £125 for trespasses committed during the disturbance. Of that sum, the king remitted over £85 and ordered that the remainder be paid to his yeoman, Bernard de Bardelia.[105] The abbot of Sibton was among the many defendants sued by Matilda de Neville for the damages to her wood at Hedenham. The litigious Robert de Tattershall was involved in a suit which included a monk of Revesby in Lincolnshire,[106] and in another action against the abbot of Jervaulx in Yorkshire.[107] The *de terris datis* rolls for Cambridgeshire and Berkshire implicated two other Cistercian houses but here the records are incomplete. The two houses were Stratford Langthorne in Essex,[108] and Beaulieu in Hampshire.[109] In another suit, the abbot of Beaulieu was charged with cutting down trees

---

99   PRO, JI 618b, m. 14.
100 PRO, JI 237, m. 4. The case was printed in Joseph Hunter, ed., *Rotuli Selecti ad res Anglicas et Hibernicas spectantes* (London, 1834), pp. 120–21.
101 PRO, KB 26/177, m. 10.
102 PRO, KB 26/175, m. 6.
103 *CPR 1258–1266*, p. 559.
104 PRO, JI 59, m. 15d.
105 *CPR 1266–1272*, p. 341.
106 PRO, KB 26/177, m. 25d. The inquest of 1265 stated flatly that the abbot of Revesby had never been against the king (*CIMC*, 1:238). This case involved a Brother Hubert of Revesby who may have been at one of the granges so commonly associated with the Cistercians.
107 PRO, KB 26/177, m. 20. The abbot appeared and denied the charge and put himself on the country (PRO, KB 26/178, m. 8d). There was no verdict. In a somewhat unusual sequence, the sheriff was ordered to conduct an inquest into the matter, but again nothing was resolved (PRO, KB 26/181, m. 5).
108 PRO, JI 83, m. 31d.
109 PRO, JI 42, m. 1.

valued at £200 belonging to a royal justice. Also named in the suit were five other clerical defendants including Alfrich de Ore, prior of the Augustinian house of Breamore.[110]

Breamore was only one of many Augustinian houses involved in the violence. Six houses in the counties surrounding the Isle of Ely were also involved. The prior of Little Leighs in Essex was among those charged with seizing the tenements of John Reyng.[111] Ralph fitz Ranulf sued Ammo de Episcal, prior of Pentney in Norfolk, for stealing his goods at Hethersett and Pickenham.[112] In another instance, the prior of Ravenstone in Buckinghamshire was among those charged with carrying off the goods of William de Gray from his manor in Stoke Goldington.[113] The prior of Fineshade in Northamptonshire was accused of harboring Ralph de Wodeward and his stolen goods during the disturbance. The prior did not deny the allegation, but asked that he should not be forced to answer since Ralph was really the principal offender.[114]

Although the Cluniacs, Premonstratensian and Gilbertine canons were much less numerous that the other congregations, there were also several instances of their involvement. For example, Walter, the prior of Castle Acre in Norfolk, was accused by William Crisp and Roger de Waterden of assaulting and falsely imprisoning them.[115] Another case involving the prior of the Cluniac house of Prittlewell in Essex provides a glimpse of the real heat generated by the conflict. Master Nicholas de Curtenay, a royal clerk, accused the prior and others of coming with force and arms to his church of Hockley, from which they expelled him. When Master Nicholas showed them a letter of protection from the king and Lord Edward, they threw it on the ground in contempt. In turn, Prior Walter denied the charge, asserting that he had acted on the authorization of the bishop of London. Apparently, this was a weak defense since the bishop was a notorious rebel. As a result, the sheriff was ordered to collect a jury, although there is no record of a decision.[116]

There are relatively few instances of involvement by the Gilbertine and Premonstratensian canons. One of these comes in a suit brought by Henry de Mersenton against the prior of the Gilbertine house of Clattercott. Henry charged that the prior had sent several canons of his house to Rodeford and that they had carried off his goods and timber and brought them to the prior's house at Wymerlachton (Wymondley, Herts.). Although the prior denied everything, the jurors of the hundred of Wardon not only agreed that he had carried off the

[110] PRO, KB 26/181, m. 24.
[111] PRO, KB 26/181, m. 14, and 15.
[112] PRO, KB 26/175, m. 3; and 182, m. 9.
[113] PRO, KB 26/174, m. 12d.
[114] PRO, JI 618b, m. 20d.
[115] PRO, KB 26/197, m. 3d; and 201, m. 17d.
[116] PRO, KB 201, m. 7d.

timber, but further charged that he had harbored enemies of the king.[117] In two
other cases, the prior of the Gilbertine house of Shouldham in Norfolk was
charged with looting.[118]

There are many more such cases involving clear acts of violence and theft
on the part of both monastic and secular clergy during the period. The cases
presented in this article have focused on some of the most important figures of
the period. Despite the incompleteness of the records, they tell the tale of a very
real violence involving substantial numbers of clerics. It may well be that
Hanawalt's conclusions concerning clerical defendants found in her study of
fourteenth-century crime tend to apply here as well. She believed that clerics
of all ranks often led gangs of criminals. Furthermore, due to their intimate
local knowledge, these clerical bandits were often able to lead their followers
to goods carefully hidden by the owners.[119] In short, just as Friar Tuck could
be a willing and active member of Robin Hood's band, so the thirteenth-century
English clergy were willing and active participants in the violence associated
with the barons' war.

[117] PRO, JI 618b, m. 5.
[118] PRO, KB 26/182, m. 5; KB 185, m. 13d.
[119] Hanawalt, pp. 136–38.

PART TWO

Medieval Families and Feuds

Deudo and the Roots of Feudal Violence in Late Medieval Castile

L. J. ANDREW VILLALON

In 1979, Professor Helen Nader of the University of Indiana published a highly provocative work entitled *The Mendoza Family in the Spanish Renaissance*, in which she radically redefined the concept of a Renaissance in Spain, moving it back in time and portraying it as a largely indigenous phenomenon rather than a mere import from Italy.[1] A lesser theme which emerges from Nader's work concerns the mitigation of feudal violence in the central Iberian kingdom of Castile by *deudo*, which she defines as follows:

> The bond of family, friendship, and vassalage that binds men together and obligates them to one another. . . . Without it, there would be a state of predatory violence, and each man would be left to fend for himself. Although *deudo* within a nuclear family was legally imposed, the *deudo* that bound friend to friend and king to vassal had to be initiated by the persons involved and required a persistent mending of the relationship.[2]

Thus, *deudo* stretched beyond simple family ties, to encompass a variety of close interpersonal relationships within the social elite. Despite this wider applicability, Professor Nader uses the term primarily to refer to those ties of blood and marriage which translate roughly as "extended kinship." Again, to use her own words,

---

[1] Helen Nader, *The Mendoza in the Spanish Renaissance* (Rutgers NJ, 1979). I should like to thank the following individuals and institutions for their assistance in the research and writing of this article: John Boswell, Judith Daniels, Dan Gottlieb, Consuelo Gutierrez del Arroyo, Donald Kagay, Sally Moffitt, Helen Nader, Ann Twinam, Thomas White, the Archivo Histórico Nacional, the Real Academia de la Historia, the Medieval Institute at Western Michigan University, Kalamazoo, Michigan, the Reference Desk and the Interlibrary Loan and Photoduplication Services of the University of Cincinnati Library System. The research which went into this article was partially financed by the Spanish Fulbright Commission and the University of Cincinnati Research Council. An earlier version was presented on 8 May 1992, at the 27th International Congress on Medieval Studies, held at Kalamazoo, Michigan.
[2] Nader, *The Mendoza in the Spanish Renaissance*, p. 69.

KINSHIP TIES [*DEUDO*] BETWEEN MENDOZA AND MANRIQUE

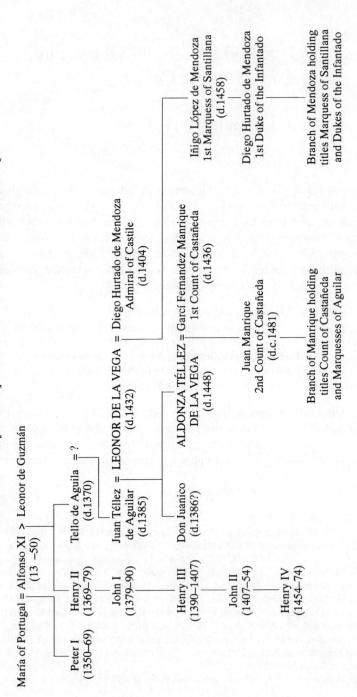

María of Portugal = Alfonso XI > Leonor de Guzmán
(13 –50)

Peter I (1350–69)

Henry II (1369–79)

Tello de Aguila (d.1370) = ?

John I (1379–90)

Juan Téllez de Aguilar (d.1385) = LEONOR DE LA VEGA (d.1432) = Diego Hurtado de Mendoza, Admiral of Castile (d.1404)

Henry III (1390–1407)

Don Juanico (d.1386?)

ALDONZA TÉLLEZ DE LA VEGA (d.1448) = Garcí Fernández Manrique, 1st Count of Castañeda (d.1436)

Iñigo López de Mendoza, 1st Marquess of Santillana (d.1458)

John II (1407–54)

Juan Manrique, 2nd Count of Castañeda (d.c.1481)

Diego Hurtado de Mendoza, 1st Duke of the Infantado

Henry IV (1454–74)

Branch of Manrique holding titles Count of Castañeda and Marquesses of Aguilar

Branch of Mendoza holding titles Marquess of Santillana and Dukes of the Infantado

This abbreviated geneology lists only: (1) the reigning monarchs of Castile during the period under consideration (with the dates they reigned) and (2) members of the House of Tello, Manrique, and Mendoza who are mentioned in this article. The names of the two women who established the ties of deudo – Leonor and Aldonza de la Vega – are fully capitalized. Symbols utilized in this chart have the following meanings: (1) "d." – the year of an individual's death; (2) "=" – a connection by marriage; (3) ">" – a non-marital connection (4) "c." – circa.

During the fifteenth century, [aristocrats] intermarried so frequently that the entire nobility . . . constituted an extended family. . . . In this situation, civil warfare was impractical, for one's enemies were also one's relatives, and it was almost unthinkable to breech deudo by killing one's relatives.[3]

There can be no denying that *deudo* is a useful concept for understanding relationships not just within the Castilian aristocracy, but within any social group. After all, of the "ties which bind," those of family are among the strongest. Nevertheless, in their emphasis on kinship as a unifying factor, useful in mitigating social violence, historians like Nader sometimes fail to give due consideration to the other side of the coin – to the way in which close family ties could set the stage for bitter property disputes, a major cause of the violence which permeated medieval life.

By focusing upon the relationship between two of the leading families of late medieval Castile, this article will attempt to demonstrate two things: (1) that kinship could as easily occasion violence as prevent it; and (2) that what may appear at first sight to be the mitigation of violence by *deudo* can turn out, upon closer examination, to be something quite different. The two families involved in this study – those of Mendoza[4] and Manrique[5] – are ones whose

---

3   Ibid., p. 105.
4   One of the most illustrious Spanish noble families of the late medieval and early modern periods, the Mendozas originated in the mountainous Basque province of Alava, in the shadow of the Pyrenees. The line, which branched off in the twelfth century from the even more ancient house of Vizcaya, came into existence when its founder began to use "Mendoza," the name of a small Basque village which his family ruled, as his patrilineal surname. Around the middle of the fourteenth century, at about the time when Alava was incorporated into the Crown of Castile (1332), the head of the house left his ancestral home and moved the family seat to new lands he had acquired on the broad meseta of Castile. His son, Pedro González de Mendoza, father of Admiral Mendoza, was the man chiefly responsible for establishing the family as one of the most important in the realm. No Castilian house has been the subject of more historical research. The most important genealogy, written in the eighteenth century, is Diego Gutierrez Coronel's *Historia Genealógica de la Casa de Mendoza*, ed. Angel Gonzalez Palencia (Cuenca, 1946). The leading twentieth-century history of the family is Francisco Layna Serrano, *Historia de Guadalajara y sus Mendozas en los Siglos XV y XVI*, 4 vols. (Madrid, 1942). The most useful work dealing with the Mendoza family in English is Helen Nader's *The Mendoza in the Spanish Renaissance*.
5   In the fourteenth century, the Manrique ranked among Castile's oldest families, having branched off from the even more ancient house of Lara. The eponymous founder of the family was the renowned Count Almerico who died in battle in 1164 and gave his name – which could be rendered in a number of ways (Almericus, Amalrico, Malriq, Manriq, etc.) – to the line descended from him. The fact that the Manrique were senior to another branch of the same family which eventually became the royal house of Castile accounts for their boastful device: "it is not we who are descended from kings, but kings who are descended from us." For the Manrique family, see Luis Salazar y Castro, *Pruebas de la Historia de la Casa de Lara* [*Pruebas*], vol. 4 of *Historia Genealógica de la Casa de Lara*, 4 vols. (Madrid, 1694–97).

relationship Nader cites as a prime example of the way in which *deudo* could mitigate intra-familial violence. By contrast, I shall suggest that the *deudo* existing between these two noble houses created more violence than it dissipated.

I

The principal kinship tie between the powerful houses of Mendoza and Manrique can be traced to a pair of late medieval women – a wealthy heiress named Leonor de la Vega and her daughter, Aldonza Téllez de la Vega.

During the troubled decade of the 1360s, Leonor de la Vega, daughter of Garcilaso de la Vega and Mencia de Cisneros, fell heir to almost all of the property of both parental lines,[6] whose menfolk had perished in the aristocratic bloodbath conducted by Pedro the Cruel. This made her a prize marital catch – a fact which did not escape the notice of Pedro's successor, King Enrique II (1369–1379), founder of the Trastámara dynasty.[7] In 1371, Enrique arranged for Doña Leonor to marry his illegitimate nephew, Juan Téllez de Aguilar, eldest son of his unreliable and recently deceased brother, Count Tello.

Both bride and groom brought extensive properties to the marriage, most of which were located in the mountainous northern region of Spain known as the Asturias de Santillana. A grant of King Enrique's, issued in 1371, had conferred upon Juan Téllez the lands of Aguilar de Campóo, Castañeda, Liébana, Pernia, and Campo de Suso.[8] For her part, Doña Leonor held a number of valleys which the Crown had bestowed upon her great uncle, Gonzalo Ruiz de

6   Coronel, 1:15–35.
7   The chronicles of Pedro I and his illegitimate half-brother, Enrique II, were both written by one of the great chroniclers of the Middle Ages, a nobleman named Pedro López de Ayala, who served first one and then the other. See Pedro López de Ayala, *Crónica del Rey Don Pedro Primero, Crónicas de los Reyes de Castilla* [*CRC*], 1, *Biblioteca de Autores Españoles* [*BAE*], 66 (Madrid, 1953), pp. 393–614; Pedro López de Ayala, *Crónica del Rey Don Enrique Segundo de Castilla, CRC*, 2, *BAE*, 68 (Madrid, 1953), pp. 1–34. For modern assessments of Pedro I, see L. J. Andrew Villalon, "Pedro the Cruel: Portrait of a Royal Failure," in *Medieval Iberia: Essays on the History and Literature of Medieval Spain*, ed. Donald J. Kagay and Joseph T. Snow (New York, 1997), pp. 205–11; Clara Estow, *Pedro the Cruel, 1350–1369* (Leiden, 1995), pp. 205–59.
8   There exist two slightly different versions of Enrique's grant to Juan Téllez, both of which originate from documents generated by a sixteenth-century lawsuit. See (1) *Pleito sobre el valle de Liébana* [*Pleito*], in Réal Academia de la Historia [RAH], Salazar M–14, ff. 141–73; and (2) *Memorial del Pleyto que sobre la propiedad del Valle de Liebana y Campo de Suso sostuvieron Luis Fernandez Manrique, II Marques de Aguilar de Campóo y Diego Hurtado de Mendoza, III Duque del Infantado* [*Memorial*] in both RAH Salazar M–67 and Archivo Histórico Nacional, Madrid [AHN], Osuna 4252, n. 4. Many of the individual documents on which this study is based are contained within one or both of these longer sources.

la Vega, in 1341.[9] In the normal course of events, their heirs could have looked forward to inheriting the combined properties, thereby dominating the Asturian region.

The marriage of Juan Téllez and Leonor de la Vega lasted for fourteen years. Then, in 1385, Don Juan took part in Castile's ill-starred invasion of neighboring Portugal and, like many of his fellow countrymen, left his bones to whiten on the field of Aljubarrota.[10] Two of the couple's offspring seem to have survived their father's sudden and violent death – an infant son, usually referred to in the documents as Don Juanico (or "little Juan"), who apparently died less than two years later, and a daughter, Aldonza Téllez de la Vega, who lived on into the 1440s.[11]

In 1395, a marriage was arranged between Aldonza Téllez and a litigious young nobleman named Garcí Fernandez Manrique,[12] head of a cadet branch of one of Castile's oldest families. Not long before the husband's death in 1436, King Juan II of Castile (1407–1453) conferred upon him the hereditary title, count of Castañeda. In the 1480s, the couple's grandson received from the Catholic Monarchs, Ferdinand and Isabel, a second hereditary title, Marquess of Aguilar.[13]

Meanwhile, Leonor de la Vega had not been left to enjoy her early widowhood in peace. There was enormous pressure on the young heiress to remarry; and by 1388 she found herself with a second husband, an ambitious and rising nobleman named Diego Hurtado de Mendoza. Mendoza enjoyed close ties with the crown prince, who, in 1390, ascended to the throne as Enrique III (1390–1407). With the succession of his royal patron, Don Diego became Lord Admiral of Castile and one of the most powerful men in the realm.[14]

From the marriage of admiral Mendoza and Leonor de la Vega came the

---

9   When Gonzalo Ruiz de la Vega died without legitimate issue, the lands passed to his brother, Garcilaso de la Vega, whose eldest son and namesake was Leonor de la Vega's father. Doña Leonor fell heir to the property when both her father and her only brother, a third Garcilaso, died at Pedro's hands. Coronel pp. 33–34; RAH, Salazar M–118, ff. 1–3v; M–119, ff. 1r–v.

10 Pedro López de Ayala, *Cronica del Rey Don Juan Primero de Castilla e de León* in *CRC*, 2, *BAE*, 68 (Madrid, 1953), p. 105. For Aljubarrota, see Thomas M. Izbicki, "The Punishment of Pride: Castilian Reactions to the Battle of Aljubarrota," *Medieval Iberia*, pp. 217–28.

11 The will of Aldonza Téllez, who died in 1443, is printed in *Pruebas*, pp. 87–90.

12 The marriage treaty, negotiated between Manrique and the bride's grandmother, Mencia de Cisneros, was signed in July 1395: RAH, Salazar T–36, ff. 159–60v.

13 Salazar y Castro, 1:485–501, 526–33.

14 Admiral Mendoza frequently appears in Ayala's *Crónica del Rey Don Enrique Tercero del Castilla e de León* in *CRC*, 2, *BAE*, 68 (Madrid, 1953), pp. 65–144 see esp. pp. 196–97, 216, 224). An early fifteenth-century author named Fernán Pérez de Guzmán, who has left us a capsule biography of Mendoza, observes "en el tiempo del non auia en Castilla cauallero tanto heredado." See Fernán Pérez de Guzmán, *Generaciones y Semblanzas* (Buenos Aires, 1947), p. 34. The document elevating Mendoza to the position of Lord Admiral is contained in RAH, Salazar M–9, ff. 76–77 (1494).

main branch of the house of Mendoza, members of which would amass in the course of the fifteenth century enormous property and numerous titles, principal among them Marquess of Santillana (1445) and Duke of the Infantado (1475). The couple's eldest surviving son was the great warrior-poet, Iñigo López de Mendoza (1398–1458), first Marquess de Santillana. Their grandson was the Cardinal-Archbishop of Toledo, Pedro Gonzalez de Mendoza (d.1495), who, for many years served as the principal adviser to the Catholic Monarchs.

In this manner was established the *deudo* – that tie of kinship – which should theoretically have drawn the houses of Mendoza and Manrique more closely together. Unfortunately, the relationship also had built into it the seeds of division in the form of a major property dispute.

Before any aristocratic match could take place, certain financial details had to be worked out – the size of the dowry (*dote*) to be settled upon the bride by her family and the dower rights (*arras*) which she would receive from her husband. Generally speaking, the larger the dowry she brought, the larger the dower she could command. As heiress to two great fortunes, Doña Leonor's dower would be a substantial one; in providing it, her first husband, Juan Téllez, had followed a very common procedure: rather than turn over the cash, he had pledged as security three of his properties – Liébana, Pernia, and Campo de Suso.[15] When Don Juan died at Aljubarrota, these properties remained in the widow's possession.

In February 1387, nineteen months after Aljubarrota, Leonor de la Vega tried to transfer this property to her daughter. Her remarriage was in the offing and she feared that her future husband might attempt to seize possession of the lands pledged for her dower. Consequently, she stated her conviction that those lands should immediately go to her daughter, Aldonza, the legitimate heir of Juan Téllez, and suggested that her dower rights might be settled by simply giving her the income for the next fifteen years.[16]

The proposed transfer never took place. Within a year, Doña Leonor married the future Admiral Mendoza and, as she had predicted, her new spouse was loath to surrender the lands. He continued to occupy them until such time as the question of ownership could be resolved in his favor. That moment came in November 1395, when his royal patron, Enrique III, duly declared that the properties had reverted to the crown and immediately regranted them to the admiral.[17]

---

[15] The dowry, which Enrique II pledged in his nephew's behalf, was 200,000 mrs. Since the bride was under twenty-five at the time of her marriage, the properties securing that dowry were originally turned over to her mother for safe keeping, in accordance with Castilian law. By the terms of the contract, whenever Juan Téllez or his heirs paid the 200,000 mrs., the properties would be returned to them: *Fuero Real*, bk. III, tit. ii, law 3; *Pruebas*, p. 677 (1387); RAH, Salazar M–14, ff. 166–67 (1387). *Memorial*, ff. 98v–101v.

[16] *Pruebas*, p. 677; *Pleito*, ff. 166r–v; *Memorial*, ff. 100v–101.

[17] *Pleito*, ff. 164v–65v; *Memorial*, ff. 106–7.

King Enrique claimed this reversion despite the presence of the grantee's daughter, Aldonza Téllez, who, as a direct descendant, was fully capable of inheriting the lands under the terms of the original grant. The king based his claim on a notorious provision written into the will of his grandfather Enrique II – the so-called "entailing clause."

Born the illegitimate son of Alfonso XI (1311–1350), Enrique II had mounted the throne only after defeating his legitimate half-brother, Pedro the Cruel, in a bloody civil war. To secure the support which had made this victory possible, Enrique had alienated a good part of the royal patrimony and, as king, had faced the unenviable task of refilling those same royal coffers which he had so sadly depleted. His most famous expedient for regaining some of the lost property was a clause which appeared in his last will, a document drawn up in 1374 but not made public until his death five years later.[18]

Although the will reaffirmed Enrique's many property grants, it saddled them with a new condition – one which made their reversion to the Crown far more likely. In Enrique's own words:

> Let these grants be held in entail [*mayorazgo*] and fixed upon the eldest child. If any holder dies without a legitimate child, let the properties then return to the crown of our realm.[19]

Thus, by a single if highly unorthodox stroke, Enrique converted into entailed estates all of the grants that he had bestowed during his reign. Furthermore, he imposed upon them much more stringent conditions for inheritance than would normally have been the case. Ordinarily, an entail granted by the Crown could be inherited by any legitimate, direct descendant of the recipient. This meant that if some future holder were to die without issue, the estates could pass to another line directly descended from the grantee. By contrast, Enrique's "entailing clause" permitted inheritance only by a legitimate descendant of the most recent holder. This meant that if any person who held the entail failed to produce legitimate progeny, the estates would escheat to the Crown. They could not pass to a collateral relative of the last holder, even if that relative had descended directly from the original recipient.

In 1395, Enrique III used this provision of his grandfather's will, a provision both hated and feared by Castile's aristocracy, to reclaim the lands of his uncle, Juan Téllez. In the new grant to Admiral Mendoza, the king explained that after the battle of Aljubarrota, the property had passed to Don Juan's infant son, Don Juanico, who had shortly thereafter died without issue. Under the terms of the "entailing clause," it had then reverted to the Crown rather than passing on to the dead boy's sister.[20] Not surprisingly, the clause was an ever-present sore

---

[18] The *Testamento de Don Enrique II* is appended to Ayala's *Crónica de Enrique II, CRC*, 2:39–44.

[19] Ibid., p. 42.

[20] The grant is contained in both the *Pleito*, ff. 164v–65v, and the *Memorial*, ff. 106–7.

point with Castilian aristocrats, many of whom held at least part of their property from Enrique II. The provision, imposed both unilaterally and after the fact, greatly diminished the inheritability of their grants, thereby suspending a "sword of Damocles" over future generations of their families. In 1390, at the *Cortes* of Guadalajara, the nobility of Castile passionately challenged the legitimacy of the clause, and ultimately prevailed upon Enrique II's son, Juan I (1379–1390), to revoke it.

Unfortunately, the royal revocation came too late to do the descendants of Juan Téllez any good. Don Juan had died in 1385, his heir, the young Don Juanico, less than two years later. At that time, the "entailing clause" of Enrique II's will was still in full force. As a result, Enrique III felt fully justified in invoking it against Don Juan's daughter, even though he appears to have waited until the 1390s to do so.[21]

Like most Castilian aristocrats, the dispossessed daughter and her husband regarded the "entailing clause" as having always been both unjust and illegal. In the opening years of their marriage, they merely bided their time, awaiting a good opportunity to regain the lost estates, if not by law then by force. During Admiral Mendoza's lifetime, such an opportunity never arose. His high position and continuing influence with the king precluded any serious challenge to his possession of the northern lands. Then, in the spring of 1404, the admiral contracted a serious illness and, within a matter of weeks, died.[22] He left as his principal heir the eldest surviving son of his marriage to Leonor de la Vega, the six-year old Iñigo López de Mendoza, who would later become the first Marquess of Santillana.[23] The succession of a minor could throw the affairs of a noble house into turmoil just as readily it could those of a kingdom. And so the admiral's death provided a golden opportunity to all those who hoped to seize some part of his estate, including his stepdaughter, Aldonza Téllez, and her husband. Aided by an internal faction which favored their cause, the couple marched in and seized the disputed properties. This initial act of aggression ushered in a period of nearly four decades during which the house of Manrique repeatedly attempted – and ultimately failed – to make good its claim through

[21] The petition of the aristocrats challenging the "entailing clause" is printed in its entirety in Ayala, *Cronica de Juan I*, p. 142.

[22] Although some authors, including Pérez de Guzmán, date Admiral Mendoza's death to 1405, primary documentation establishes beyond all doubt that he actually died the preceding year. This discrepancy has already been noted by other important scholars who have studied the family's history: see Salazar y Castro, 3:503–4; José Amador de los Rios, *Vida del Marqués de Santillana* (Buenos Aires, 1947), pp. 23, 101.

[23] An earlier will, drafted in 1400, identified the admiral's principal heir as a son named Garcia, and left only a minor share of the estate to the boy's younger brother, Iñigo López. However, according to the will drawn up on 5 May 1404, when Admiral Mendoza lay dying, Iñigo López had become the major heir, leading one to conclude that, in the intervening period, death had claimed the older brother: AHN, Osuna 1762 (1400) and Osuna 1762 (1404); reproduced in Layna Serrano, 1:298–310.

the use of force. Three times, members of the family or their supporters occupied part of the disputed property, only to be forced on each occasion to hand it back to the Mendozas. Several of these attempts to seize the property more or less coincided with outbreaks of violence on the national level, as the Manriques used disturbed conditions in Castile in order to mask their own illegal activities.

The changing relationship during these decades between Leonor de la Vega and her daughter, Aldonza Téllez, illustrates just how a property dispute of this sort could effectively cancel the kinship ties out of which it had arisen. In the years immediately after the death of Juan Téllez, mother and daughter had been on good terms. Doña Leonor had tried (albeit unsuccessfully) to transfer the Asturian lands to Aldonza. Then came that series of events which precipitated the quarrel – starting with the mother's remarriage to Admiral Mendoza around 1388 and culminating in the admiral's death in 1404.

Thereafter, as the years passed and the pair repeatedly clashed over the northern valleys, relations became ever more strained until, in 1432, as the mother lay dying, she dictated a last will completely disinheriting her daughter.[24] In Leonor de la Vega's own words, "I declare her [Aldonza] to be a stranger and I disinherit her in everything I possess."[25] In the will, Doña Leonor leaves no doubt that this estrangement had grown out of the fight for property:

> the said Doña Aldonza was very ungrateful to me in my lifetime and did me many grave and atrocious injuries and dishonored me in word and deed. [She] and her husband wished to dispossess me. They took from me by force and against my will many of my goods and properties and they fomented against me many malicious lawsuits over their possession.[26]

Clearly, the bitterness of the Mendoza-Manrique property dispute now far overshadowed the *deudo* out of which it had emerged, a fine illustration of how kinship often tended to divide rather than unite.

---

[24] One of Spain's most famous chroniclers, Hernando del Pulgar, states that Leonor de la Vega died while her son, Iñigo López de Mendoza, was still only an infant, testimony to the fact that even the most accomplished of chroniclers occasionally err: see Hernando del Pulgar, *Claros Varones de Castilla* (Madrid, 1954), p. 37.

[25] AHN, Osuna 1762, n. 2 (1432). The secondary literature contains some confusion as to precisely whom it was that Doña Leonor disinherited. This is due in large measure to José Amador de los Rios, a prominent literary critic of the nineteenth century, whose biography of the first Marquess of Santillana confused Doña Leonor's daughter, Aldonza Téllez de la Vega, with her stepdaughter, Aldonza de Mendoza, and alleged that the latter rather than the former had been disinherited: Amador de los Rios, pp. 50–1. However, a careful reading of the passage of the will leaves no doubt as to whom Doña Leonor intended to exclude. Nevertheless, confusion on this point continues. See, for example, Rogelio Pérez Bustamante, *Sociedad, Economía, Fiscalidad y Gobierno en las Asturias de Santillana (S. XIII–XV)* (Santander, 1979), pp. 73–74.

[26] AHN, Osuna 2762, n. 2 (1420).

II

The property quarrel begun in 1404 would drag on not only for decades, but for generations. While the violent phase ended in 1445, to be followed by a hiatus of more than half a century, the quarrel would pick up again in 1510 when the Manriques brought their suit into the Castilian courts. Not until 1577, after the original trial and two appeals, did the Royal Council finally issue its definitive sentence, favoring the house of Mendoza.[27]

Nevertheless, despite the considerable significance of this dispute to both families, the extent to which it dictated their relationship with one another must not be overestimated. To neither of these great noble houses was any one property dispute an all-consuming matter. Between outbreaks of violence there were long periods of inactivity, during which each family went about its other business, seemingly oblivious to the unresolved problem. They interacted peacefully enough, and even intermarried. Nor did their disagreement over this one block of property dictate to either party just how it would line up in Castilian politics. On the contrary, on various occasions, the two families found themselves allies on the national level, even at moments when engaged in bitter conflict over the northern lands.

Faced with these facts, it is tempting to fall back upon "ties of kinship" (or *deudo*) as an explanation for why two such families could co-operate on the national level, despite their deep and abiding division over property. This is precisely the temptation to which Professor Nader yields in her book. By contrast, I would argue that the historian should be somewhat less eager to fall back upon the explanation of kinship. Instead, he or she should carefully examine all of the circumstances, to be certain that there were not factors other than kinship better able to account for what happened.

The second part of this article will attempt to illustrate this point by focusing closely upon the activities of the two families during the third and final outbreak of violence in their dispute over the northern lands, an episode which closely coincided with one of the major political crises of fifteenth-century Castile.

In the years between 1438 and 1445, Castile experienced political turmoil unequalled since the civil wars which had brought Enrique II to power nearly a century earlier.[28] Like most of the lesser disturbances that troubled the reign

---

27 For a complete account of this dispute, see L. J. Andrew Villalon, " 'The Law's Delay': The Anatomy of an Aristocratic Property Dispute (1350–1577)" (Ph.D. diss., Yale University, 1984).

28 The Castilian political crisis of the 1440s is extensively covered in the chronicles of the period. In compiling my treatment of the event, I have utilized the four most prominent: (1) *Crónica del Serenisimo Principe Don Juan, Segundo Rey deste Nombre en Castilla y en León*, in *CRC*, 3, *BAE*, 68; (2) Pedro Carillo de Huete, *Crónica del Halconero de*

of Juan II, this major crisis centered around his royal favorite, the Constable of Castile, Alvaro de Luna. After ruling Castile for nearly three decades, Constable de Luna would end on the block, a victim of the king whom he had long served. However, in 1438, that event lay fifteen years in the future, and de Luna still controlled both his king and the kingdom. Since 1429, he had faced no serious challenge to his authority. Yet large segments of the Castilian aristocracy regarded the constable with equal measures of fear, hatred, and jealousy; and resistance to his rule was never far beneath the surface. All that was needed was the proper spark.

In August, 1438, Pedro Manrique (a prominent nobleman from a different branch of the same noble house) escaped from Crown custody and fled to the estates of a close friend. To head off any royal attempt to retake him, the fugitive and his host gathered around them their relatives and friends. From the start, these rebellious nobles demanded the removal of Constable de Luna, whom they imagined to be at the root of all their troubles. Their stand on this matter guaranteed them widespread support from their class. One after another, disgruntled Castilian aristocrats flocked to their banner and before the year's end most of the nobility had entered into a coalition dedicated to de Luna's overthrow.

Meanwhile, the branch of Castile's royal family which for some decades had ruled the neighboring kingdoms of Aragon and Navarre saw in the crisis an opportunity to regain Castilian lands confiscated from them during the last anti-de Luna uprising.[29] In 1439, two of these so-called *infantes*[30] of Aragon – King Juan of Navarre and his younger brother, Enrique – returned to Castile, where they quickly assumed leadership of the aristocratic uprising. In 1440, they were joined by their sister, the Queen of Castile, along with her son, the future Enrique IV (1454–1474).[31]

Backed by a formidable military array, the coalition seized royal cities, dispatched letters of defiance to the constable, and eventually declared him an outlaw. When the king resisted this attack on his favorite, the rebels seized his person and, in 1441, forced him to approve a sentence which stripped de Luna of power, permanently banished him from public life, and turned the governing

Juan II (Madrid, 1946); (3) Lope Barrientos (Bishop of Avila), *Refundición de la Crónica del Halconero* (Madrid, 1947); (4) *Crónica de Alvaro de Luna* (Madrid, 1940).

29 *Crónica de Juan II*, pp. 462–65; *Crónica de Alvaro de Luna*, p. 93.

30 The word *infante* refers to the son of a king (the female form is *infanta*). The so-called *infantes of Aragon* were the sons of Fernando of Antequera, a younger brother of Enrique III of Castile who, as a result of the Compromise of Caspe (1412), became the first Trastámara monarch of Aragon. Despite the removal of their branch of the family into Aragon, the *infantes* contined to play a major role in Castilian history throughout the first half of the fifteenth century.

31 Prince Enrique was the eldest son of King Juan II and his queen, María of Aragon, daughter of Fernando of Antequera and the sister of the *infantes* of Aragon with whom her royal husband had so often found himself in conflict.

of the kingdom over to a regency council, largely controlled by the Aragonese *infantes*.

Despite its initial success, the coalition met the fate of most such attempts at collective action undertaken by medieval aristocrats: its leaders soon began to bicker with one another over the spoils of victory. Late in 1443, the heir to the Castilian throne, Prince Enrique, angered by the preponderant share of power which had fallen to his Aragonese cousins, did a political about-face. Rallying around him other nobles discontented with the leadership of the Aragonese *infantes*, he entered into secret negotiations with the faction supporting Constable de Luna. These political maneuverings eventually led to a new alliance between Prince Enrique, the constable, and their respective allies – an alliance dedicated to freeing the king and breaking the power of the *infantes*.

In summer 1444, the conspirators finally went public, freeing the king and forcing the remaining members of the once dominant anti-de Luna coalition either to withdraw to their estates or retreat into Aragon. During the spring of 1445, the Aragonese *infantes* re-entered Castile and, at the head of their now much-diminished following, made one final bid to regain power. On 19 May, the two sides clashed near the town of Olmedo where the forces of the anti-de Luna coalition were soundly defeated by the backers of King Juan, Prince Enrique, and Constable de Luna. Although, for some months after the battle, hostilities dragged on in a desultory fashion, the crisis finally ended with the rebellion snuffed out, the *infantes* again driven from the realm, and the constable firmly re-established in power.

This turbulent episode in Castilian history coincided with a resurgence of private violence in the Asturias de Santillana, as enemies of the house of Mendoza, acting in the name of the Manriques, once again seized control over the disputed lands. Despite this, the two families appear to have followed a similar path through the national crisis. Early on, both joined the anti-de Luna coalition – the Manriques in 1439, the Mendozas in the following year. Both remained part of that coalition until 1444. Then, within a matter of weeks, both did an abrupt political about-face, joining the prince and the constable in their new alliance.

The question naturally arises: what are we looking at here? Is this a case of kinship ties taking precedence over the property quarrel? Are the two families putting aside their material differences to form and reform their alliances according to the dictates of *deudo*? The answer requires close scrutiny of the motives and actions of both families during these crisis-filled years.

For their part, the Mendozas had enjoyed good relations with the monarchy throughout the 1430s, culminating in 1437 in the king's appointment of Iñigo López de Mendoza as Captain-General of all Castilian forces on the Moorish frontier.[32] Nevertheless, there remained lurking in the background potential for

---

[32] *Crónica de Juan II*, pp. 512, 524–25; RAH, Salazar M–25, ff. 150–60v.

serious friction between King Juan and his powerful vassal, once again, over questions of property, for, during that same decade, the crown found itself enmeshed in several Mendoza property disputes, either in the role of judge or, worse yet, of litigant.

Among the questions of property entrusted to several specially-appointed royal judges was the dispute over the northern valleys, which had once again taken a violent turn around 1430. In 1433, in order to prevent the two sides from resorting to the battlefield, the Crown re-opened its inquiry into the unresolved dispute. A leading royal secretary was assigned to the task of collecting relevant documents and interviewing witnesses. The fruits of his search were then turned over to a pair of royal councillors, whose commission it was to sift through this evidence and dictate a settlement. After five years of sluggish deliberation, they finally handed down a relatively innocuous sentence, returning the property to Mendoza possession, while maintaining intact the Manrique right to seek further redress in the regular courts of Castile. Although this restoration of the *status quo* by the special panel did not satisfy either party, neither found it so unpalatable as to precipitate a break with the Crown.[33]

Unfortunately, the cautious approach adopted in the dispute over the northern valleys was not imitated in the handling of another Mendoza case. This case involved the lands in the Asturias de Santillana which Leonor de la Vega had inherited from her forebears and which had after her death passed into the hands of her eldest son, Iñigo López de Mendoza.

Since the beginning of the fifteenth century, aggressive royal officials in the region had repeatedly tried to extend their jurisdiction into these seigneurial lands of the de la Vegas, despite the strenuous objections of Doña Leonor, her husband Admiral Mendoza, and, later on, their son Don Iñigo. The most recent episode had come early in the 1430s, when a *corregidor*,[34] newly appointed by the Crown, began to meddle.[35]

To make matters worse, Juan II had chosen this moment to confer upon Juan

---

[33] AHN, Osuna 1762, n. 2 (1432); Osuna 1790, n. 8 (1430); Osuna 1799, n. 3 (1431). RAH, Salazar M–9, ff. 57r–v (1431); Salazar M–23, ff. 71v–73; Salazar M–92, ff. 267v–71v (1445).

[34] A royal official assigned to represent the Crown in a town or district. On behalf of the Crown, such an official wielded extensive judicial, administrative, and financial powers within the region entrusted to his care.

[35] This royal challenge to Mendoza jurisdiction over the lands once held by the de la Vegas gave rise to a property dispute between the family and the Crown which was every bit as complex and protracted as the dispute between the houses of Mendoza and Manrique over Liébana and Campo de Suso. Most of my information concerning this dispute comes from a series of documents preserved in the Real Academia's Salazar Collection, the most important of which are (1) a summary of the case entitled *Memorial del Pleyto del Duque del Infantado con el fiscal de su Magestad, y los valles de las Asturias de Santillana*; and (2) an untitled compendium of the relevant documents: RAH, Salazar M–118, ff. 1–66v; M–119, ff. 1–15.

Manrique, second Count of Castañeda, lordship over eight hundred vassals living in the nearby valley of Toranzo.[36] The grantee was the eldest son of Garcí Fernandez Manrique and Aldonza Téllez de la Vega who had assumed the leadership of his family in 1436, thereby becoming Mendoza's chief rival in the Asturias de Santillana.

In 1437, Iñigo López de Mendoza drafted a petition to the Crown, in which he complained of both the royal encroachments upon his seigneurial jurisdiction and the Toranzo grant. This, in turn, forced King Juan to initiate special inquiries into each of these sensitive matters.[37] It was at this juncture that the king chose Iñigo López to take command on the southern frontier. Realizing that his absence might adversely affect the handling of his cases, the new captain-general accepted the royal commission only after receiving a royal pledge that all legal disputes would be held in abeyance until his return.[38]

Mendoza's campaign of 1438 against the Moors yielded some notable successes, including the capture of Huelma. Nevertheless, due to the fast-developing political crisis in Castile, the king soon ordered his captain-general to cut the war short and patch up the best truce he could with the enemy.[39]

Despite his victories, Mendoza did not hesitate to comply with these royal instructions to make peace, having good reasons of his own to get back to the north as quickly as possible. For the royal promise given him upon his departure had not been kept. Juan II had ordered the judges to proceed with their inquiry into the Toranzo grant, despite Mendoza's absence. In December 1438, their deliberations ended with an announcement that this grant of eight hundred vassals to Manrique would be sustained, Mendoza's objections to the contrary notwithstanding.[40] Meanwhile, yet another royal official introduced even more sweeping claims on behalf of the Crown against the de la Vega lands.[41] All this was done with at least the tacit approval of the king.

Not surprisingly, Iñigo López de Mendoza deeply resented this betrayal of his interests. Upon returning to Castile, he rode directly to his estates without putting in the customary appearance at court. He soon learned that his judicial troubles were not the only ones he would have to confront. Seizing upon the

---

36 RAH, Salazar M–119, ff. 2v–4.
37 Mendoza's petition, along with many of the other documents relevant to these proceedings, is reproduced within a much longer document issued by Juan II in January, 1448, spelling out the settlement which recognized Mendoza claims to jurisdiction over the Asturian properties inherited from the House of de la Vega: RAH, Salazar M–118, ff. 17v–18 (1448).
38 RAH, Salazar M–25, ff. 150r–v (1437).
39 *Crónica de Juan*, 2:534–35, 547; Pulgar, p. 40.
40 RAH, Salazar M–119, f. 3. Gaspar Ibañez de Segovia, Marqués de Mondejar, *Historia de la Casa de Mondejar escrita para el Marques de Valhermoso, por el de Mondejar, su abuelo*, a manuscript in RAH, Salazar B–73, see esp. f. 194v.
41 RAH, Salazar M–119, f. 3v.

chaotic state of Castile, his opponents in the northern valleys had once again rebelled. After taking control of Liébana, the principal town in the region, and murdering Mendoza's bailiff, the rebels appealed for help to the Count of Castañeda, who, in turn, lent his own prestige and that of his mother, Aldonza Téllez, to their rebellion.[42]

Mendoza's troubles quickly propelled him into the anti-de Luna coalition. In the spring of 1439, while serving as the Crown's captain-general, he had frustrated the coalition in its attempt to seize an important frontier town.[43] But in January, 1440, having returned north to find his own affairs in disarray, he joined the other disgruntled aristocrats,[44] signed their violent denunciation of the constable, and, with the aid of friends and vassals, occupied the royal city of Guadalajara.[45] Although gravely wounded in a battle with pro-de Luna forces, he recovered in time to endorse the sentence providing for the constable's permanent banishment, and, for a time, he served on the new royal council, dominated by the *infantes* of Aragon.[46]

Some months before Mendoza deserted the Crown and joined the anti-de Luna coalition, his young rival, the Count of Castañeda, had already made the move.[47] As a result, Mendoza and Manrique now found themselves on the same side, but for reasons which apparently had nothing to do with their *deudo*. Mendoza's presence in the coalition resulted from his belief that the Crown, influenced by the royal favorite, had betrayed his interests in the Asturias.

The reason that the Count of Castañeda had joined is harder to fathom. Perhaps it reflected the close attachment his father had once had to the *infantes* of Aragon. Perhaps it was a valid case of *deudo* in operation – *deudo* not with his cousin Mendoza, but with a senior branch of the house of Manrique, in the person of Pedro Manrique, the man whose escape had touched off the crisis. Whatever may have been his reasons, Juan Manrique had joined the anti-de Luna coalition quite sometime before Mendoza, and therefore not because of any kinship ties existing between the two of them.

As already indicated, this coalition against de Luna ultimately became the victim of its own success. Removal of the constable dissolved the cement which had held it together. A serious rift soon developed between the *infantes* of Aragon and Crown Prince Enrique. As a result, the prince met secretly with the bishop of Avila, a staunch partisan of Constable de Luna, and the two men

---

[42] AHN, Osuna 1811, n. 1. RAH, Salazar M–92, ff. 267v–71v.

[43] Huete, p. 284.

[44] AHN, Osuna 1860, n. 3 (1440).

[45] *Crónica de Juan II*, pp. 560–62, 574.

[46] Ibid., pp. 578, 599, 609; Huete, p. 423.

[47] In 1439, the count and his younger brother, Gabriel Manrique, Grand Commander (*comendador mayor*) of Castile in the Military Order of Santiago, joined the rapidly spreading rebellion: *Cronica de Juan II*, pp. 552–55.

worked out an agreement.[48] In March, 1444, the constable secretly endorsed this agreement, but reserved his public adherence until such time as the prince and the bishop could muster additional support.[49]

By then, the prospects of finding that support had greatly improved.[50] Waiting in the wings were the constable's old followers, who had simply been biding their time for the right opportunity to resurface. Other Castilian nobles were becoming restive at the domineering attitude of the Aragonese *infantes*. Some of these men, whose grievances against crown or constable had driven them to join the opposition, might now return to the fold if those grievances were redressed. One such figure was Iñigo López de Mendoza.

In a series of secret negotiations, Don Iñigo made it clear that the family's support could be had for the right price – the price being a readjustment in the Asturian region more favorable to Mendoza interests.[51] Early in July 1444, Prince Enrique won over the house of Mendoza with two promises: first, to surrender all royal claim against the de la Vega lands; secondly, to bestow upon Don Iñigo lordship over one of the principal towns in the region, a place called Santillana del Mar.[52] Less than a month later, the king, having in the meantime escaped from his captivity, confirmed the bargain.[53] In 1445, the king capped these earlier concessions by conferring upon Iñigo López de Mendoza the double title Marquess of Santillana and Count of Real de Manzanares.

Within weeks of having won over Mendoza, the Crown also gained the support of his bitter rival in the property dispute, the young count of Castañeda.[54] The count's change of heart also appears to have resulted from a "royal buy-out." In other words, he too switched sides because it was made worth his while to do so. In August 1444, King Juan not only reaffirmed the Toranzo grant issued six years earlier, but substantially sweetened it by turning over to the Manriques additional crown vassals living in three other Asturian valleys.[55] As a result of these separate "transactions," both Mendoza and

---

48 *Crónica de Juan II*, p. 614; Huete, pp. 449–550.

49 *Crónica de Juan II*, p. 615; Huete, p. 446.

50 *Crónica de Juan II*, pp. 614–21.

51 Ibid., p. 620. The bishop of Avila carefully sounded out Don Iñigo through two fellow conspirators – the Count of Alba and that nobleman's uncle, the archbishop of Toledo. As members of the house of Toledo, they had long enjoyed close ties with the Mendozas. In response to this clandestine overture, Mendoza sent his second son as an emissary to Prince Enrique carrying the message that his support could be had, under the proper circumstances.

52 AHN, Osuna 1784, n. 6 (1 and 2).

53 The royal confirmation is dated 28 July 1444, at the siege of Peñafiel. Three and a half years later, the monarch reaffirmed this arrangement: AHN, Osuna 1784, nos. 1 and 2; RAH, Salazar M–118, ff. 12–19v.

54 *Crónica de Juan II*, pp. 614–15, 620, 622.

55 RAH, Salazar M–118, ff. 19v–20v. In the words of the Crown: "I confer upon you this irrevocable grant of the vassals which I have in the valleys of Gaña, Ruynasa, Sant Vicente, and Toranzo, in the region known as the Asturias de Santillana; excepting [from

Manrique again found themselves fighting on the same side. Once again, however, their presence there seems to have had nothing to do with their bonds of kinship.

In fact, there is one further and even more telling indication that *deudo* played little or no role in motivating either family. Having separately won over to the new alliance both Mendoza and Manrique, the Crown was now hard pressed in keeping them from each other's throats over the issue of the northern valleys! In November, 1444, a royal-sponsored attempt to mediate the outstanding quarrel broke down when Mendoza refused to have anything to do with the proceedings.[56] In the aftermath, both sides began preparing to move into the Asturias de Santillana in force. The prospect of an armed clash between two of its allies, in the depth of the national crisis, forced the Crown once more to intervene.

Juan II summoned both noblemen to appear before him, in order that they might air their differences in the presence his entire council and other members of the alliance. When it still proved impossible to reach a compromise, the king simply reimposed the *status quo ante*, just as his special judges had done a few years earlier. Possession of the valleys would be restored to the house of Mendoza. At the same time, the right of the Manriques to seek redress through the regular judicial system would be preserved. Finally, both the Count of Castañeda and his mother were ordered to withdraw their backing from the rebels within the valleys, who claimed to be acting in their name.[57] In June 1445, abandoned by the house of Manrique, the rebellion in the Asturias finally collapsed.[58]

Although the houses of Mendoza and Manrique moved through the political crisis of the 1440s more or less in tandem, their appearance first on one side and then on the other had little if anything to do with their kinship ties. At the root of their actions were other, more tangible concerns. Like all great nobles of the period, they had many "irons in the fire." They did not define family interests solely in terms of one property dispute, however important and longstanding it may have been. Despite their conflict over the northern valleys

---

this grant] those other valleys in the Asturias which I have given to my vassal, Iñigo López de Mendoza . . . and also excepting any vassals which the said Iñigo López might have in these four valleys."

[56] *Pruebas*, pp. 90–91; *Pleito*, f. 150. Although the agreement to submit to binding arbitration bears the endorsement of the Count of Alba, who claimed to be acting for Iñigo López de Mendoza, it is highly questionable that the count had received any authorization to make such a commitment. All other evidence from this period indicates that Mendoza was in no mood to compromise. What is more, when the house of Manrique introduced this document into their suit many decades later, Don Iñigo's descendants vociferously argued that their ancestor had refused to take any part in the negotiations.

[57] AHN, Osuna 1811, n. 1; RAH, Salazar, ff. 268–69v.

[58] RAH, Salazar M–92, ff. 267v–71v; B–73, ff. 197v–99 (Mondejar MS).

and the abiding dislike for one another which seems to have grown out of it, the two families did not hesitate to become political allies when it suited their overall interests to do so. Let me close this article with my reworking of an old and well-known aphorism: "Blood may indeed be thicker than water, but soil often proves to be thicker than both."

The Iberian *Diffidamentum*:
From Vassalic Defiance to the *Code Duello*

DONALD J. KAGAY

The words of John of Salisbury, the brilliant philosopher of the late twelfth century who had witnessed human violence at its most frightening when his master, Thomas à Becket, was murdered in 1191, may serve as an opening chord for this, and all, investigations of mankind's darker side: "nothing is more harmful to man than man."[1] Despite the destructive potential of its individual members, human society expends much of its energy and resources in trying to sublimate, or at least channel, such vehement behavior. This paper will trace one such societal mechanism for the control of violence – the challenge or defiance – from its feudal origins to a form with clear influence on the modern world. The investigation will focus on the states of Christian Iberia, most particularly the realms which comprise the Crown of Aragon – Catalonia, Valencia and Aragon.

To understand the language of violence by challenge for Spain and much of the rest of western Europe, one must look to the seed-bed of feudal institutions: the kingdom of the Merovingians and the empire of the Carolingians. If the essential features of European feudalism (lordship, vassalage, and the oaths of homage and fealty which bound two parties to pledged allegiance and responsibility) emerged under Frankish rule,[2] so did the means by which feudal ties could be broken. While the feudal relationship was clearly tipped in favor of the lord, the vassal was allotted some clear points of defense by feudal custom. Thus if a lord tried to kill or unjustly imprison his man, committed adultery with his wife, or failed to defend him before the law or on the battlefield as he had sworn to, the vassal could unilaterally declare the feudal bond shattered.[3] He did so by engaging in the *exfestucatio*, a ritual which reversed the ceremony of fealty. This rite consisted of breaking a stick or twig and hurling it at the feet

---

1 John of Salisbury, *Policraticus: The Statesman's Book*, trans. Murray E. Markland (New York, 1977), p. 151.
2 See Susan Reynolds, *Fiefs and Vassals: The Medieval Evidence Reinterpreted* (Oxford, 1994), pp. 75–114, for a reconsideration of even this premise.
3 David Herlihy, ed., *The History of Feudalism* (New York, 1970), p. 87, nos. 77, 104; F. L. Ganshof, *Feudalism*, trans. Philip Grierson (1961; repr., New York, 1964), p. 98.

of the offending lord. With the possibility of violent exchanges inherent in such ceremonies, the rupture of feudal ties eventually came to be carried out by letter or proxy.[4] These documents of defiance mark the real starting point for the manipulation of violence in medieval Iberia.

With the tenth century, "public" structures were crumbling all over the remnants of the Carolingian empire. In Catalonia, a new era of "militarism" based on the myriad of castles which dominated and, in fact, gave the region its name, was consolidated by feudal relations which lent security and power to both lord and vassal.[5] The obligations which linked the two were recorded in a feudal pact or *convenientia*.[6] While such documents set out a contract of sorts between lord and vassal,[7] they clearly reflected the inferior legal status of the vassal who could scarcely attempt to gain redress for his grievances with his *senior*, but rather had to opt for the formal infringement of the *convenientia* itself. This cancellation of a vassalic loyalty which had been pledged in the oath of homage or *affidamentum* was announced to the lord and the land in general with the vassal's proclamation of a *diffidamentum* or formal divestment of all connections to the lord.[8] This breach naturally implied the vassal's surrender of all castles granted by the lord along with their dependent territories, revenues and all other fiefs. Though such a procedure was specified by feudal custom and such written codes as the *Usatges of Barcelona*, the *Fueros of Aragon*, and *Furs of Valencia*, aggrieved vassals hardly saw matters in this way. They often retained fiefs even after breaking faith with their lords as a point of leverage for reaching a final arbitrated solution or simply because they claimed full tenure for these holdings since they or their families had held them for over thirty years – the Visigothic prescriptive limit for uncontested ownership.[9] In such cases, the offended lord had several options before the law. He could issue

---

4   Marc Bloch, *Feudal Society*, trans. L. A. Mangon, 2 vols. (Chicago, 1964), 1:228–29; Jean-Pierre Poly and Eric Bournazel, *The Feudal Transformation, 900–1200*, trans. Caroline Higgitt (New York, 1991), pp. 62–63; Reynolds, p. 371; Ganshof, p. 99.

5   Honofre Manescal, *Sermo vulgarament anomenat del serenissim Senyor Don Jaume Segon* (Barcelona, 1603), f. 12; Pierre Bonnassie, *La Catalogne du milieu du Xe à la fin du XIe siècle: Croissance et mutation d'une société*, 2 vols. (Toulouse, 1975–76), 2:741–44.

6   Thomas N. Bisson, "Feudalism in Twelfth-Century Catalonia," *Structures féodales et féodalisme dans l'occident et mediterranéen (Xe–XIIIe siècles)*, Colloque International Organisé par le Centre de la Recherche Scientifique et l'École Française de Rome, October 1978 (Paris, 1983), pp. 176–77.

7   Walter Ullmann, *The Individual and Society in the Middle Ages* (Baltimore, 1966), p. 65.

8   Eulalia Rodón Binué, *El lenguaje técnico del feudalismo en el siglo XI en Cataluña* (Barcelona, 1957), pp. 12–14, 80; Luis Garcia de Valdeavellano y Arcimus, *Curso de história de los instituciónes españoles de los origenes al final de la edad media* (Madrid, 1968), pp. 324, 401.

9   *Monumenta Germaniae Historica [MGH]*, *Leges Nationum Germanicarum Legum* sectio 1: *Leges Visigothorum* (Hanover, 1902), bk. II, tit. 1, chap. 20; bk. V, tit. 1, chap. 4; bk. X, tit. 2, chaps. 3, 6, 63, 209, 339, 392–94; P. D. King, *Law and Society in the Visigothic Kingdom* (Cambridge, 1972), pp. 93, 101, 156, 205.

a "public accusation" (*reptamentum, riepto*) against his vassal and settle the matter through judicial means, normally by champions in the wager by battle.[10] Such a peaceful and relatively civilized method was not the road most often taken because of a simple quirk of all medieval legal systems – without a general punitive force to bring all disputants before the law, whether royal or seigneurial, the over-mighty subject was more than willing to remain behind the strong walls of his castle and openly defy his lord. From the lordly side, then, the vassal's *diffidamentum* could only be viewed as a declaration of war and was treated as such.[11] Suffering such open "treason" (*bausia*) at the hands of his trusted subordinate, the lord felt that it was both his right and duty to try to reclaim the fief or castle and hold it until the traitor came to his senses.[12]

The response to the *diffidamentum* could thus fall within the realms of adjudication or military vengeance depending on which path the challenged party took. Despite the sovereign's role as the high judge of the land, many an offended Aragonese or Catalan lord trusted to his own strong arm to gain justice and some measure of vindication from the issuer of the challenge. If he wished to remain within the limits of the law in gaining such satisfaction, he turned to the private arena of judicial combat (*torna, batallia*). In an attempt to prevent the defiance from becoming grounds for vendetta, Catalan, Aragonese, Valencian, and Navarrese law all interposed a ten-day cooling off period. During this time, any violent acts exchanged between the principals made them traitors before law and "at the mercy of the king." This respite was also used to lay out the conditions under which the struggle would take place. The site of the combat, the allotment of expenses, and the formal determination of what victory and defeat would mean in the settlement of the initial disputes were all to be agreed upon before the combatants took the field. If the principals were of different ranks, champions of the same class would be chosen. Thus the horror, at least to aristocratic sensibilities, of lesser men entering the lists against their betters was removed. While the challenged party normally had the choice of weapons, the battle was customarily fought out with sword and shield. Nobles fought on horseback while townsmen and peasants normally fought on foot; swords were used by the first group and quarterstaff by the second and third. None seemed to fight in special uniform or sporting a distinctive haircut as in England.[13] To assure that the whole process was not in

10 Joan Bastardas, ed., *Usatges de Barcelona: El codí a mitjan segle XII* (Barcelona, 1984), pp. 73, 124–26, 144, 146–48, arts. 26, 89, 111, 114; Donald J. Kagay, trans., *The Usatges of Barcelona: The Fundamental Law of Catalonia* (Philadelphia, 1994), pp. 71, 87, 92–93.

11 Rodón Binué, p. xvii.

12 Joannis de Socarraris, *In tractatum Petri Alberti canonici Barchinonensis De consuetudinibus Cataloniae inter dominos & vassalos* (Barcelona, 1551), pp. 596–97; Josep Rovira i Ermengol, ed. *Los Usatges de Barcelona i commeracions de Pere Albert* (Barcelona, 1933), pp. 200–4; *Usatges*, trans. Kagay, p. 42.

13 Henry Charles Lea, *Superstition and Force* (Philadelphia, 1866); pts. 1–2 repr. as *The*

vain, guarantors were appointed from each side who would post sizeable sureties with a local official or clergyman. If the decision rendered by the battle was not adhered to by one of the parties, this "earnest money" was forfeit to the other.[14] With all these arrangements, a quasi-legal structure was fashioned so disputes of a violent world might be brought to a mutually acceptable conclusion. The challenge (*desafiament* in Catalan and *desafio* in Aragonese and Castilian), though still firmly rooted in feudal practice, also gave members of all classes the opportunity to force settlements on the field of *batallia*. Given the political impotence of rulers when this form took shape in the early Middle Ages, a victory in judicial battle, like survival of the ordeal, marked one as favored by a higher court – that of the Almighty.[15]

This "direct sort of wild justice" spread across Europe with the encouragement of Charlemagne and his successors, and quickly entered the realm of law and jurisprudence. The "battle" was thus defined by a twelfth-century English code as "a single combat between two men to prove the rightness of their case – and whoever won was understood to have proven his case."[16] Despite its widespread use throughout the Continent and in England by the thirteenth century, the "barbarous foreign custom" of wager by battle was looked on as a judicial perversion and threat to both papal and royal power.[17] Even with such direct attacks, the battle could not be killed outright and remained as an adjunct to established adjudication until modern times.[18] In the Iberian states, sword justice was marginalized by allowing only the peasantry and urban proletariat to settle disputes by such violent means.[19] Eventually its semi-legal character

---

Duel and the Oath, ed. Edward Peters (Philadelphia, 1974), pp. 186–87; M. T. Clanchy, "Highway Robbery and the Trial by Battle in the Hampshire Eyre of 1249," *Medieval Legal Records Edited in Memory of C. A. F. Meekings*, ed. R. F. Hunnisett and J. B. Post (London, 1978), p. 34; Frederick Pollock and Frederick William Maitland, *The History of English Law before the Time of Edward I*, 2 vols. (Cambridge, 1968), 2:633–34.

14   Francesch Carreras i Candi and Siegfried Bosch, "Desafiaments a Catalunya en el Segle XVI," *Boletín del Real Academia de Buenas Letras de Barcelona [BRABLB]* 16 (1933–6): 46–47; José Luis Lacruz Berdejo and Jesús Bergua Camón, "Fueros de Aragón," *Anuario de Derecho Aragonés* 2(1945): 313–15, 319–20, arts. 249, 253, 262; Rodón Binué, pp. 39–41, 245–46; Mauricio Mohlo, ed., *El Fuero de Jaca* (Zaragoza, 1964), pp. 166, 190, arts. 2, 29; Manuel Dualde Serrano, ed., *Fori Antiqui Valentiae* (Madrid-Valencia, 1950–67), p. 246, bk. 129, tits. 8–10.

15   Lea, p. 104.

16   *Encyclopedia Britannica*, 11th ed., 29 vols. (London, 1910), 8:642; James P. Gilchrist, *A Brief Display or the Origins and History of Ordeals, Trials by Battle and Chivalry or Honour and the Decision of Private Quarrels by Single Combat* (London, 1821), pp. 25–26; A. J. Robertson, ed. and trans., *The Laws of the Kings of England from Edmund to Henry I*, 2 vols. (Cambridge, 1968), 2:633–34.

17   William Stubbs, *The Constitutional History of England and its Origin and Development*, 3 vols. (Oxford, 1874), 1:616; Lea, pp. 140–65; George Nelson, *Trial by Combat* (New York, 1891), pp. 14–15, 313–14.

18   Clanchy, p. 29; Jens Rohrkasten, *Die englischen Krazeugen, 1130–1330*, Berliner Historiche Studien, 16 (Berlin, 1990).

19   Lea, pp. 146, 151, 214. For a Muslim view of *battalia*, see *An Arab-Syrian Gentleman*

was steadily encompassed by another form, the *duellum* or duel in which man challenged and fought man to finally settle grievances and gain vengeance – all without a shred of legality. Unlike the wager by battle, then, the duel made no claims to legal existence, but stood as "an affront to the law." Despite its wholly private nature, however, the duel still laid claim to certain judicial formats of the *batallia*, among them the challenge which called an adversary to the field of honor where his insulting words might be defended or retracted. Though royal and town law in all the Crown of Aragon had long attempted to provide public procedures for the settlement of such potentially explosive arguments,[20] men ultimately relied on their own martial prowess to safeguard their honor, the importance of which was expressed by such late medieval voices as that of the Castilian poet Jorge Manrique who observed that, "the life of the reputation is more glorious than physical and finally eternal life."[21] With this ethereal view of human honor as a backdrop, it is hardly surprising that the duel had a long and volatile history in later medieval Iberia, and was so connected with the protection of *honor* that the challenge became synonymous with the duel itself.[22] The ritual of exoneration also retained its feudal overlay with the understanding that the opponents would not engage in hostilities for ten days after the initial affront and the statement of the challenge. In fact, some of the most illustrious defiances of later medieval Iberia centered on this "cooling-off" period.

The possibilities of the *diffidamentum* were not lost on the monarchies of the Iberian states or their European neighbors. Thus, when Charles of Anjou, the French sovereign of Sicily, eventually saw the island come under the control of the Aragonese king Pedro III (1276–1285) in 1282–1283, he proceeded to proclaim that his rival was a traitor both to feudal law and to their friendship since he had not given ten days prior warning before the invasion of the island. With his own honor at stake, Pedro agreed to meet Charles and a band of hundred retainers in the lists with a band of equal number. This small battle, much like those of later tournaments, was to take place in the neutral English territory of Bordeaux with its lord, King Edward I of England, as referee.[23] Within the Iberian Peninsula proper, the *desafio* was also used to

and Warrior in the Period of the Crusades: Memoirs of Usāmah Ibn-Munqidh, trans. Philip K. Hitti (1929; repr., Princeton, 1987), pp. 167–68.

20 Jaime Caruana Gómez de Barreda, ed., *El fuero latino de Teruel* [*FLT*] (Teruel, 1974), p. 345, art. 425; *Usatges*, pp. 64, 103, arts. 17, 70; *Usatges*, trans. Kagay, 80, 90; Ambrosio Huici Miranda and Maria Desamparados Cabanes Pecourt, eds., *Documentos de Jaime I de Aragón* [*DJ*], 4 vols. (Valencia, 1976–82), 2:115, 132, docs. 338, 351.

21 François Bellaçois, *The Duel, its Rise and Fall in Early Modern France*, ed. and trans. Trista Selous (New Haven CT, 1990), p. 213.

22 Ibid., p. 33; Julio Caro Baroja, "Honour and Shame: A Historical Account of Several Conflicts," trans. R. Johnson in *Honour and Shame: The Values of a Mediterranean Society*, ed. J. G. Peristiany (1966; repr., Chicago, 1974), pp. 1–137.

23 Lea, pp. 105–6; Bernat Desclot, *Chronicle of the Reign of King Pedro III of Aragon*, trans. F. L. Critchlow, 2 vols. (Princeton, 1928), pp. 103–18, chaps. 31–32.

personalize international rivalries. For example, in 1361 after several seasons of Castilian campaigning against the Crown of Aragon, the King of Castile, Pedro I (1350–1369), formally challenged his cousin and archenemy Pedro IV of Aragon (1336–1387) to single combat to determine the fate of the belea-guered city of Valencia.[24] Surely the most significant defiance of the era was that delivered by the English sovereign Edward III (1329–1377) to his lord, the French king Philip VI (1328–1350). Though this *diffidamentum*, like those mentioned above, never resulted in the proposed single or conscribed combat, it did signal an era of intermittent war which would engulf England, France and the Spanish states for the next century.[25]

The challenge was thus a procedure fraught with manifold dangers and repercussions, many of which the involved parties could not anticipate. The rules of the challenge, however, were well known. The challenge in such disputes remained tied to the public accusation and painted the adversary as a faithless violator of sworn commitments. To shield his honor from such charges, the defied party generally reacted by declaring the challenger to be a *calumpniator* or perjurer both because he was spreading lies and might also be infringing feudal ties which bound them.[26] Though, by law, such differences should have been settled in a royal tribunal, the results of due process were often too lengthy and expensive and so combatants sought out a neutral site and referees to see that the duel was conducted fairly.[27] By the later Middle Ages, this format of challenge, combat agreement, and duel transcended the disputes of lords and vassals. Instead, they were used by men of all classes, even the peasantry, to safeguard their dignity and that of their families.[28]

With the long history of the *desafiament* in Catalonia and *desafio* in Aragon and Castile, it seemed only logical that Spain would become one of the influences on the regularization of duelling forms with the emergence of the *code duello* in the later decades of the fifteenth century. Drawing from the terms of tournament combat and duel agreements, the code laid out proper grounds for the honorific battle and detailed procedures which followed from the challenge.[29] As the duel of the later medieval centuries still wore the raiment of a feudal heritage, so did the duellist – in both academic theory and popular imagination. Many an Iberian and European knight agreed whole-heartedly with the poet and visionary Ramon Lull who claimed that knights

---

[24] Clara Estow, *Pedro the Cruel of Castile, 1350–1369* (Leiden, 1995), p. 215.

[25] Eduard Perroy, *The Hundred Years War*, trans. W. B. Wells (New York, 1965), pp. 92–93.

[26] Victor Kiernan, *The Duel* (Oxford, 1986), pp. 32–34; Frederick R. Bryson, *The Point of Honor in Sixteenth-Century Italy: An Aspect of the Life of the Gentleman* (New York, 1935), pp. 24–26; idem, *The Sixteenth-Century Italian Duel* (Chicago, 1938), pp. 6, 18–19.

[27] Lea, p. 229.

[28] Carreras i Candi and Bosch, p. 47, n. 2; Kiernan, *Sixteenth-Century Italian Duel*, p. 15; Alfred Vaigts, *A History of Militarism* (1937; repr., New York, 1959), p. 70.

[29] Richard Barber, *The Knight and Chivalry* (New York, 1970), pp. 173–76.

were to be honored by all other classes since they, in fact, personified the law.[30] Even such law codes as the *Usatges of Barcelona* saw the sovereign's court as a site for the honoring of nobles and, in fact, a place where "new knights" were made.[31] Though imagination seldom squared with the lives many knights led, it pointed clearly to the way nobles thought they should defy each other, all in the defense of honor. The ideal challenge and resultant duel could scarcely fail to become a model for knightly readers who consumed chivalric romances much as we do soap operas. Following the adventures of such courteous heroes as Tirant lo Blanc or Amadis of Gaul, readers saw each and every duel carried to completion by the solemnized actions of its participants. Thus, the hero, who seems to give offense to other great men on almost every page, is consistently challenged – normally by an extremely courteous letter *(lletra de batalla)* – and so he had the right to choose weapons.[32] Not only did fictional kings know of these combats but often served as referees for them.[33] Though the embodiment of territorial law, the sovereign in the chivalric mirror of late medieval romance was more than willing to relinquish control over adjudication simply to see knightly exoneration fulfilled. In the real world of early modern Iberia, however, the Crown grew increasingly protective of its legal prerogative and repeatedly attacked the "quasi-justice" which the duel represented. Surely no literary figure of the era better represents the chasm between romantic imagination and hard-headed reality than does Don Quixote. The Knight of Sad Countenance is time and again battered for the issuance of a formal challenge by a world that did not recognize its existence. In the end, he had to admit there was no place for the duel or even the knight to fight it.[34]

If reawakened chivalry gave the duel a new lease of life as the last years of the Middle Ages slipped away, then the emergent doctrine of the magnanimous gentleman who was to selflessly right public wrongs militated against the customarily jealous vengeance afforded by the duel.[35] Thus, while this "sustained illusion and apparition of honor,"[36] – to use Francis Bacon's words – was even treated with ambivalence within the realm of chivalry, it was barely

---

[30] Ramon Lull, *The Book on the Order of Chivalry* in *The History of Feudalism*, pp. 315, 341–42, chaps. 3, 8.

[31] *Usatges*, pp. 136–38, art. 103; *Usatges*, trans. Kagay, pp. 90–91.

[32] Joanot Martorell and Marti Joan de Galba, *Tirant lo Blanc*, trans. David H. Rosenthal (New York, 1984), p. 96, chap. 71b; Edward T. Aylward, *Martorell's Tirant lo Blanch: A Program for Military and Social Reform in Fifteenth-Century Christendom*, North Carolina Studies in the Romance Languages and Literatures, 225 (Chapel Hill NC, 1985), pp. 136–80.

[33] *Tirant lo Blanc*, pp. 79–81, 95–96, 263–64, chaps. 62, 64–65, 71a–b, 77, 107, 150; Arthur B. Ferguson, *The Indian Summer of English Chivalry: Studies in the Decline and Transformation of Chivalric Idealism* (Durham NC, 1960); idem, *The Chivalric Tradition in Renaissance England* (Washington, 1986), p. 96.

[34] Bellaçois, p. 40.

[35] Ferguson, *Chivalric Tradition*, pp. 96–98.

[36] Ibid., p. 144.

tolerated within the realm of royal or municipal law. From the vantage point afforded by the statute law of the entire Spanish *ancien régime*, the duel was branded as acceptable or unacceptable only by the timing and intent of the challenge which brought it into being. The defiance was allowed among nobles to settle a number of offenses including ambush, battery, wounding, murder or insults to a man or his family. Such disputes were clearly "the concern of the King and Kingdom." They had to be registered before at least three witnesses and then the proper royal official also had to be notified. These cooler heads were to determine if the substance of the dispute was worthy of a duel. Those whose vehemence led them to dispense with this "express form" of challenge and duel were publicly proclaimed traitors and exiled for up to two years.[37] With the accession of Isabella of Castile and her marriage to Fernando of Aragon in 1469, Iberian royal authority turned an increasingly unkind eye on the duel as a social institution outside its authority. The Catholic Kings began to exert control by outlawing the profitable business of copying or delivering defiances for another.[38] They also required that the manufacture, sale and possession of all arms be approved and registered by the Crown. Duels carried out secretly without royal approval were harshly punished by royal law through fine, exile or even death.[39] Eventually, with the enforced absolutism of the Bourbon monarchy, the Spanish duel was totally forbidden by the Crown on 16 January 1716.[40] Unlike France, Italy or England, where the reign of the challenge would hold dominance for centuries, the death knell of the formal duel in Spain reflected a growing prejudice against it even among the nobility. The *desafio* was under mounting pressure, suffering from the raucous lampoons in such picaresque novels as *Lazarillo de Tormes* and in a whole range of cloak and dagger comedies. More serious clerical attacks were mounted against "the cruel, bloody, barbarous and heathen . . . law of the duel" which brings "honor only to the devil" and "directly opposes the laws of Christianity." Despite this opposition, the formal challenge and duel were as much ridiculed as vilified in the literary world of the *siglo de oro*. By contrast, in the real world, many Spaniards of the later Middle Ages showed by their actions agreement with the dictum of St. Thomas Aquinas that "nothing in human

---

37 Antonio Xavier Pérez y López, *Teatro de la legislación universal de España y Indias*, 28 vols. (Madrid, 1791–98), 10:307–10, 314–17, 325, 327–29, 331–32.

38 Ibid., 10:332–33.

39 *Constitucions y altres drets de Catalunya compilats en vertut del capitol de cort lxxxII de las Corts per la S. C. Y. R. Senyor del Rey Don Philip IV, nostre senyor celebradas en la ciutat de Barcelona* (Barcelona, 1704), pp. 439–46, bk. IX, tit. 19, laws 1–9; tit. 22, law 1; *Llibre dels quatre senyals del General de Catalunya continent diverses capitols de corts, ordinations, declarations, privilegis y cartas reales fahents per lo dit General* (Barcelona, 1634), app. 1; Bellaçois, pp. 34, 96.

40 Pérez y López, *Teatro de la legislación*, 10:333–40; Don C. Seitz, *Famous American Duels* (New York, 1929), p. 3.

affairs is greater than honor" and its defense.[41] Despite this, the Peninsula seemed to became infertile ground for the duel largely as the result of the drive for racial and societal unity centering on "purity of blood" (*liempieza de sangre*). The frenzy of duelling in other European countries was replaced in Spain by a distinctly Hispanic mania – that of the *corrida de toros*.[42]

If Spain of the fourteenth century knew nothing of chivalry, as the chronicler Jean Froissart claimed, it quickly learned, becoming an important site for chivalric rite and literature in the process.[43] The success of an emerging Spanish state, marked by the conquest of Granada in 1492, drove chivalry from its place of prominence and replaced much of its influence with an increasingly intrusive bureaucracy and professionalized military.[44] Despite the withering of chivalric realities in the period after the fall of Granada and the discovery of America, their spirit would remain a clear influence in the delineation and defense of personal honor. As the duel was hemmed in and finally outlawed in Spain, the ordered violence of the field of honor was replaced by a bloody vengeance, often carried out by hired killers.[45] Even though the duel died away, the defiance lingered on as a relic of a bygone age. Losing its earlier function of initiating the duel process, the *desafío* of Hapsburg Spain did nothing more than announce one's hostilities against another. Yet it made no attempt to specify when the axe would fall. One seeking to avenge his honor needed only to post a "letter of defiance" in some public spot like the door of a church, the town gate, or next to a public thoroughfare and then he could proceed to stalk his victim at leisure with some semblance of legality. In fact, the posted challenge was utilized if such disputes ever came to litigation both as a defense by the challenger and a charge by his intended victim. In such a judicial spotlight, the cruel inefficiency of the challenge was also highlighted. It was not unknown for a person suffering an affront from a total stranger to mistake

---

[41] Bellaçois, pp. 34–38; C. A. Jones, "Honour in Golden Age Drama: Its Relation to Real Life and to Morals," *Bulletin of Hispanic Studies* 35–36(1958–59): 202, 205; Otis H. Green, *Spain and the Western Tradition: The Castilian Mind in Literature from "El Cid" to Calderón*, 4 vols. (Madison, 1968), 1:20–21; Henry Sieber, *Language and Society in La Vida de Lazarillo de Tormes* (Baltimore, 1978), pp. 34–35.

[42] Bellaçois, pp. 37–39. Spanish critics of the *tauromaquia*, such as "Generation of '98" author Eugenio Noel, sounded much the same objections as royal law of the *siglo de oro* did against the duel, saying that the *corrida* was a neutral zone where the law of the state could not penetrate and only the barbarous and suicidal force of the matador prevailed: Eugenio Noel, *Escritos Antitaurinos*, ed. Eugenio Muñoz Mesonero, Temas de España, 59 (Madrid, 1967), pp. 86–88.

[43] Roger Boase, *The Troubadour Revival: A Study of Social Change and Traditionalism in Late Medieval Spain* (London, 1978), pp. 77, 118.

[44] Maurice Keen, *Chivalry* (New Haven CT, 1989), pp. 288–89.

[45] Bellaçois, p. 38. Bartolomé Bannassar, *The Spanish Character: Attitudes and Mentalities from the Sixteenth to the Nineteenth Century*, trans. Benjamin Keen (Berkeley, 1979), pp. 214, 234–35; J. H. Elliott, *The Revolt of the Catalans: A Study in the Decline of Spain (1598–1640)* (Cambridge, 1963), p. 52.

the identity of his adversary and defy someone with a similar surname.[46] Hispanic law remained largely undecided about the challenge and its judicial merit even after the 1716 prohibition of the duel. With Philip V's final ban of 1723 on the private "satisfaction of each grievance or injury," the final page of the Iberian *desafio/desafiament* was turned.[47] This is not to imply that assault or murder – all in the name of wounded honor – immediately ceased as a feature of the Iberian social landscape.[48] Such acts, whether preceded by a challenge or not, were simply viewed by royal law as felonious activity, no matter the status of those who committed them.

In Spain and in all European states molded by feudal relations, the *diffidamentum* has lived on in the way in which nations or national groups interact with each other. Though the defiance came into being as a largely vassalic mode of resistance against the oppression of lords and a means to prove one's innocence before the law at the expense of one's adversary, such scholars as Sidney Painter and Walter Ullmann assert that it effectively laid the groundwork for the modern right of resistance which a citizen can claim against an unjust government, thus forming one of the cornerstones of modern democracy.[49] Besides this heritage of liberty, the *diffidamentum* stands as an analogy for how the modern world manages war and peace. Though it was supposed to act as a peaceful means for the separation of parties tied by feudal alliance, the defiance always acted as a signal for impending war. As this process of feudal defiance was transmuted first into the wager by battle and later into the duelling challenge, hostilities were effectively "civilized" by a set of rules which were ultimately reinforced by royal or clerical authority. It was hoped that violence bound up with rules was violence limited.[50] Unfortunately, the attempt to hem in "the severe and atrocious character" of personal and national violence by such Spanish legists as Vitoria[51] did not succeed. Instead, public war and private violence alike seemed justified by the mere adherence to the formality of the challenge. From such a turbulent arena, the disquieting horizon of modern times, when a declaration of war is often interpreted as *carte blanche* for inflicting atrocities against entire enemy populations, is clearly discernible.

---

[46] Carreras i Candi and Bosch, pp. 51–61.

[47] Bellaçois, pp. 63–64.

[48] Marcelin Defourneaux, *Daily Life in Spain in the Golden Age*, trans. Newton Branch (Stanford CA, 1970), pp. 30–31.

[49] Sidney Painter, *Feudalism and Liberty*, ed. Fred A. Cazel Jr. (Baltimore, 1961), pp. 258–59; Ullmann, pp. 64–66; Harold J. Berman, *Law and Revolution: The Formation of the Western Legal Tradition* (Cambridge MA, 1983), pp. 306–7, 533.

[50] Irnaus Eibl Eibesfeldt, *The Biology of Peace and War: Men, Animals, and Aggression*, trans. Eric Mosbacher (New York, 1979) pp. 95–96; Maurice R. Davie, *The Evolution of War: A Study of its Role in Early Societies* (New Haven CT, 1929), pp. 293–96.

[51] Francisco Vitoria, *De Indis e de jure belli relectiones*, trans. John Pawley Bate, The Classics of International Law, 7 (Washington, 1971), p. 171.

Criminal Settlement in Medieval Castilian Towns

THERESA M. VANN

In 1893, Frederick Jackson Turner proposed that the western frontier had shaped American character and institutions by acting as the source of democratic ideas and movements.[1] According to Turner, the promise of individual liberty on the frontier drew energetic individuals from the cities, who utilized the resources of the frontier to open up markets for the industrial East. In addition to feeding the growth of the East, frontier liberties provided a source for American popular political movements, thus shaping a unique American democracy. The underpopulated frontier also served as a "safety valve" for criminal passions and violence found in crowded eastern cities. But when the 1890 United States Census announced the closing of the frontier, it marked the end of American expansion and the conclusion of the first phase of American history.

Turner's thesis has subsequently been tested, challenged, and revised by three generations of American scholars. But to this day his frontier model remains a subject of academic discourse.[2] And even though Turner stressed the role of the frontier in shaping a unique American character, his thesis has been adopted by Spanish historiography to interpret the role of the reconquest of the Iberian peninsula in the formation of modern Spain. Claudio Sánchez-Albornoz stands out as the main proponent of the application of the Turner thesis to the medieval Iberian, specifically Castilian, frontier. In numerous books and articles he stressed the settlement of the frontier by free men, equals

---

1   Frederick Jackson Turner, "The Significance of the Frontier in American History," American Historical Association, *Annual Report for the Year 1893* (Washington DC, 1894), pp. 199–227. This was Turner's address to the 1893 meeting of the American Historical Association. It has since been reprinted in anthologies: see Ray Allen Billington, ed., *The Frontier Thesis: Valid Interpretation of American History?* (New York, 1966), pp. 9–20. Turner wrote other articles and monographs discussing his thesis, including *The Frontier in American History* (New York, 1920).

2   The most recent commentary on the longevity of the Turner thesis is by Patricia Nelson Limerick, "Turnerians All: The Dream of a Helpful History in an Intelligible World," *AHR* 100(1995): 697–716. She notes that even Turner presented a half-hearted antithesis to his famous thesis.

in a society that lacked feudal structures, and he attributed the formation of Castile to frontier warfare.[3]

Sánchez-Albornoz employed the Turner thesis in order to argue that freedom, and possibly even democracy, existed on the medieval Castilian frontier. His influence upon a generation of historians has led to an almost uncritical adoption of the Turnerian concept of the medieval frontier as a safety valve for Castilian society, which has manifested itself in the idea that the medieval Iberian monarchs encouraged criminal settlement on the frontier. Since historians of medieval Spain lack the kind of crime statistics available to American historians, they rely almost entirely upon the codified customs of the municipal tribunals, called *fueros*, to support the idea of the frontier as a refuge for violent criminals who would assist in the monarchy's scheme of protecting the kingdom and continuing the reconquest. Certainly repopulation of the frontier was a major concern of the Castilian monarchy; this, however, does not mean that the kings abdicated royal control over justice. A re-examination of the eleventh- and twelfth-century Castilian foral evidence that scholars usually advance to support the idea of the frontier as a place of refuge for criminals indicates the contrary. The monarchs of Castile-León tried to prevent violence because a peaceful kingdom was necessary for the defense of the realm and the continuation of the reconquest.

The idea of criminal settlement in New Castile is an attractive one, based upon the simple logical premise that the monarchs wanted experienced killers staffing the municipal militias. But the assumption that the Castilian monarchy abetted the escape of criminals to the frontier in order to provide it with both settlers and a militia contradicts the general trend of Castilian royal law. The proof usually produced for criminal settlement in Castile comes from isolated sections of the *fueros*, which are cited to indicate that murderers traveled freely to the southern frontier. It is worthwhile to restate the Turnerian arguments for criminal settlement and to examine how the formation of customary law encouraged a modern interpretation that substantially contradicts medieval legal concepts.

The advocates of criminal settlement base their assertion on one clause in one *fuero*. José María Lacarra, whose work has stressed the themes of popular settlement, has stated that the municipal code of Sepúlveda, issued in 1076 by Alfonso VI of Castile-León (1072–1109), gave sanctuary to murderers, thieves, and other criminals, and opened up Extremadura to criminal settlement.[4] This is based on a clause in the *fuero* that states: "If any man from Sepúlveda should

---

3 See especially Claudio Sánchez-Albornoz, "The Frontier and Castilian Liberties," in *The New World Looks at its History*, ed. Archibald R. Lewis and Thomas F. McGann (Austin, 1963), pp. 27–46. Also see idem, *España, un enigma histórico*, 2 vols. (Buenos Aires, 1956), 1:16–33.

4 José María Lacarra, "Las ciudades fronterizas en la España de los siglos XI y XII," in *Colonización, parias, repoblación y otros estudios* (1963; repr., Zaragoza, 1981), p. 99.

kill another [man] from Castile and escapes to the Duero, no man should follow him."[5] Following a Turnerian line of reasoning, the *fuero* of Sepúlveda thus became a medium which made the frontier a legally-sanctioned refuge for murderers and other criminals, where they could exercise their natural homicidal tendencies against Muslims instead of their fellow Castilians. Therefore, the Castilian monarchs consciously permitted violent criminals from the towns to move to the frontier in order to defend the kingdom from outside enemies. Since the conclusion of the *fuero* of Uclés (1179) named the *fuero* of Sepúlveda as that town's ancillary code, criminal settlement was also apparently welcomed by the towns of New Castile, which lay along the Tagus frontier in the Kingdom of Toledo and were under the dominion of the Order of Santiago.[6]

Lacarra's theory about the role of the *fuero* of Sepúlveda in the criminal settlement of all of New Castile has been accepted by others, such as Manuel González Jiménez, who has postulated that criminal settlement was permitted in 1076, then lapsed until 1310, when Fernando IV revived it by granting settlement rights in Gibraltar to all wrongdoers except traitors.[7] González cites the work of James Powers to connect the migration of murderers to the frontier with recruitment for municipal militias.[8] Although Powers does not say that municipal militias obtained recruits from the criminals who fled to the frontier, he does note that the judicial penalty of exile permitted persons guilty of violent crimes to make a new start in frontier settlements, where one of the obligations of citizenship was service in the municipal militia.[9] And Heath Dillard has

---

5 Emilio Saez, ed., *Los fueros de Sepúlveda* (Segovia, 1953), p. 46, no. 13: "Et si aliquis homo de Sepuluega occiderit alium d[e Castella et fugier usque ad Duero, null]us homo persequatur eum."

6 Milagros Rivera Garretas, *La encomienda, el priorato y la villa de Uclés en la Edad Media: Formación de un senorío de la Orden de Santiago* (Madrid, 1985), pp. 238–39: [29] "Et super hoc quod scriptum est concedo vobis toto illo foro que fuit datum a Sepulvega in tempore qua populata fuit, foras iactada arrova et almudes in die de mercado et alcavara de carniceros, quia istas III causas se prendidit rex ad profectum senior de villa."

7 Manuel González Jiménez, "Frontier and Settlement in the Kingdom of Castile (1085–1350)," in *Medieval Frontier Societies*, ed. Robert Bartlett and Angus MacKay (Oxford, 1989), p. 72. Also see the text in Miguel Angel Ladero Quesada and Manuel González Jiménez, "La población en la frontera de Gibraltar y el repartimiento de Vejar (siglos XIII y XIV)," *Historia, Instituciones, Documentos* 4(1977): 237. "Mandamos é defendemos firmemente que todos aquellos que se fueren para Gibraltar, é que sean y vecinos y moradores quier que sean golifantes ó ladrones, ó que hayan muerto homes, ó otros homes qualesquier malhechores que sean, ó muger casada que se fuya á su marido, ó en otra manera qualquier, que sean y defendidos y amparados de muerte, e que los que y estubieren é moraren en la villa ó en su termino que ninguno non sea osado de les faser male ninguno, non seyendo ende ome trahidor que dió castillo contra su señor, quebrantó tregua ó paz de rey ó leva muger de su señor, que estos que non sean y amparados, mas que hayan aquella pena que merecen."

8 González, pp. 54–55.

9 James F. Powers, *A Society Organized for War: The Iberian Municipal Militias in the Central Middle Ages, 1000–1284* (Berkeley, 1988), p. 204.

found examples in twelfth-century Aragonese royal *fueros* where frontier towns extended clemency to murderers and to abductors of women, presumably because women were scarce in frontier society and the authorities hoped that the pair would establish a family on the frontier.[10]

Lacarra has formulated a very influential theory, one that has found wide acceptance because we are conditioned to accept Turner's model about the role of the frontier as a safety valve. In comparison, pre-Turnerian nineteenth-century legal scholars such as Francisco Martínez Marina recognized the importance of the *fuero* of Sepúlveda to the development of Castilian foral law, yet did not comment upon any mechanism within it that permitted criminal settlement.[11] Undoubtedly, each generation uses its own experience to pose new questions and to create a new interpretation of the past; this is what separates the historian from the antiquarian. But no one has ever asked if the *fuero* of Sepúlveda functioned according to Turner's "safety-valve" theory, as Lacarra claims. Lacarra's theory can be tested in several ways: through the meaning of the law itself, the transmission of the text of the *fuero*, and the transmission of the *fuero* to the Castilian frontier via Uclés.

It should be understood that the *fuero* of Sepúlveda was not issued to the entire kingdom, but to a specific locality. In general, a town's initial *fuero* (also known as a *carta-puebla*) established the qualifications for settlers and the conditions under which settlement could take place. These initial *fueros* were brief, and therefore some directed the municipality to consult another law code for directions in unforeseen matters. A settlement might receive a subsequent code if conditions in the town changed substantially enough to require modification or expansion of the original *fuero*. Although the towns borrowed *fueros* or parts of them from each other, any similarity among the foral laws of frontier towns occurred because of proximity or the origins of its settlers; once the legal tradition of the town was established, it was not changed. Each medieval Iberian frontier functioned according to its own customary laws, creating different legal zones.[12] Thus the *fuero* of Sepúlveda would have functioned within the jurisdiction of the tribunal of Sepúlveda. It would not have any meaning outside the jurisdiction of Sepúlveda's tribunal unless the monarch specifically named it as an ancillary code to another town with similar customs.

The basis for all Castilian law was the seventh-century Visigothic code known as the *Liber iudicum*. During the twelfth century, the monarchs of

---

[10] Heath Dillard, *Daughters of the Reconquest: Women in Castilian Town Society, 1100–1300* (Cambridge, 1984), pp. 138–39, cites several *fueros*, most of them issued by Alfonso I of Aragon, to support her contention that frontier family values ranked abductors with murderers as the criminal settler of choice.

[11] Francisco Martínez Marina, *Ensayo histórico-critico sobre la legislación y principales cuerpos legales de los reinos de Leon y Castilla*, 2 vols. (Madrid, 1834), 1:118–84.

[12] See Robert I. Burns, S. J., "The Significance of the Frontier in the Middle Ages," in *Medieval Frontier Societies*, pp. 318–19, 324, for the differences in law between Valencia, Aragon and Catalonia.

Castile-León granted the *Liber iudicum* to towns in León and to the city of Toledo; in the thirteenth century it was translated into the vernacular and entitled the *Fuero juzgo*.[13] The *Liber* represented the force of written law, which gave the Castilian monarchs a mandate to keep order within the kingdom and to retain punishment of criminals as a royal prerogative. The *Liber* justified the monarch's authority by stating that before a king could consider waging a war of conquest, he must put his kingdom at peace and remove all internal contentions.[14] The law was his weapon in this quest. By enforcing the law, the king gained the support of his subjects in all his military endeavors.[15]

The thirteenth-century *Siete Partidas* and its compiler, Alfonso X, fully developed the concept of a peaceful kingdom whose law-abiding members co-operated in the defense of the realm under the direction of its head. The king put the kingdom at peace before undertaking expansion.[16] Nowhere in the *Siete Partidas* does Alfonso state that criminals should be permitted to join militias. Alfonso does note that at some indeterminate "ancient" time (a phrase borrowed from his model, the fourth-century author Vegetius) knights were selected from men like butchers because butchers were used to blood and killing living animals, but more recent commanders preferred that their knights should have good habits and virtues.[17] Alfonso himself says that no traitor, criminal, or condemned man could be dubbed a knight; in fact, Alfonso expected honor and morality from his foot soldiers as well.[18] Neither did Alfonso's other code, the *Fuero Real* advocate exiling dangerous criminals to frontiers in order to provide personnel for militias, but instead ordered the execution of the murderer and the confiscation of his goods on behalf of the Crown.[19]

Therefore, royal and written law, which had its roots in the Roman legal

---

[13] See Alfonso García-Gallo, *Manual de historia del derecho español*, 2 vols. (Madrid, 1984), 1:376–77.

[14] Gustav Friedrich Haenel, ed., *Lex romana Visigothorum* (Leipzig, 1848), bk. I, tit. 2, l. vi.

[15] Real Academia de la Historia, ed., *Fuero Juezgo* (Madrid, 1815), p. 3. Also see Samuel Parsons Scott, ed. and trans., *The Visigothic Code (Forum judicum)* (Boston, 1910), pp. 6–7.

[16] See García-Gallo, 1:702, no. 1246, for a discussion of the fifteenth-century concept of the maintenance of peace and of law by the monarch.

[17] Alfonso X, *Siete Partidas*, 3 vols. (Madrid, 1802), Partida 2, tit. XXI, l. 2. Vegetius, *Epitoma rei militaris* (Leipzig, 1885), bk. I, 7, p. 11, advised excluding all those who followed "womanly" occupations such as weaving, fishing, and baking from joining the corps.

[18] Alfonso X, *Siete Partidas*, Partida 2, tit. XXI, l. 12.

[19] Alfonso X, *Fuero Real*, ed. José Muro Martínez (Valladolid, 1874), pp. 148–49, bk. 4, tit. 17, lines 2, 4. Law 2: "El que mate a otro a traicion o con alevosía, sea arrastrado, y despues ahorcado; y el Rey haya todos los bienes del traidor, y la mitad de los del alevoso, siendo la otra mitad para los herederos del mismo. El que mate en otra forma sin derecho, muera ahorcado, hayan todos sus bienes sus herederos, y no pague el homicidio."

tradition, firmly supported the punishment of criminals and did not encourage their relocation to the outskirts of society. Was the trend in customary law, then, contradictory to written law? The answer would be no. The contents of the *fuero* of Sepúlveda from 1076 do not suggest that the frontier was deliberately structured as a violent place. The *fuero* penalized homicides, establishing monetary damages for murder and placing a higher value on the lives of citizens than of non-citizens. The clause Lacarra cites as proof for criminal settlement stated that if any man of Sepúlveda should kill a Castilian, and then fled to the Duero, no man should pursue him.[20] A later clause says that if the murderer is killed before he reaches the Duero, this act is to be treated as a homicide, for which the killer would have to pay a fine of 300 *sueldos*, a prohibitive amount.[21] Despite the claims Lacarra makes for them, these two laws are not about criminal settlement on the Muslim frontier. Instead, they were intended to prevent blood feuds, which were a real problem affecting the peace of Castilian towns, and to define the jurisdictional limits of the municipality. The Duero river was to the north, not the south, of Sepúlveda, and in the *fuero* it functions as a clearly-defined geographical boundary outside of the municipality's district. A similar concept is found in a later, more extensive *fuero* that the town of Sepúlveda re-compiled around 1300, which said that if a personal enemy of a citizen should settle in the town then the two parties should swear to keep the peace.[22] The fluidity of movement within Castile required Sepúlveda and other towns to enact similar laws to preserve the peace if two different parties to a feud which had originated elsewhere migrated to the same town. A *fuero* given to Dos Barrios in 1192 contained a similar provision which stipulated that if two enemies should settle in the town, they had to swear to discontinue their dispute.[23]

These *fueros* kept peace within the town by providing an amnesty for new settlers. In no way can we assume that the new settlers were murderers, or even violent criminals. They might be relocating for other reasons, such as relief from debts, as found in the *fuero* of Cuenca (c.1191), which in addition to protecting new settlers from blood feuds also absolved them from debts and other financial claims incurred elsewhere.[24] All *fueros* imposed punishment for

---

20 Saez, *Los fueros de Sepúlveda*, p. 46, no. 13.
21 Ibid., p. 47, no. 18: "Siquis homo quomodo hic nominauimus quesierit [sequere suo omiziero et de] Duero in antea lo mataret, CCC solidos pectet et sit omiziero."
22 Feliciano Callejas, *Fuero de Sepúlveda* (Madrid, 1857), p. 21. tit. 14: "Si el que enemigo fuere ante que Spulvega se poblase, viniere poblar a Sepulvega, e y fallare su enemigo, de el uno, al otro fiadores de salvo a Fuero de Spulvega e finquen en paz; e el que fiadores non quisiere dar, sáquenlo de la villa e de todo su término."
23 Derek W. Lomax, *La Orden de Santiago (1170–1275)* (Madrid, 1965), p. 264: "Tod inimigo qui uinier poblar a Dos Barrios si el otro inimigo uiniere poblar despues, non pueble sin amor del que uino primero, ningun uezino quel recibier in sua casa a porsabidas, e lo podieren firmar, pectet x morauedis."
24 Rafael de Ureña y Smenjaud, ed., *Fuero de Cuenca* (Madrid, 1935), bk. 1, chap. 1, nos. 10 (or 8), 120, 121: "Omnibus etiam populatoribus hanc prerogatiuam concedo, quod

such crimes as murder, robbery, assault, and theft, as the kings tried to limit private justice by instituting public prosecution of crimes.[25] The penalty, though, was still understood to be a matter between the family of the victim and the accused, although the courts collected a portion of the fine. The gradual development of royal prosecution in the twelfth and thirteenth centuries meant that the Crown increased its authority by assuming responsibility for punishing malefactors. The thirteenth-century *Libro de los fueros de Castilla* included murder among the crimes that the king ought to prosecute.[26] The *Fuero Real* (c.1252–1284) treated murder of an enemy in a blood feud as a homicide, punishable by a fine of 500 *sueldos*, but not by execution.[27] Nevertheless, by the thirteenth century, the convicted criminal was understood to be an enemy to the entire municipality, not just the family of a victim. The town would brand him a traitor and employ the penalty of exile to remove him from society.[28] In consequence, any citizen of the city was able to kill him with impunity, his house could be torn down, and his goods could be destroyed or confiscated. The exile might still be necessary as a penalty to prevent violence from erupting in the municipality, since with the expansion of prosecution the entire community could attack the criminal for his crime.

Not only did the concept of criminality change, but also the text of the *fuero* of Sepúlveda may have been adulterated with interpolations from Aragonese legal sources. The *fuero* of Sepúlveda itself does not survive in its original form, but in a text from the late eleventh century, which was confirmed in 1110

quicumque ad concham uenerit populari, cuiuscumque sit condicionis, id est, siue sit xristianus, siue maurus, siue iudeus, siue liber, siue seruus, ueniat secure, et non respondeat pro inimicia, uel debito, aut fideiussura, uel herencia, uel maiordomia, uel merindatico, neque pro alia causa, quamcumque fecerit, antequam concha caperetur. Et si ille, qui inimicus fuerit antequam concha caperetur, conche uenerit populari, et ibi inimicum suum inuenerit, det uterque fideiussores de saluo ad forum conche, ut sint in pace. Et qui fideiussores dare noluerit, exeat ab urbe adque a termino suo."

25 José Orlandis, "Las consecuencias del delito en el derecho de la alta edad media," *Anuario de Historia del Derecho Español [AHDE]* 18(1947): 69. Richard M. Fraher, "Preventing Crime in the High Middle Ages: The Medieval Lawyers' Search for Deterrence," in *Popes, Teachers, and Canon Law in the Middle Ages*, ed. James Ross Sweeney and Stanley Chodorow (Ithaca NY, 1989), pp. 212–33, finds an overall increase in penalties due to the influence of Roman Law in the twelfth and thirteenth centuries.

26 Galo Sánchez, *Libro de los fueros de Castilla* (1924; repr., Barcelona, 1981), p. 59, tit. 117: "Titulo delas cosas que el rey deue pesquirir. Estas tres cosas deue el rey pesquirir auyendo querellosos: de muger forçada, et de omne muerto sobre salua, et de quebrantamiento de camino. Mas sy algun omne se querellar de otro omne quel firio de fierro o de punno o de otrea qual ferida se quier, auyendo testigos, e non murier de aquel colpe, esto deue correr por el fuero et el rey non lo deue pesquirir."

27 Alfonso X codified the *Fuero Real* as a uniform municipal code. The law on homicide (Martínez, *Fuero viejo*, pp. 148–51 [tit. 17]) indicate that in this code Alfonso X imposed a penalty of a fine, not exile or execution.

28 See Eduardo de Hinojosa, *El Elemento Germánico en el Derecho Espanol* (Madrid, 1915), p. 70.

by Alfonso I "the Battler" of Aragon (1104–1134) and Queen Urraca of Castile (1109–1126). The possibility for changes and emendations of the lost original exists. Bernard Reilly suspects that this copy contains later interpolations, but that it also comprises the text issued by Alfonso VI's chancery in 1076.[29] The *fuero*'s confirmation by Alfonso I of Aragon also suggests the introduction of Aragonese customs, especially since Alfonso I is linked to other Castilian *fueros* that are also cited as proof that murderers settled the frontier.

Indeed, if there is a trend towards criminal settlement in twelfth-century Castilian *fueros*, it seems likely that it was introduced by Alfonso I instead of his father-in-law, Alfonso VI. For example, the text of a *fuero* that Alfonso VI granted to Medinaceli in 1094 gave immunity to murderers who settled there. But the original text of this *fuero* does not survive.[30] The clause in question comes from the text of the *fuero* of Carcastillo, which Alfonso I of Aragon appended to Alfonso VI's *carta-puebla* in 1129. The text says that if "a man from other lands who committed homicide should come to Carcastillo to settle, [the townsmen] should assist him as much as they can."[31] Alfonso I's settlement charters to other Aragonese border towns granted immunity from prosecution to criminals who fled to the frontier settlements. Once the new settler arrived, however, he was liable for any crimes committed in the new town. For example, Alfonso I issued a *fuero* that exempted murderers who fled to Marañon from the *homicidium* that they owed their pursuers – but only if the pursuers did not want to collect.[32] Later, in 1142, Count Ramon Berenguer III of Barcelona issued a similar *fuero* to Daroca, in Zaragoza.[33] Alfonso I's *fueros* to Belchite (1119) and Cáseda (1129) promised outright that murderers would

---

[29] See Bernard F. Reilly, *The Kingdom of Leon-Castilla under Queen Urraca, 1109–1126* (Princeton NJ, 1982), pp. 323–24, for a brief description of the earliest copy of the *fuero* of Sepúlveda, which came from the later twelfth century and was possibly copied from Alfonso VI's document. Ibid., p. 323, n. 31, Reilly cites Saez's edition as establishing that Castilian law was different from Leonese law and that it provided the foundation for tracing Castilian movement into the trans-Duero region. Also Saez, 45–51. Bernard F. Reilly, *The Kingdom of Leon-Castilla under King Alfonso VI, 1065–1109* (Princeton NJ, 1988), p. 119, n. 6, reaffirms his contention that Alfonso VI's chancery issued the text of the *fuero* of Sepúlveda in its current form.

[30] See Alfonso García-Gallo, "Los fueros de Medinaceli," *AHDE* 31(1961): 9–16, for the transmission of the text of the *fuero* of Medinaceli.

[31] Tomás Muñoz y Romero, ed., *Colección de fueros municipales y cartas pueblas* (Madrid, 1847), 469–70: "Homine qui fuerit homicida de alteras terras, et venerit a Carocastellis populare, adjuvent illum cantum meliorem poterint." For a more recent edition, see Luis Javier Fortun Perez de Ciriza, "Colección de 'fueros menores' de Navarra y otros privilegios locales," *Principe de Viana* 165(1982): 297–98.

[32] Fuero de [F]Marañon (1124–1134), Muñoz, p. 498; Ciriza, p. 303: [27] "Et, si omicida uenerit primitus in Maraione et suos omicieros veneri[n]t post eum, colligant eum. Et, si noluerint colligere eum, exeant foras." This law does assume that a judgement made elsewhere is valid in Marañon.

[33] FDaroca, Muñoz, p. 536: "Si quis in Darocam populare venerit, et inimici eius venerint post eum, aut colligant eum, aut eiiciatur de villa."

not be pursued.[34] But these laws taken out of context are misleading. As in the Castilian *fueros*, Alfonso I wanted to discourage the continuation of blood feuds on the frontier. He granted a free pardon for all past deeds, but he expected his subjects to behave well from that point on. The same *fuero* of Cáseda applied the *fuero* of Soría to anyone who killed a citizen or an outsider, imposing upon the malefactor a fine of 300 *sueldos*.[35] Although the citizen-murderers of Marañon were not held responsible for acts against outsiders committed within the town limits, they would be fined for murdering a fellow-citizen.[36] Marañon's customs embody tribalism, since the town did not prosecute its citizens for murders committed elsewhere. As noted above, the town's *fuero* did leave it open for other municipalities to collect the *homicidium* for their citizens, for obviously Marañon considered the murderer responsible only to the town or family of his victim, not to any larger, national group. Likewise, Sepúlveda valued the lives of its citizens over the lives of non-citizens.

The possibility of corrupted text exists even in modern editions of *fueros*. For example, Muñoz's printed text of Alfonso VII's *fuero* to the town of Lara in 1135 seems not only to permit criminal settlement, but also to foster an image of the untamed frontier: "Homicierum qui in Lara fecerit homicidium et in Lara populaverit non se prehendet cum suos inimicos."[37] But in a later edition prepared by Martínez Díez, the same law clearly protects settlers who had killed someone during a war from becoming involved in blood feuds: "Omiziero qui in guerram fecit omicidium et in Lara populauerit, non segudent eum suos inimicos."[38] Clearly some transcriber mistook *in guerram* for "in Lara," even though elsewhere in the *fuero* there are clear penalties for homicides within the settlement.

---

34 FCáseda, Muñoz, pp. 474–75; Ciriza, p. 299: ". . . [Si fuerit] homicida et fecerit iniuria, veniat ad Casseda et sedeat solutus et non petet aliquid. Qualecumque malum fecerit non respondat ad ullo homine pro illo et, si requisierit illum, pectet mille solidos ad regem.";
FBelchite, Muñoz, 413: "Ego quidam Adefonsus, Dei gratia, imperator, facio hanc cartam firmationis, et liberationis, ad totos homines, qui sunt in Belgit, et in tota illa honore de Galinsangiae populati, et in anteea ibi populaverint, mando et affirmo ad totos homines de tota mea jurisdictione, homicidios, latrones, et malifactores, postquam ad Belgit, vel in illa honore alia de Galinsangiae, venerint populare et ibi populaverint, ut non habeant resguardo de nullo homine per nulla malefacta, sed sedeant ibi ingenui et liberi sine ullo cisso malo . . ."

35 Ciriza, p. 299: "Homo de Caseda, si hociderit hominem de foras, pectet XXX solidos ad foro de Soria. Si occiderit suo vecino, pectet XXX solidos."

36 Ciriza, 302: [5] "Et, si homo de Maraione occiderit alium hominem foras de villa, non habeat nullum pectum. Et, si uicino ad uicino occiderit in villa pectet XXX solidos. Et, si aliquis homo de foras de villa que non fuerit uicino occiderit homine de Maraione, pectet quingentos solidos."

37 Muñoz, p. 521.

38 Gonzalo Martínez Díez, *Fueros locales en el territorio de la provincia de Burgos* (Burgos, 1982), p. 141, art. 30.

So far the intent of the *fuero* of Sepúlveda and the transmission of the text do not support Turnerian interpretations; the final test is its application to Uclés and the rest of the Castilian frontier. In 1085, almost ten years after Alfonso VI granted the *fuero* of Sepúlveda, he reconquered the city of Toledo and extended the line of the Castilian frontier to the Tagus river. Alfonso VI did not introduce the *fuero* of Sepúlveda in Toledo, where the *Liber iudicum* formed the root of law. The towns of the kingdom of Toledo then received some sixty-eight supplementary *fueros* between the eleventh and the thirteenth centuries, of which the *fuero* of Uclés was only one.[39] And even in Uclés, the reference to the law of Sepúlveda is specific to markets, not to homicide. The other *fueros* of Toledo make no reference to the *fuero* of Sepúlveda, and it apparently had little influence there.[40] Thus, the transmission of this law to the Toledan frontier is suspect, since Toledo customs were not similar to or based upon Sepúlveda. Criminal settlement seems to be an interpolation from Aragonese law. And, unlike Aragonese law, Castilian settlement charters do not readily support the idea of criminal settlement. Lacarra, realizing that the foral evidence from Toledo did not support his initial assertion, later postulated that the fame of the cities of New Castile, especially Toledo, was sufficient to attract settlers without having to serve as a refuge for murderers and thieves.[41]

Toledo's *fueros* present their own issues concerning the moral probity of new settlers. Two Toledan *cartas-pueblas* are on occasion cited as proof of criminal colonization: the *fuero* of Oreja (1139) and the *fuero* of Ocaña (1156). These towns, located close together in the hinterlands of Toledo, were colonized by the same groups of settlers who borrowed legal precedents from each other. Alfonso VII issued the *fuero* of Oreja immediately upon the recapture of the town, and it seems, as a matter of military strategy, that the king had to populate the area immediately.[42] The particular law cited as proof of criminal

---

39 This estimate is based on the *fueros* listed for the identified towns in the kingdom in Tomas Muñoz y Romero, *Diccionario bibliografico-histórico de los antiguos reinos, provincias, ciudades, villas, iglesias y santuarios de España* (1858; repr., Madrid, 1973) and in Ana Maria Barrero García and María Luz Alonso Martín, *Textos de derecho local español en la Edad Media* (Madrid, 1989).

40 Alfonso García-Gallo, "Aportación al estudio de los fueros," *AHDE* 26(1956): 431–32, n. 131.

41 José María Lacarra, "Acerca de la atracción de pobladores en las ciudades fronterizas de la España cristiana (siglos XI–XII)," *En la España Medieval* 2(1982): 490–91.

42 Alfonso stated in the preamble that he intended to encourage settlers to come to the town, so that it would not be lost to the Muslims through Christian weakness. See Carmen Gutiérrez del Arroyo, "Los fueros de Oreja y Ocaña," *AHDE* 17(1946): 654–57: "Quia Dei subueniente potentia ego Adefonso Hispanie imperator baronum meorum suffultus auxilio castellum Aurelie quod Toletum et circa manentem prouincia fere in solitudinem redegerat, mauris qui illud possidebant expulsis, acquisiui ne acquisitum, mauri per impotentiam christainorum et incuriam iterum recuperare ualeant omnibus illis qui ad idem castellum populandum uenerint foros et terminos dignum donare censui."

settlement permits individuals below the rank of count who had incurred the king's wrath, or *ira del regio*, to come as settlers without fear of reprisal.[43] In a similar manner, the law of Ocaña permitted the sheltering of exiles there.[44] The same provisions are not found in other *fueros* given to Toledo and its countryside, nor were they promulgated in later versions of the *fueros* of Oreja and Ocaña.

Hilda Grassotti speculates that these two *fueros* reflect Alfonso VII's policy between 1139 and 1156 of sending discontented followers to the Toledan frontier in order to preserve the internal peace of his kingdom. The exiles, whom Alfonso VII encouraged to populate Oreja and Ocaña, may have been murderers, thieves, or violent criminals, but their chief characteristic was that they were former or discontented vassals who had incurred the king's wrath. As Hilda Grassotti has observed, the wrath of the king was a specific penalty incurred by vassals who had displeased the king through disobedience or treachery and who, as a consequence, were expelled from royal service, breaking the ties of vassalage.[45] Not only was the vassal exiled, but his lands and goods were confiscated.[46] However, the vassal could still serve the king by fighting the Muslims, and such pardons as those Grassotti cites from the *fueros* of Oreja and Ocaña provided the vassal with an opportunity to regain the royal grace.[47] These clauses may reflect an immediate problem within Alfonso VII's court in 1139 rather than local customs. Rodrigo González de Lara had led a revolt against Alfonso VII in Asturias, in 1130. Alfonso put down the revolt and made Rodrigo González the military governor of Toledo, apparently to separate him from his power base, not to unleash his martial talents against the Muslims.[48] By contrast, when Alfonso finally undertook campaigns in the hinterlands of Toledo, he installed in the city a trusted retainer, Rodrigo Fernández de Castro.[49]

Finally, there is the undeniable fact that Europeans exiled criminals to colonies and frontiers for the good of the country, a practice that spanned the fourteenth to the nineteenth centuries. González Jiménez argues that this trend originated in Spain with the *fuero* of Sepúlveda, and that even though criminal settlement lapsed on the Toledan frontier, it revived with the privilege which

---

[43] Ibid., 655: "Quisquis uero, exceptis comitibus et aliis potestatibus que regios honores possideant, iram regiam ita ut eum exheredet aut de sua terra exire iubeat, incurrerit, ad Aureliam si populator ibi fieri uoluerit, securus ueniat, et qui tunc princeps et dominus illius Aurelie castelli fuerit ipsum tali modo sine timore recipiat."

[44] Ibid., p. 658: "Et toto inimico foras inde traditor qui sedeat amparado in Occania et lo alcayde qui lo amparet."

[45] See Hilda Grassotti, "La ira regia en León y Castilla," in *Miscelanea de estudios sobre instituciones castellano-leonesas* (Bilbao, 1978), pp. 3–132, esp. pp. 17–22.

[46] Ibid., p. 29.

[47] Ibid., p. 84.

[48] Manuel Recuero Astray, *Alfonso VII, Emperador* (León, 1979), p. 103.

[49] Ibid., p. 163.

Fernando IV gave to Gibraltar in 1310 and continued with the privilege of the *homicianos*, given to Tarifa around 1320.[50] Fernando IV's privileges quite clearly permit several types of fugitives to settle on the frontier, including "vagabonds" (*golifanes*), thieves, murderers and women fleeing their husbands. Traitors, however, were excluded from this general amnesty and were not accepted as settlers. Once the fugitives had settled in Gibraltar, they were then accountable for any crimes they committed there.[51] It is clear from the work of Timothy Coates that this is part of a fourteenth-century legal trend both to ensure settlement and to cleanse the kingdom of wrongdoers. But it is debatable if a clear legal chain exists from 1076 until 1310 encouraging criminal settlement on the frontier, especially since a close examination shows that the *fuero* of Sepúlveda did not implement such legislation. The medieval concept of customary law did not admit of national programs or agendas, but functioned entirely on the local level.

Therefore, according to the foral evidence, not all frontier lands provided amnesty to murderers in the eleventh, twelfth, and thirteenth centuries. The evidence does not support the suggestion that Castilian foral law was shaped in order to encourage criminal settlement on the frontier. This does not mean that criminals never migrated to the frontier: we lack the statistical proof for criminal settlement for twelfth- and thirteenth-century Castile. The application of Turner's "safety-valve" theory to medieval Castile, which argues that violent and criminal Castilians were directed to the southern frontier, where they could start over and fight against Muslims, is a modern paradigm. Invoking the myth of the American frontier, it suggests that violence was consciously channeled out from the settled part of the kingdom to its boundaries, where it could then be exercised against Muslims and not against fellow Christians.

But we cannot automatically assume that the frontier was settled by criminals. Indeed, the arguments put forward for this assumption do not stand up to close scrutiny. Not all exiles were violent criminals, nor did Castilians believe that a successful private murder was a pre-requisite for serving in a municipal militia. Admittedly, customary law was slow to recognize the criminal as a menace to the entire society. The foral law acted to preserve the peace of the town from blood feuds, and eventually written law, codified by Alfonso X, reserved the punishment of criminals to the monarch. This punishment precluded amnesties for frontier settlement. In all, we are guilty of confusing tribal loyalties with modern concepts of criminality. We must reconsider our attitudes towards medieval frontier settlement, and discard, if possible, the Turnerian notion of the frontier as a "safety valve."

---

[50] Ladero Quesada and González Jiménez, p. 214.
[51] Ibid., p. 238: "Todo homo qualquier malfechor que sea, salvo trahidor, segund dicho es de suso que en Gibraltar morare año y dia, quier que sea vecino quier no, que le sea perdonada la nuestra justicia, salvo faciendo el maleficio en la dicha Gibraltar."

PART THREE

Public Control and Private Violence
in Early Modern Times

The Language of Violence in the Late Italian Renaissance: The Example of the Tuscan Romagna

JOHN K. BRACKETT

When Jacob Burckhardt sought to illustrate what he regarded as the particular nature of the *vendetta* in volume two of *The Civilization of the Renaissance in Italy*, he rustled through his notes for an example from Acquapendente, today developed as a water sports resort, complete with a giant water slide, in the Romagna. Undoubtedly while repressing an inward shudder, the Swiss historian then wrote of a feud resulting in the deaths of thirty-six persons, which had begun with the accidental death of a youth at the hands of two companions while watching cattle in the mountains. The father of the dead boy killed the young man who took him to his son's grave, and served his liver – *à la* Hannibal Lecter – to the boy's father.[1] Through this and other examples, Burckhardt was interested in a tentative exploration of what, after Gertrude Himmelfarb, we might call the "moral imagination" of the Italians as they stood on the threshold of modernity; he wished to illustrate the excesses of unrestrained egoism to which poor and rich alike were prone when it seemed, to him, that Renaissance Italians had no moral compass after having thrown aside the obscuring veil of Christianity.

Exploration by historians, anthropologists, and sociologists continues into the form and meaning of factional violence and vendetta in Italy, but few have attempted to follow in Burckhardt's footsteps by investigating the connection between violence, imagination and society. Some have used a functional model viewing the feud as a means of social control, a way of containing violence which allows social structures to remain intact. Lately, factional violence and vendetta have been of interest to historians of Italy concerned with the development of the modern state. Traditionally, political history has focused on the extension of power from the center to the periphery; recently Osvaldo Raggio, Angelo Torre, and myself, among others, have used factional violence as a lens

---

1 Jacob Burckhardt, *The Civilization of the Renaissance in Italy*, 2 vols. (1929, repr. New York, 1958), 2:430.

for reversing the focus, to look from the periphery inward.[2] Especially interesting is Angelo Torre's study of the Langhe region in the seventeenth and
eighteenth centuries, which argues that factional violence, comprehended as
coded behavior, can thus be read as a "language," the "idioms" of which are
expressive of shifting local power arrangements. Edward Muir's study of the
vendetta in Friuli during the late Renaissance is fascinating as well, but for a
different reason. Muir has been drawn to explore the origins and the "poetics"
of notably brutal acts of violence.[3] While making no overt moral judgements
about his subjects, he is close to Burckhardt in his interest in the origins of
extreme violence in the imagination of feuding Friulians.

My aim is to follow up on the initiatives of Torre, Muir and Burckhardt by
taking some soundings into the moral imagination of the violence-prone in the
Tuscan Romagna, reorganized by Cosimo I in 1542 as a province of the
Florentine Grand Duchy. I agree with Angelo Torre that the violence of the
vendetta constituted a language in the sense mentioned above; that is, that the
act was not an end in itself, but above all was meant to convey meaning to one's
enemies. Reading this type of violence as an idiom of power relations at any
particular time demonstrates that violence changes and adapts to local circumstances; it is thus historical. Researching both the vocabulary of violence and
its poetics will demonstrate that concepts of honor and shame played a key role
in instigating and shaping violence in this mountainous, rural society separated
from Florence by the sharply arching wall of the Appennines.[4]

The difficult region of mountain and seacoast known as the Tuscan Romagna was notorious for the violence of its inhabitants. It is well known, for
example, that Niccolò Machiavelli warned his contemporaries that its men
were heavily armed, skilled, and not reluctant to use their weapons. During a
term as governor of the Romagna, his friend, Francesco Guicciardini, never left
his quarters without the accompaniment of a large bodyguard. The violence and
political instability of the entire region have economic roots according to John
Larner and P. J. Jones.[5] Hard-pressed to extract sustenance, let alone wealth

2   Osvaldo Raggio, *Faide e parentele: lo stato genovese visto dalla Fontanabuona* (Torino,
    1990); Angelo Torre, "Faide, fazioni e partiti, ovvero la ridefinizione della politica nel
    feudi imperiali delle Langhe tra sei e settecento," *Quaderni Storici* 63(1986): 775–810;
    John K. Brackett, "Aspects of the Local Reaction to the Extension of Criminal Justice
    in the Tuscan Romagna, 1537–1609," in *Instituzioni e Società in Toscana nell' Età
    Moderna* (Rome, 1994), pp. 245–56. Each of these studies focuses on local resistance to
    attempts at control from the center, and on manipulation, especially of the criminal
    justice system, by local factions. Raggio goes the farthest in rejecting the reality of the
    "state" in favor of family- and clan-based power.
3   Edward Muir, *Mad Blood Stirring: Vendetta and Faction in Friuli during the Renais-
    sance* (Baltimore, 1993).
4   J. G. Peristiany, ed., *Honour and Shame: The Values of Mediterranean Society* (London,
    1965). Still a classic set of studies on the role of honor and shame in the societies of the
    Mediterranean basin.
5   John Larner, *The Lords of Romagna: Romagnol Society and the Origins of the Signorie*
    (New York, 1965); idem, "Order and Disorder in Romagna, 1450–1500," in *Violence*

from modestly fertile terrain, the Romagnoli were forced to resort to smuggling salt, foodstuffs, cloth and other items to make ends meet. It seems to have been around the need to control roads and trails to facilitate this illicit traffic that much of the region's factionalism crystallized,[6] though much more work needs to be done before this argument can be fully confirmed.[7]

My material has been drawn from the archive at Terra del Sole which became in 1579 the seat of administration and criminal justice for the entire province into at least the nineteenth century. Included are fighting words exchanged between those engaged in pursuit of the vendetta, and between other persons whose conflicts appear to be unconnected with factional feuding. Despite the well-known difficulties of working with criminal court documents, these records remain an indispensable source for the social historian. In them, the "little people" speak, though they do so through filters; they do not always speak the entire truth, thus it is often necessary to attempt to read their silences.[8] We begin by establishing a taxonomy of violence.[9]

It requires a leap of imagination for members of a highly literate culture like ours to understand language and thought processes in a pre-literate, or partially literate one, such as that of sixteenth-century Romagna. In contemporary

and Civil Disorder in Italian Cities, ed. Lauro Martines (Berkeley, 1972), pp. 39–71; P. J. Jones, *The Malatesta of Rimini and the Papal State* (Cambridge, 1974).

[6] Cesarina Casanova, *Comunità e governo Pontificio in Romagna in età moderna* (Bologna, 1981), pp. 20, 71.

[7] Muir argues convincingly that factional violence in Friuli was transformed into more socially acceptable duelling by the late sixteenth century as Venice worked institutional changes which defused violence as a political option. Raggio argues that it was immigration to the Americas in the nineteenth century that ended feuding in the Genoese territories. In the larger cities of Italy, such as Florence, it was institutional "reform" under the Medici principate, and the rush to aristocracy of the principate, which ended feuding. Interestingly, duelling was more written on and discussed than practiced in Tuscany, since the Grand Dukes did not approve of such behavior on the part of their aristocrats. My reading of the records of the Otti de Guardia e Balia for 1537–1609 indicates that Florentine aristocratic men resorted to informal street confrontations to settle their affairs of honor, which effectively criminalized the activity. See John K. Brackett, *Criminal Justice and Crime in Late Renaissance Florence, 1537–1609* (New York, 1992).

[8] On the problems of reading criminal court documents, see Thomas Kuehn, "Reading Microhistory: The Example of Giovanni and Lusanna," *Journal of Modern History* 61(1989): 512–34. Kuehn's article makes a valid argument in taking some historians to task for the "naive" use of these records, but is incorrect in the assessment of Gene Brucker's *Giovanni and Lusanna: Love and Marriage in Renaissance Florence* (Berkeley, 1986), which is anything but naive in its reconstruction of the pertinent ecclesiastical court process.

[9] Walter Ong, *Orality and Literacy: The Technologizing of the Word* (London, 1982), pp. 8–9. For sociolinguistics, see: Joshua A. Fishman, *The Sociology of Language: An Interdisciplinary Social Science Approach to Language in Society* (Rowley MA, 1972); Peter Burke and Roy Porter, *The Social History of Language* (Cambridge, 1982); Peter Burke and Roy Porter, *Language, Self and Society: A Social History of Language* (Cambridge, 1991).

western society, most people of varying levels of class are schooled to read at least at some rudimentary level, in the rationalized, standardized structures of national language. It is true that even today in Italy many still grow up with more exposure to a spoken dialect than to the national language. Such was the rule rather than the exception in the Romagna of Machiavelli's time, when the construction of the national language was a project only recently underway. The literate elites of the Romagnol towns, for example, consisted of notaries whose highest reading skills involved memorization of a few Latin formulas necessary to fulfill their client's needs. They did not exhibit any great proficiency in Latin or vernacular literature. The Romagna had neither the resources nor the need to produce the high level of literacy present in a major city such as Florence. Consequently, as the literary theorist, Walter Ong, has convincingly argued, it is not that pre-literate people are less intelligent than contemporary Europeans or Americans, but that they think differently. All thought is, to some extent, analytic, in that it organizes bits of material into various levels and combinations of components. But abstractly sequential, classificatory, explanatory examination of phenomena is impossible without reading.[10] This is so because the extenuation of precision and nuance achievable in written texts cannot be sustained in oral form. In the absence of reading, knowledge is constantly repeated, and often allegorized, to be remembered. In pre-literate societies, the utterance of words is a form of action – words have power. It is not surprising then to find them encoded in the criminal statutes of Florence and Castrocaro alike, prohibitions against the implementation of various types of insult through words, gestures and acts considered as assault – a continuum of communication as action.[11] In a literate society, there is a sharp distinction drawn by law between words and actions. But the statutes of Castrocaro–Terra del Sole, for example, criminalized use of words like: "bandit" (*predo*); "thief" (*fur*; *furfante*); "prostitute" (*meretrix*); "pimp" (*ruffiano(a)*). Violations brought fines of as much as 10 *lire* if such words resulted in the rupture of a formal peace between feuding families, leading to death.[12] The use of these words and others like them constituted an attack upon honor. While these examples do not exhaust the list of insulting words, they do establish principles of classification, which are the attempt to identify the recipient as "other," as outcast through deployment of the negative side of some of the dualities that

---

10 Ong, pp. 8–9.
11 Brackett, *Crime*, pp. 113–14; Archivio Storico di Castrocaro, Terra del Sole [ACTS], *Statuta et Ordinamenta Terrae Castrocarii*, 1513, III, "Libro de Maleficiis," ff. 58r–v, rubric 7. Of course such laws were common everywhere in Italy.
12 Anna Maria Enriquez, "La vendeta nella vita el nella legislazione fiorentina," *Archivo Storico Italiano* [*ASI*] ser. 7, 19(1933): 85–146, 181–223. In Florentine territory the vendetta had legal status; its violence was regulated through mediatory procedures, making it in effect a separate legal system. I refer also to a conversation with Andrea Zorzi, who has completed a *tesi di dottorato* at the University of Florence that deals with the vendetta in fourteenth-century Florence.

define the values of Mediterranean societies: honest man/thief (good/evil) and decent or "honest" woman/whore (pure/unclean).[13]

The reader will forgive me if the atmosphere turns a bit blue from the taxonomy that follows.[14] First, we can discern differences in the words used by men to insult women: for example, *puttana ruffiana* meant "whore procuress", that is, a woman who was completely outside of the accepted bounds of sexual behavior – the target first sold sex for money and then caused other women to do the same, and lose their honor as well. A "cow" (*vacca*) – as distinct from "milk cow" (*mucca*) – which had some positive sexual connotation – was used for agricultural labor. Thus the reference was to women of easy virtue garnished with the charge of physical ugliness and deformity brought on by constant labor.[15] *Sbudellata* was a term for evisceration which came from the butchery of animals and meant that the woman was "gutless." Interestingly, this term was not used to insult men.[16] "Pig" (*porca*) again emphasized physical deformity, but also sex – voluptuousness gone bad. A *poltrona* was a lazy woman not disposed to work or care for herself. Such a person was a social parasite because she did not carry her own weight. The capacity to work, to join in the community's common endeavor to survive, was a part of the gender definitions of both men and women, and thus a target of insult.

Men used the following sorts of words to insult each other. If a man looked on another as especially incorrigible, he called him "both a donkey and a lazy person" (*asino e poltrone*) or a "highwayman, or a violent sneak outside of society and at war with it" (*ladrone di strada*). If he wished to cast doubt on his enemy's legitimacy and family stature, he would call him a "son of a bastard" (*figlio del bastardo*). To throw doubt on his loyalty to family and faction, he might call his adversary "a traitor" (*traditore*). To insult the lack of control his enemy had in his own household and over his own wife, he could call him "a cuckold, vituperous pimp" (*becco cornuto vituperoso ruffiano*). To add emphasis to his enemy's sexual insecurity, he might call him an "ugly

---

13 Anton Blok, "Rams and Billy Goats: A Key to the Mediterranean Code of Honour," *Man: The Journal of the Royal Anthropological Institute*, n.s. 16, no. 3 (1981): 430–1. The symbolic pattern representing the code according to Blok is as follows:

rams/billy goats	pure/unclean	
sheep/goats	strong/weak	
honor/shame	good/evil	
men/women	silence/noise	virility/feminity

14 ACTS, *Libro Criminale non descritti*, f. 171 (1580–81); f. 172 (1580–81); f. 175 (1581–82); f. 180 (1582–83), *Libro Criminale descritti*, f. 178 (1581–82), f. 187 (1583–84). The examples cited in the text are drawn from these volumes of cases.
15 Ministro della Pubblica Istruzione, Emilio Broglio, *Novo Vocabolario della Linguage Italiana Secondo L'Uso di Firenze* (Florence, 1897), q.v. "vacca," "mucca."
16 Ibid., s.v. "sbudellata."

prick" (*beccaccio*)[17] who "doesn't have what it takes to be a decent man in the community" (*non l'haveva de huomo da bene*).[18]

In socio-linguistic terms, such insults are parts of a specific type of "speech event" – a set of time-worn role relationships in which such customary responses are not only expected but demanded. Such words are thus not random utterances. A type of social situation is thus created, ready-made with its own glossary of appropriate language.[19] In Tuscan society, the use of such words presented the targeted man with a choice: respond with violence or accept public dishonor. When men insulted women, however, the women were reminded of their subordinate place in the social order, since violence was not expected of them. Even under provocation of insult, women were defined as passive and could only respond with words. The woman's role as sexual subordinate to man was thereby made clear, for it was only in the eyes of men that women could have honor. When men – usually men of the same social level – confronted each other, the aim of the insult was to provoke the opponent either to violence or silence through various angles of attack on his "manhood."

But the honor of an entire family or clan could also be attacked through insult, testing its "manhood." An instructive encounter occurred in the piazza of Modigliana on 12 February 1582, when Giovanni d'Antonio Cimetti and Cecchino di Bernardo were confronted by Bastiano Meletti, son of Messer Domenico Meletti, a cobbler to whom the two owed payment for a pair of shoes. They had promised to deliver a pig as payment, but had not yet repaid their debt, and Bastiano, tired of waiting, was now talking up for his father. As Giovanni and Cecchino passed his shop, Bastiano called out to them that they had held off his father long enough with words, and that now was the time for deeds (*venire alli fatti*).[20] Giovanni responded promptly with: "You're lying through your throat" and Cecchino chimed in with "you thief" (*deli furfante*); then "Do you dare call our family liars and insult us on the piazza" (*Hai ardimento contra dici parentado senza rispettarci su una piazza*). The verbal confrontation then turned physical as these men were joined by other family members in combat with swords and cudgels. Cooler heads intervened before anyone was killed or seriously injured. Later that same month, the same men engaged each other in another brawl.[21] By December 1583, then, the court, in possession of a fuller transcript of the testimony than that which survives today, decided that after Bastiano said "but it seems to me that the two of you have screwed us and tricked us many times" (*ma mi pare ci haverete tutti due*

---

17 Salvatore Battaglia, *Grande Dizionario della Lingua Italiana* (Torino, 1961).
18 See note 14.
19 Fishman, pp. 33, 38–39.
20 ACTS, *Libro Criminale descritti*, 181 (1582–83), 22 February 1582, ff. 348v–349v. (Old style: the Florentine new year began on 15 March.)
21 ACTS, *Libro Criminale descritti*, ff. 349v–50r (2 March 1582).

uccellato tante volte et maschato), nothing that Giovanni or Cecchino said thereafter was punishable, so provocative had Bastiano's words been.[22]

Among men, certain individual words or spontaneous expressions could precipitate a violent reaction, but they did not pose the clear and unavoidable challenge contained in other, more formulaic expressions typically the way of thinking in oral cultures.[23] As Muir has noted, the expression "you are lying through your throat or through your teeth, as we might say" (*ti menti per la gola*) was an insult that could not be redressed by a further exchange of words.[24] In one instant, it unmasked the naked hostility of both parties through a call to put aside the social niceties, the everyday dissimulations that made social life possible. In a "theatrical society"[25] such as that of Italy, or more broadly – according to Ong – in oral cultures, speech is never informal, but always agonistic, formulaic and performance-oriented.[26] Men and women in such societies are always on guard – always challenging or preparing to rebuff a verbal thrust. Consequently, it can be said that such societies are always acting, always throwing up a shield against the world. Even when such actions become ritualized within an entire class, the same kind of individual motivations remain.[27] To have maximum effect, the more publicly given an insult the better, since it was in public places that male honor, especially, was treated and contested. All public "domains" were the natural habitat for such jeering and probing language, and in early modern Tuscany, the most public of places was the central piazza, where men passed and gathered to do business. But certain forms of violence were themselves intended to communicate, to serve as speech acts when a violent act expressed such depths of hatred and contempt as could only be communicated symbolically in a grand gesture.[28]

Rare cases of horrendous acts of violence constituted the maximum degree of expressiveness of the language of violence. An instance taken from Monte Vecchio, which occurred on 1 May 1583, provides us with a particularly florid episode of a very active and bloody feud between the Monsignani, their allies the Lanini, and the Fabbri clans.[29] Under cover of darkness thirteen Fabbri men lay in ambush for two members of the Lanini on their way from Premilcuore to Castrocaro to buy grain. The killers had hidden for days in an agricultural worker's house awaiting their prey. When they finally appeared, the Fabbri

---

[22] ACTS, *Libro Criminale descritti*, 187 (1583–84), ff. 4–5.

[23] Ong, pp. 8–9.

[24] ACTS, *Libro Criminale descritti*, 173 (1580–81), 30 April 1580 (old style: the Florentine new year began on 15 March), ff. 13r–v.

[25] Peter Burke, *The Historical Anthropology of Early Modern Italy* (Cambridge, 1987), introduction.

[26] Ong, pp. 110, 140–41.

[27] Robert C. Davis, *The War of the Fists: Popular Culture and Public Violence in Late Renaissance Venice* (New York, 1994), p. 131.

[28] Fishman, pp. 38–39.

[29] ACTS, *Libro Criminale descritti*, 181 (1582–83), 10 May 1583, ff. 368v–69r.

opened fire with arquebuses, killing both Lanini men. Then, they stripped the
bodies of clothing and cut off the heads of their enemies, carrying them away
"with the greatest scorn and hatred throwing them to dogs."[30] This case was
terminated in Terra del Sole's court and called up to Florence by the Eight on
Public Safety. The desecration of the corpses was unusual; I have read many
cases of murder and mayhem but nothing like this. I checked back through the
earlier instances of vendetta between these families and found that in the
incident immediately preceding this one, the two ambushed Lanini were the
only participants not to have received some form of punishment from a court
judgement in favor of the Fabbri. In fact, then, the murders seem to have been
intended to supplement the actions of the Florentine criminal justice system,
which the Fabbri judged deficient in this case. The desecration of the corpses
was calculated to create a debt versus the Lanini and the Monsignani clans
through the emotional shock that would accompany news of the deed. In
addition, the very public nature of the affront to community standards of
decency – the Fabbri did not attempt to hide what they had done – emphasized
in dramatic fashion the deep hatred that the Fabbri felt towards their enemies,
but it also highlighted their frustration ultimately, since the Monsignani faction
had been extremely successful at piling up Fabbri dead in their encounters. To
respond, the Fabbri took violence to the level of poetry, attempting to achieve
in symbolic form the victory that was unachievable in reality.

Ultimately much of the vocabulary of violence is rooted in various kinds of
competition: it is often directly or indirectly sexual in content and expressive
to a limited extent of the gender relations between men and women, emphasiz-
ing the inferiority of women; or it stems from competition between men of all
social levels over honor, which could only be gained at someone's expense,
thus demonstrating just how valued violence was as a way of winning esteem.
I also believe that some of the floridness of some acts of extreme violence –
such as Burckhardt's example – was calculated to create a "debt" that the other
side would be hard-pressed to match, let alone surpass. The extreme mistreat-
ment of a corpse dishonored the deceased, the family and the faction.

Violence in the largely pre-literate culture of the sixteenth-century Tuscan
Romagna did constitute a language, since Romagnoli did not distinguish as
neatly between words and actions as modern industrial societies do. For them,
the boundaries were considerably blurred; words and actions had near equal

---

30 Muir, p. 194: "Carnival, vendetta and hunting were distinct activities, but in the act of
killing and in talking and writing about killing the boundaries among the three blurred,
so that a vendetta could easily become a carnival riot or adopt the cultural trappings of
the hunt." Muir, pp. 215–46, makes the case that throwing parts of human corpses to
dogs replicated part of the ceremonial of the hunt in which parts of the killed prey were
thrown to hunting dogs. An incident in the Friuli examined by Muir is strikingly similar
to the murder that I have elucidated. Hunting was of course an activity familiar to the
men of the Romagna, as it was to Friulians.

communicative power. But the level of their expression was tied to their sense of the concreteness of things and the world. The vocabulary of violence measured men and women according to the commonest everyday standards: sexual attractiveness or lack thereof; an ambivalent sense of their own sexuality especially of its carnality; willingness to work or not; in comparison to useful but physically repulsive animals which they kept in their homes or saw wandering the streets. Affairs of honor contracted in this public arena were initiated by stock expressions whose meaning and implications were understood by all, including trained jurists. The poetic peaks of feud violence represented the clumsy attempts of pre-literates to ascend to the realm of bloody symbolism to avenge actual grievous injury.

Artificial Antagonism In Pre-Modern Iran: The Haydari-Ne'mati Urban Factions

JOHN R. PERRY

I

Iran was not established as a nation state until the beginning of the sixteenth century, when Shah Ismâ'il and his successors of the Safavid dynasty gained power over the area comprising the Iranian plateau from eastern Anatolia and Iraq (the limits of the Ottoman empire) to the Hindu Kush in eastern Afghanistan, bordering the nascent Mughal empire of India. Technically, Safavid Iran was as much a multi-ethnic empire as its neighbors, comprising large numbers of Persians and Turks and smaller numbers of Arabs, Pashtuns, Kurds, Baluch and others. Frontiers fluctuated from one war to the next; religious affiliation, within the majority of Muslims, was divided between the antagonistic Sunni and Shi'a sects; and regional, tribal, class and other loyalties meant more to most subjects than the abstraction that was the state. Nevertheless, the early Safavid shahs succeeded in imposing Shi'ism as the state religion on most of their subjects, consolidating their territory, and conducting diplomatic relations on more or less equal terms not only with their "oriental" rivals but with contemporary European powers, including England, France, Genoa, Venice and Russia. Persian language and literature was established as the main vehicle of the country's culture, and the cult of the shah characterized the Iranian polity for both natives and foreigners. It is clear that from at least 1600 we are dealing with an ideologically unified, territorially delimited and culturally solidified nation in which local loyalties were being subordinated, or harnessed, to central political and economic interests.

Traditionally, Iran's political culture has centered around two groups: (1) the nomadic pastoralists, tribally organized, who generally furnished the ruling family and the core of the military; and (2) the cities, which provided the economic and administrative infrastructure. Indigenous historians have always tended to write for and of the former. Consequently, the social, political, commercial and religious life of the cities of the Eastern caliphate and its Iranian successor states has to be gleaned piecemeal from the *obiter dicta* of

local historians and geographers and foreign travelers, or extrapolated from
modern anthropological and sociological studies. The urban dynamics of
pre-modern Islamic polities, especially of the Iranian region, have attracted
serious scholarship only in the last few decades, and still have a long way to
go: even now, new manuscripts are being discovered and known sources are
being re-read for new purposes. Furthermore, fieldwork – though boasting
some excellent and innovative approaches by both Western and Iranian scholars – has been patchy and interrupted. In such a situation, theory tends
periodically to outstrip data, and documentation of the more vernacular and
fluid urban phenomena is tantalizingly inexact.

The best known of the factors in urban communal identity, solidarity,
competition and conflict in pre-modern Iran may be summarized as follows.
Religion was, and has remained, probably the most visible and ostensibly most
significant of these factors. Before the establishment of state Shi'ism, adherents
of rival religious communities – the four rites (*mazhab*) of the Sunna, or the
four principal sects of Islam (Sunna, Imami or "Twelver" Shi'a, Isma'ili or
"Sevener" Shi'a, and Kharijites) – could often be found living in their own
quarter or ward (*mahalla*) of a city, with their own mosque, bazaar, shrine(s)
and other communal centers. Sectarian disputes could escalate into riots or
pogroms, either internally motivated or aggravated by more widespread disorder or by enemy invasion. For example, the Mongols often found their task of
selective extermination facilitated by communal bigotry.[1] From Safavid times
on, most Iranian cities had a majority of Shi'i citizens; Christian, Jewish and
Zoroastrian communities would have adjacent and separate quarters or villages. Conduct of the many and varied Shi'i religious festivals could indeed
lead to conflict and violence, as we shall see, but the causes and pretexts were
other than sectarian.

Of the official bodies involved in structured social interaction from at least
1600 until the present century, the most important were the *asnâf*, or guilds.[2]
As self-governing corporations of artisans, shopkeepers and traders, the Iranian
guilds exercised traditional religious and ceremonial functions and were a
channel for voicing political demands. They yielded nothing in terms of
pageantry and clout to their analogues in Europe. Though not in themselves
competing factions, their activities provided a framework within which social,
political and local antagonisms might be expressed. In particular, they controlled the employment and periodically co-opted the leisure time of a majority of

---

1   Hossein Mirjafari, "The *Haydari-Ni'mati* Conflicts in Iran," trans. and adapted by J. R.
    Perry, *Iranian Studies* 12/3–4(1979): 135–37. This article, as a pioneering study of the
    Haydari-Ne'mati factions, includes more detailed accounts of events that are summa-
    rized or alluded to in the present article, and full citations of original Persian and Arabic
    sources and field informants.
2   See Willem M. Floor, "Asnâf," *Encyclopædia Iranica*, ed. Ehsan Yarshater, 2 vols.
    (London, 1987), 2:772–78.

the city's young males. Other social organizations that occasionally rose to prominence with similar or overlapping functions were mystical and dervish orders (*tariqât*) and associations of young men (*fotovva*, *'ayyâr*, *luti*, *dâsh*, *mashdi*, *pahlavân* and other terms).

Discussion of the genesis and ethos of this last phenomenon, which at its broadest includes Indo-European sodalities and modern street gangs, is particularly problematic in the case of pre-modern Iran. They have been characterized as everything from chivalric paramilitary *Männerbünde* in the style of the knights of the round table, to social bandits *à la* Robin Hood's merry men, to unregenerate rent-a-crowd street thugs.[3] In Iran, these associations of young men have invariably been organized around the individual *mahalla*, where the *zurkhâna* or traditional gymnasium functions as a clubhouse. Solidarity is publicly expressed during religious holidays by congregating in and marching *en masse* from the *mahalla*, with banners and accoutrements, to join the general procession. Emulative rivalry between wards often erupts into violent conflict, or in cases where a ceremonial rite such as a *hosayniya*, a *ta'ziya* (religious play) or other ritual is performed in common between several wards, the bands of young men may represent a traditional grouping or alliance of city wards.

II

The factional conflict that forms the subject of this inquiry, though connected at several points with the factors identified above, is not identical or analogous to any of them. The striking thing about it is its apparent arbitrariness and lack of overt motivation. Briefly stated, from at least the early Safavid period up until the present century, a number of cities and towns of Iran were perceived as being divided into two groupings of adjacent wards, one known as Haydari and the other as Ne'mati or Ne'matollâhi, the respective (male) inhabitants of which would profess mutual contempt and antagonism, and would periodically clash in massive street fights. The origin of the terms, which evidently came from personal names, and of the antagonism was not generally known to the participants, and was not, it seems, the object of much speculation; the topography and composition of the *mahalla* groupings that made up the Haydari-khâna and the Ne'mati-khâna (as the rival districts were known), though they remained constant, were apparently irrelevant; and membership in one of these factions corresponded to no other social, political or sectarian affiliation.

---

[3] See Willem M. Floor, "Guilds and Futuvvat in Iran," *Zeitschrift der Deutschen Morgenländischen Gesellschaft* 134(1984): 106–14; idem,"The *Lutis*, a Social Phenomenon in Qajar Persia – A Reappraisal," *Die Welt des Islams* 13(1971): 103–20; Claude Cahen and W. L. Hanaway, Jr., " 'Ayyār," *Encyclopædia Iranica* 3:159–63.

A summary of the instances known and comments by observers will clarify the dimensions of this phenomenon, while magnifying the fundamental problem.

As early as 1571, the Italian traveler Vicentio D'Alessandri reported that the nine wards of Tabriz (the Safavid capital up until 1555) were divided between the Ne'mati and Haydari factions, five belonging to one and four to the other, and in a state of permanent feud. His statement also implies that the feud pre-dated the establishment of the Safavid dynasty in 1502.[4] Chardin, visiting Iran a century later, confirmed this situation in Tabriz and asserted that by the fifteenth century the factions divided "toute la Perse."[5] He provides a more circumstantial account of the feud in Isfahan:

> The village of Ispahan was divided in two quarters, one named *Joubaré Neamet Olahi* which faced to the east and the other named *Dere-dechte Heideri*, which faced to the west ... These two quarters are properly like two factions which enter into the suburbs and the territory of the village. In effect, all the villages of Persia were thus found divided.[6]

On holidays and other occasions of public assembly, the one party would attack the other to secure precedence, and on ordinary days the wrestlers and young toughs of each side hurled challenges at each other. Sometimes, pitched battles ensued on the old square, with hundreds fighting on either side. The participants were always of the lower classes, and, although they fought only with sticks and stones, there were always a few killed and many injured.

Another French traveler, Tavernier, who made six journeys to Iran in the course of the seventeenth century, confirmed Chardin's picture in respect to Isfahan and added that on festive occasions the two factions would bet heavily on the bull- and bear-baiting, cock-fighting and other popular sports.[7] In Qazvin, which served as the Safavid capital from about 1555 until 1588, Shah 'Abbâs's astrologer records two incidents during the year 1003 of the Hijra (AD 1594): a fight between the Haydari and Ne'matollâhi factions that took place "by royal decree" in the public square, victory going to the "Mir Haydari" faction; and a second fight that was ordered at a local shrine.[8] Other occasions on which Shah 'Abbâs instigated such clashes for his personal

---

4 Charles Gray, trans., "Narrative of the Most Noble Vicentio D'Alessandri," in *A Narrative of Italian Travels in Persia*, Hakluyt Society, ser. 1, vol. 49 (London, 1873), p. 224. The names of the factions appear here as Nausitai and Himcaivatu.

5 Sir John Chardin, *Voyages*, 2 vols. (Amsterdam, 1711), 2:316.

6 Chardin, 8:11–13: "La Ville d'Ispahan est divisée en deux quartiers, l'un nommé *Joubaré Neamet Olahi*, qui regarde l'Orient, & l'autre nommé *Dere-dechte Heideri*, qui regarde l'Occident ... Ces deux quartiers ... sont proprement comme deux Factions, qui engagent avec elles les Faubourgs & le territoire de la Ville ... En effet, tous les villes de Perse se trouvent ainsi divisées."

7 Jean Baptiste Tavernier, *Les Six Voyages* (Paris, 1677), 1:396.

8 Mirjafari, p. 147.

amusement are reported by Pietro della Valle in 1617.[9] On the other hand, observers occasionally noted bloody – and sometimes futile – attempts by the shah's troops or the local authorities to quell spontaneous Haydari-Ne'mati clashes that got out of hand. One such incident occurred as recently as 11 June 1975 in the town of Ardakân in Fars province.[10]

Although essentially a plebeian phenomenon, the Haydari-Ne'mati split automatically applied to patricians who resided in one or other of the faction-alized neighborhoods. The Qâjâr prince Mas'ud Mirzâ Zell al-Soltân, newly appointed governor of Isfahan in 1882, was surprised by an outbreak of factional rioting and asked his aides what it was all about. He was apprised of the history of the factions and of the fact that "in accordance with the division of the city, Your Highness is a Haydari"; whereupon he was delighted and exclaimed, "Since I'm to be a Haydari, let's give the Ne'matis hell!"[11]

The feud could also be used for more serious partisan or political purposes. In Dezful during the second half of the nineteenth century there were Haydari-Ne'mati riots instigated by rival regional powers outside the city itself: Shaykh Khaz'al, who supported the Ne'matis, and the Bakhtiyâri khans, who favored the Haydaris.[12] At Ardabil during the Constitutional Revolution of 1906, two rival regional revolutionary councils (*anjoman*) were set up because the leader appointed by the provincial revolutionary council in Tabriz belonged to the Ne'mati faction. The two sides finally brought in tribal allies from outside the city, erected barricades and shot at each other.[13] The division noted by Chardin at Isfahan survived until at least the 1950s among the villages of Jolga-ye Ru-dasht, the region east of the city, where the landowners were able to use these animosities to provoke fights in order to improve their access to water or otherwise extend their authority.[14]

Noted by many observers of the Haydari-Ne'mati conflicts is the regularity, even cyclical nature, of their occurrence and other ritual, ceremonial and sporting features. In Shiraz during the nineteenth century, where five of the eleven wards were Haydari and five Ne'mati (the Jewish quarter fell outside this scheme), pitched battles would be held three or four times a year.[15] According to an attaché of the British Legation:

---

[9] Pietro della Valle, *Voyages dans la Turquie, l'Egypte, la Palestine, la Perse, les Indes orientales et autres lieux*, 6 vols. (Rouen, 1712–45), 3:42.

[10] Engelbert Kaempfer, *Am Hofe des persischen Grosskönigs*, ed. W. Hinz (Leipzig, 1940), pp. 110–11; Tadeusz Judasz Krusinski, *The History of the Late Revolutions of Persia*, 2 vols. (London, 1750), 1:91; Mirjafari, p. 155.

[11] Mirjafari, p. 148.

[12] Willem M. Floor, "The Political Role of the *Lutis* in Iran," in *Modern Iran*, ed. Michael Bonine and Nikki Keddie (Albany, 1981), p. 90.

[13] Mirjafari, p. 152.

[14] Ibid., pp. 154–55.

[15] Ibid., pp. 149–50.

Once a week, on Friday, the inhabitants of the two divisions of the population called Hyderi and Neametali, repair to the open ground beyond the city walls, and engage in a skirmish with slings and stones; an exercise which is not infrequently followed by a close fight with swords and daggers.[16]

Violence was expected, and duly occurred, during the major religious holidays that involved processions and gatherings. At Isfahan, in the elaborate ceremonials attending the annual Feast of the Sacrifice (*'Id-e Qorbân*), a universal Muslim holiday observed as late as the middle of the last century and a tradition from Safavid times, the two factions played a conspicuous role. Of six "sharers in the camel" (*mucha-dâr*) who were to have parts of the sacrificial beast there were to be three Haydari and three Ne'mati. During the parade, each "sharer" was preceded by an entourage from the city and the outlying villages, which numbered more than a thousand. At the head of the parade marched the "ruffians" (*lutis*), followed by armed riders, actors in the Moharram religious play, musicians, bearers of standards and banners, etc. The factions proceeded separately from their own quarters and came together in the main square. From there, they would parade past the provincial governor and across the river to the slaughtering ground. Despite extra guards and troops, there would always be clashes when the rival groups met at intersections and during the dividing of the sacrificial meat. Thirty to forty were injured and three or four killed every year.[17]

The principal Shi'i holiday, which commemorates the massacre of the Imam Hosayn and his adherents at Karbala in 680, falls one lunar month after the Feast of the Sacrifice, on the tenth of the month of Moharram, a day known as *'âshurâ*. Though this is a day of solemnity and solidarity for all Shi'ites, the emotions generated by the mourning rituals for the martyrs, the inflammatory sermons, the catharsis of the passion plays (*ta'ziya, shabih-khâni*), and the rivalry between wards in staging processions and plays, have repeatedly been observed as causes of Haydari-Ne'mati violence – particularly since many of the *lutis*, apprentices and other young men of the rival *mahallas* were members of the bands of flagellants or actors in the religious play.[18]

Despite the intermittent bloodshed, the Haydari-Ne'mati conflict characteristically adhered to certain norms of personal violence. A Qâjâr historian notes explicitly that casualties on either side during these periodic battles did not give rise to retaliation.[19] Thus, it was not technically a feud – a mechanism of which depends on cyclical vengeance growing out of past outrages. Each

---

16 Robert Grant Watson, *A History of Persia from the Beginnings of the 17th Century* (London, 1866), p. 110.

17 Mehdi Keyvani, *Artisans and Guild Life in the later Safavid Period* (Berlin, 1982), pp. 259–62.

18 Kaempfer, p. 111; Sir John Malcolm, *A History of Persia*, 2 vols. (London, 1829), 2:429; Mirjafari, pp. 153–54.

19 Hâji Mirzâ Hasan Hosayni Fasâ'i, *Fârsnâma-ye Nâseri*, 2 vols. (Shiraz, 1933), 2:22.

clash between Haydaris and Ne'matis appears to have been viewed as a discrete event without appeal to atavistic insult or an "eye for an eye."[20] Descriptions of the "feud" in modern times reveal a generally low level of personal violence, actual bodily harm being replaced by ritual insult, hazing, or a symbolic "counting coup." At Ardakân near Yazd, marriages were never contracted between Haydari and Ne'mati families and some Haydaris regarded the Ne'matis as ritually unclean (najes) and would not visit the bathhouse in their neighborhood.

Clashes within the rival mahallas (as distinct from set-piece battles or riots on holidays) emphasized territoriality. On the ninth of Moharram, a number of men from each of the rival neighborhoods at Ardakan near Yazd would tour their neighborhood with a donkey and a saddlebag, clashing a pair of cymbals, to collect contributions of food and money for the next day's mourning rituals. If the two factions met at the boundaries, a fight would likely ensue. Anyone visiting the other faction's hosayniya would have to demonstrate respect by kissing the kelak, a platform in the center of the courtyard, and would be forced to do so if he refused.[21] Malcolm noted that during clashes in Moharram,

> if they force their opponents from their houses, they do not enter or plunder them, but make a mark on each door with a hatchet, as a token of victory.[22]

The active participants in fights seem to have been men only, and there is no mention of women or children of the enemy faction having been harmed. Scurrilous characterizations were circulated in order to demonize the opposition. For example, at Ardakân of Yazd, the Ne'matis maintained that one could recognize a Haydari boy by the fact that if he were to be picked up while urinating and moved a few paces away, he would involuntarily return to the same spot and continue.[23]

III

The ultimate origins of this factionalism can be traced with some certainty. The Ne'matis (Ne'matiya, Ne'matollâhi[ya]) began as a cult that grew up around the well-known poet and mystic of Kerman, Sayyed or "Shah" Ne'matollâh Vali (died c.1430). In a similar manner, the Haydaris ([Mir] Haydariya) are

---

[20] Ibid. Krusinski contradicts this to a degree, claiming that the urban moieties he calls Pelenk and Felenk were forbidden to intermarry or eat together, and that each one killed by the enemy during their Moharram clashes was counted a martyr and an incitement to further bloodshed. This still does not necessarily argue a systematic, rather than merely an ad hoc, reaction.

[21] Mirjafari, pp. 153–54.

[22] Ibid.

[23] Mirjafari, p. 154.

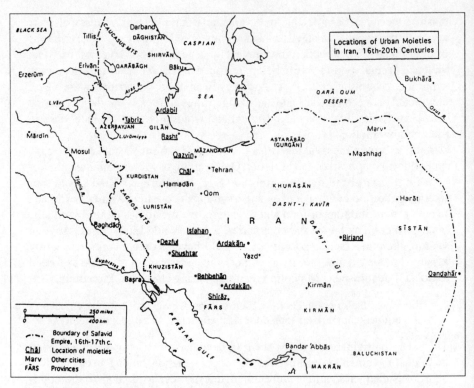

Locations of urban factions in Iran, sixteenth to twentieth centuries

presumably named after the followers of a less celebrated Sufi dervish, Soltân or "Mir" Qotb ol-Din Haydar Tuni of Tabriz (died c.1426). Alternatively, it is possible that they were named after either a different Qotb ol-Din Haydar, a resident of Zâva, or Sôltan Haydar, the founder of the Safavid dynasty.[24]

Shah Ne'matollâh himself was a Sunni, but his successors came to profess Shi'ism early in the Safavid period as a result of marriage alliances with that dynasty. Mir Haydar was an Imami Shi'i. Though their respective mystical schools or Sufi orders originated at opposite ends of Iran some two generations before the rise of the Safavids, it appears that the disciples of both leaders soon gained a following among the citizenry of Tabriz. Their original antagonism probably took the form of a Sunni-Shi'i sectarian dispute. Thereafter, the urban factions spawned by this doctrinal or cultic clash survived and expanded without motivation other than their eponymous labels. The Haydaris and Ne'matis thus give the appearance of being rioters without a cause, or artificially-created antagonists, to both native and foreign observers.[25]

---

24 Mirjafari, pp. 137, 141–42; see also Floor, "The *Lutis*," pp. 400–81, n. 14.
25 Several of the European travelers mistakenly attribute the origins of the factions to two

The following cities and towns (or villages near them) came to be divided between Haydari and Ne'mati factions after the later fifteenth century: Ardabil, Tabriz, Qazvin, Rasht, Isfahan, Ardakân (Fars), Shiraz, Dezful, Shushtar, Behbehân, Ardakân (Yazd), Birjand.[26] A glance at the map of Iran, and a moment's reflection on the course of empire from about 1500 to 1800, will show that most of these are prominent Safavid centers: Ardabil, the family's home; Tabriz, Qazvin and Isfahan, the successive capitals; Gilan, Fars and Khuzestan, western provinces chosen for economic development by the shahs. Tehran, which did not attain prominence until the early nineteenth century, under the Qâjâr dynasty, is absent from this list, as are cities in the east (Mashhad, Kerman) which were of little importance in the Safavid period. A notable exception to the pattern is Birjand, in southern Khorasan. But on balance, the evidence indicates that this dichotomy was spread by the Safavid ethos and the social disruptions it occasioned. Among them were an enthusiastic (at times, fanatical) Shi'i fervor imposed rapidly on a variegated population; urban expansion and consolidation through commerce; and politico-economic centralization of a regionally and ecologically diverse land (achieved partly by systematic deportation of populations from one part of the country to the other).

The cultural and psychological profile of Iran's urban society between about 1450 and 1850 is strikingly similar to that of late medieval Europe as characterized by J. R. Hale, as the scene of "increasing immigration from country to towns producing an insecurely employed proletariat and the beginnings of a well-defined criminal class."[27] Pastimes of both rich and poor were violent, and casualties were expected. Spectacles, such as animal combats, public executions and judicial torture, were common in real life and imitated in mystery and morality plays. Yet at the same time, it was "an age kindly to cretins, not ungenerous in providing hospitals, [and] sympathetic even to voluntary indigence."[28] To this, may be added a penchant for city-wide religious gatherings, pageants and processions, including bands of penitents or

secular rulers. A misunderstanding could have arisen from the dervishes' sobriquets ["sultan" (*soltân*), "emir" (*mir*), "king" (*shâh*)]. Not only European but even Persian writers sometimes assert that the factions owed their invention to a sovereign (usually identified as Shah 'Abbâs), who decreed that his cities should be arbitrarily so divided in order to diffuse the chance of a concerted popular revolt. Krusinski follows this Persian view, adding that 'Abbâs tried to institute a similar pair of factions in the Afghan city of Qandahar when he conquered it, but that these factions ceased to exist when Qandahar was recaptured by the Mughals (Mirjafari, pp. 137–43, 158, n. 17; Chardin, 2:316; Ange de Saint-Joseph (Joseph Labrosse), *Souvenirs de la Perse safavide et autres lieux de l'Orient*, trans. and ed. Michel Bastiaensen (Brussels, 1985), pp. 186–87; Krusinski, pp. 91–93).

26 Floor, "The *Lutis*," p. 401, n. 16, for references not cited in the present article (esp. Rasht, Gilan, Mazandaran, Birjand).

27 J. R. Hale, "Violence in the Late Middle Ages: A Background," in *Violence and Civil Disorder in Italian Cities, 1200–1500*, ed. Lauro Martines (Berkeley, 1972), p. 33.

28 Ibid., p. 24.

flagellants and the display of banners and other badges of association. In Iran, as in Italy, nobles tended to reside not on country estates but in the cities, where they were more available as patrons of or participants in such events.

IV

In conclusion, the study of the Haydari-Ne'mati factions is revealing on several levels and has some similarities with other instances of group violence in medieval and modern times.[29]

The ritualized and ludic characters of the Persian factions are similar in some aspects to the circus factions of early Byzantium, the competing political and social bands of such medieval Italian cities as Florence, Venice and Siena, and even to soccer hooligans and inner-city gangs of modern times. Such groups, though developing in widely-differing historical contexts, shared certain general structures: (1) they normally marked themselves off from society and other groups of young men by distinctive clothing and speech, (2) the members underwent initiations which reflected the transition into the organization and, by extension, into manhood, (3) many of them were composed of lower middle or lower class males with little social status, (4) the solidarity of these groups, though psychological and social in origin, eventually took a political cast which was feared, but manipulated, by the ruling powers, and (5) the groups acted within a ritualized nexus that, like an extended group language, defined manhood through its defense and search for glory in distinctly violent terms. For contrasting features of the Haydari-Ne'mati and other factional moieties refer to the following table:

	HN	TF	CF	SH
Retention of original motivation	–	x	x	x
Overt political agenda/new motivation	–	x	–	–
Flagrant badges/shibboleths	?	x	x	x
City-wide territorial division	x	–	–	–

HN – Haydari-Ne'mati, *TF* – Tuscan factions, *CF* – circus factions,
SH – soccer hooligans

29 Alan Cameron, *Circus Factions: Blues and Greens at Rome and Byzantium* (Oxford, 1976); Bill Buford, *Among the Thugs* (New York, 1991); David Herlihy, "Some Psychological and Social Roots of Violence in the Tuscan Cities," *Violence and Civil Disorder*, p. 140; J. K. Hyde, "Contemporary Views on Faction and Civil Strife in Thirteenth- and Fourteenth-Century Italy," *Violence and Civil Disorder*, p. 290; Robert C. Davis, *The War of the Fists: Popular Culture in Late Renaissance Venice* (New York, 1994); Gene Brucker, *The Civic World of Early Renaissance Florence* (Princeton NJ, 1977), p. 15; E. G. Dunning, "Football in its Early Stages," *History Today* 13(1963): 838–41.

Though the Persian groups might sport distinctive clothing or use exaggerated accents in certain contexts,[30] they did not do so to signal their status as Haydari or Ne'mati. Instead, they did little to mark themselves off from the larger Persian society. Ethnically and religiously they, like the majority of the Safavid realm, were all Iranian and Shi'ite. What, then, accounts for this long record of attack and counterattack? At their most prosaic level, the factions owed their existence to the pressures inherent in the passage from adolescence to manhood. This time of transition was also mirrored in the work lives of many of the faction members who had just begun long and difficult apprenticeships in the craft guilds. Such stress, coupled with the solidarity found in neighborhood and labor associations, could trigger violent outbursts – all to defend prestige and "turf" and to gain glory, which, though fleeting, might even extend beyond one's social circle. The pool of frustrated youths which filed into the ranks of the factions thus shared with similar medieval and modern groups "a bloated code of maleness, an exaggerated, embarrassing patriotism [and] a violent nationalism."[31]

The course of faction violence was acted out on the public stage of Persian society but was often diverted by many of these selfsame social forces. As a matter of course, religious spectacles brought factionalized citizens within the public spaces of Persian cities. The jostling over who would take precedence in the processions connected with such festivals was the normal trigger for violence between the two groups. In other public occasions, such as country fairs and sporting matches, violence between the factions could and indeed was expected to erupt over betting or disputed calls. Such outbursts were seldom random but seemed to be brought into being by the very institutions of Safavid society. As has been noted in connection with the so-called Religious Riots in medieval Europe, the violence of the Haydari and Ne'mati seemed "timed to, and a curious continuation of, the rite."[32]

In reality, the Safavid ruler and the realm's upper classes depended on the predictable clashes of the factions. Shah 'Abbâs, it is said, commanded the factions to fight for his entertainment, and on other occasions he "sometimes intervened to incite the two factions and, having brought them satisfactorily to blows, nimbly quit the field and sat at a window watching the ensuing battle and its dismal consequences."[33] When the shah was absent from Isfahan, the mayor of the city (kalântar) made no real effort to prevent Haydari-Ne'mati affrays because so much profit accrued to his office from them.[34]

Despite the broader political implications of faction violence, it was by no

---

[30] Kaempfer, p. 110; Floor, "The Lutis," p. 109.

[31] Buford, p. 262.

[32] Natalie Zemon Davis, "The Rites of Violence: Religious Riot in Sixteenth-Century France," Past and Present 59(1973): 72.

[33] Della Valle, 3:42.

[34] Chardin, 8:13.

means unlimited but was muted on several levels. Though small brawls often spread to true street battles, the Haydari and Ne'mati largely rejected the escalation of violence to enemy families and associates that was so characteristic of the vendetta. Instead, they seemed to have restricted it to the public arena. Even the laying of ambushes against one's adversaries was seen as dishonorable.

There is no doubt that the Safavid establishment of state Shi'ism and active promotion of vernacular urban celebrations fostered a sense of broader community which would emerge as Iranian nationalism. Yet the lack of religious or sectarian enemies in Persian communities, coupled with the absence of competitive, organized sports beyond the individual city quarters, demanded an alternative outlet for youthful aggression. Urban conflict on such a scale had the extra advantage of causing trouble for the authorities and damage, or at least anxiety, for the ruling class. For many pre-modern Iranian communities, a different neighborhood and a half-remembered affiliation with the supporters of a vanished dervish cult were apparently enough to legitimize antagonism between populations who were otherwise exactly the same. To borrow from Bill Buford's observation on modern gang behavior: violence creates the cause which creates the violence.[35] The group cause constitutes a higher authority which absolves the individual of all doubt and guilt. Once such an authority is firmly established, we know only too well how far it is capable of suspending people's inhibitions and sanctioning conduct normally considered criminal and inhumane. For the span of its useful life, however, the factionalized urban violence in Safavid and post-Safavid Persia remained true to its original purpose and functioned within the impenetrable walls of custom. The artificial antagonism of the Haydari and Ne'mati, then, centered on a regular bid for temporary glory within strict rules of engagement. In this way, war became sport and sport, war.

[35] Buford, p. 116.

Crime and Punishment in the Fifteenth-Century Portuguese World: The Transition from Internal to Imperial Exile[1]

TIMOTHY J. COATES

Introduction

Crime and criminality in Portugal in the late Middle Ages and the early modern period are subjects which remain virtually unexplored. Perhaps the principal reasons for this are the widely-dispersed and fragmentary nature of the surviving legal documentation[2] and the nearly-complete absence of monographs or synthetic studies on aspects relating to criminality (for example, the courts, vagrancy, the galleys) in the early modern Portuguese Empire.

The purpose of this article is to outline the first major transition in punishment which occurred in the Portuguese world: the shift from the exclusive use of internal exile sites to the concurrent use of overseas locales during the first century of Portugues° overseas exploration from 1415 to 1498. In particular, this article focuses on the Portuguese Crown's use of the punishment of exile to its Atlantic islands – the Azores, Madeira, Cape Verde, São Tomé and Príncipe – as well as to selected sites along coastal Africa from the straits of Gibraltar to the Cape of Good Hope during the first century of Portuguese maritime exploration.

The period from 1415 to 1498 is significant in maritime terms since it was the period of trial and error during which the Portuguese reached South Asia

---

1   The research for this article was made possible by grants awarded by the History Department and Graduate School of the University of Minnesota and Calouste Gulben-kian Foundation. This essay was first presented on the panel "The Early Portuguese Overseas Empire" at the *American Historical Association* National Convention in January, 1994. I am grateful for the suggestions made at that time, particularly from Professor Dauril Alden, the commentator on that panel.
2   For a discussion of surviving legal documentation in Portuguese archives, see Timothy J. Coates, "Sources in Portuguese and Goan (India) Archives and Libraries (1500–1755): A Guide and a Commentary," in *Discovery in the Archives of Spain and Portugal: Quincentenary Essays, 1492–1992*, ed. Lawrence J. McCrank (New York, 1993), pp. 291–318.

in 1498 and South America only two years later in 1500. This same period is central for understanding evolving Portuguese legal traditions; these were refined at home, tested in the first overseas areas, and, eventually, put into place on a global basis from Nagasaki to the interior regions of the Amazon. Furthermore, this period is significant in that it marks the first steps of the unique blending of criminals, the courts, penal exile, the military, and maritime discovery. This process was directed throughout the fifteenth century by the state's courts alone; the courts of the Holy Office of the Inquisition did not begin to use exile as a criminal punishment until the 1540s.

The beginnings of European, more specifically Portuguese, overseas expansion in North and West Africa during the fifteenth century have been discussed from a variety of viewpoints and with emphasis placed on distinct, but related, aspects. Blake[3] as well as Diffie and Winius[4] tend to view this as a commercial dispute between Portugal and Spain as well as between the Iberians and the Ottomans and their allies. Oliveira Marques and Magalhães Godinho have suggested the quest for wheat and gold as the motivation for Portuguese interest in this region.[5] Boxer and other maritime historians such as Armando Cortesão and Damião Peres[6] have outlined the Portuguese experience in this region charting the African coastline and becoming familiar with navigation using the southern stars and new wind and ocean currents. Teixeira da Mota deals with those same issues as well as the social interaction of the Portuguese with the peoples of West Africa, particularly in (modern) Guinea Bissau.[7] Verlinden concentrates on feudal and newly-emerging forms of land grants which developed as a result of Portuguese occupation of the Atlantic islands.[8] Saunders discusses one aspect at the core of this early immigration, both forced and free: replacing lost manpower in Portugal with African slaves.[9]

Criminals exiled to this region are yet another aspect of the century-long process of the Portuguese in the South Atlantic. How these criminals were

---

3   John W. Blake, *West Africa: Quest for God and Gold, 1454–1578* (London, 1977).
4   Bailey W. Diffie and George D. Winius, *Foundations of the Portuguese Empire, 1415–1580* (Minneapolis, 1977).
5   A. H. de Oliveira Marques, *Introdução à História da Agricultura em Portugal: A questão cerealífera durante a Idade Média* (Lisbon, 1978); Vitorino Magalhães Godinho, *História Económica e Social da Expansão Portuguesa* (Lisbon, 1947); and idem, *A Economia dos Descobrimentos Henriquinos* (Lisbon, 1962).
6   Armando Cortesão, *History of Portuguese Cartography* (Lisbon, 1969); Luís de Albuquerque, *Astronomical Navigation* (Lisbon, 1988); Damião Peres, *História dos Descobrimentos Portugueses* (Oporto, 1982).
7   A. Teixeira da Mota, *Mar Além Mar: Estudos e Ensaios de História e Geografia* (Lisbon, 1972).
8   Charles Verlinden, *The Beginnings of Modern Colonization*, trans. Yvonne Freccero (Ithaca NY, 1970).
9   A. C. de C. M. Saunders, *A Social History of Black Slaves and Freedmen in Portugal* (Cambridge, 1982), p. 48.

sentenced, collected, and used overseas, while the Portuguese state balanced its internal and imperial manpower requirements, are the central issues in this essay. The fifteenth-century Portuguese state had four models to extract what service it could from criminals: forced colonizers, sources of labor, soldiers, and cultural intermediaries.

Criminals Sentenced and Collected: The Legal System

By the early fifteenth century, the Portuguese legal system had evolved into a sophisticated national bureaucracy, directed by the Crown in Lisbon. Each of the principal cities in the kingdom (Map 1) had an elected local justice (*juiz ordinário*) who presided over minor cases. His was also a court of the first instance for more serious offenses. Crown-appointed judges, known as *juizes da fora* (lit. "judges from outside"), exercised jurisdiction in the larger towns and cities. These university-educated justices presided over cases involving serious offenses and served as courts of the second instance. This system was intended to further a unified, national legal code (see below) in the face of local interests, hence, the royal appointment of the judges. Above the *juiz da fora*, each district had a superior judge or *corregedor* who presided over all cases in his district or *comarca*. All of these courts sentenced the guilty, who could also plead their cases before the Appeals Court in Lisbon. The outline of this system was put in place by King Dinis (1279–1325) and his son King Afonso IV (1325–1357).[10] Although there were some additions and modifications, its basic structure remained in place during early modern times.

Portuguese law was codified during the reigns of three different monarchs and updated with subsequent royal orders. In terms of the interrelated tasks of building the early modern nation state and exploring the unknown waters of the Atlantic – not to mention the supporting scientific and technical developments which made the latter possible – the fifteenth century was a dynamic time in Portugal. It is no coincidence that the first of the three major legal collections developed during the period under scrutiny: the *Ordenações Afonsinas*, which was issued in the middle of the fifteenth century (c.1454). The publication in 1521 of the second great legal collection, the *Ordenações Manuelinas*, followed the discovery of the sea route to India by only twenty-four years.[11]

Sentences of exile, the most frequent punishment handed down by the courts, were classified into seven levels, ranging from simple banishment from

---

10 Ruy de Abreu Torres, "Juízes" and "Juízes da Fora," in *Dicionário de História de Portugal* [*DHP*], ed. Joel Serrao, 7 vols. (Oporto, 1992), 3:416–18.

11 The *Ordenações Manuelinas* were only replaced a century later with the *Ordenações Filipinas*, published in 1603, which remained the basic legal text in the Portuguese Empire throughout early modern times. For an overview of the history of these three legal codes, see Mário Júlio de Almeida Costa, "Ordenações," *DHP*, 4:441–46.

town to loss of nationality and perpetual exile abroad.[12] Exemptions were given to the nobility. Specifically, they were never to serve in the galleys.[13] In theory, penal exile was exclusively for the nobility; service in the galleys was exclusively for commoners. Although members of the nobility did not find themselves in the galleys, commoners more often than not found themselves serving overseas as soldiers.[14]

Broadly speaking, crimes in Portugal punished by exile and possible fines[15] can be classified into three categories: minor, serious, and absolutely unpardonable. Minor infractions usually resulted in internal exile to one of the exile cities noted on Map 1, or perhaps a few years overseas, particularly to one of the north African *presidios*, mentioned below. These garrisons were the first overseas regions where the Portuguese established a presence; providing sufficient manpower was a constant problem. One of the most fundamental distinctions in modern law – that between civil and criminal cases – was deliberately blurred by the Portuguese. When the courts deemed it expedient, criminal sentences of exile were abandoned and fines substituted. Internal exile, the most lenient form of this punishment, was an early and frequent victim to substitution by fine.[16] A list of more "serious" crimes provides a fascinating

---

12 "There are different types of exile: for life, for as long as pleases the King, to the galleys, or to a specific place for a given time, or away from town or the *termo*." Joaquim José Caetano Perreira e Sousa, *Primeiras Linhas sobre o Processo Criminal* (Lisbon, 1827), p. 219.

13 *Ordenações de D. Manuel I* (Lisbon, 1565), bk. 3, tit. 3, and bk. 5, tit. 40.

14 The issue of the punishment of *degredo* being reserved for the nobility is commented upon in both T. H. Elkiss, "On Service to the Crown-Portuguese Overseas Expansion: A Neglected Aspect," *Journal of the American Portuguese Society* 10:1(1976): 51, n. 14, and (as cited by Elkiss) in Alexander Marchant, "From Barter to Slavery: The Economic Relations of Portuguese and Indians in the Settlement of Brazil, 1500–1580," *The Johns Hopkins University Studies in History and Political Science* 60(1942): 59–60, n. 36. However, while in legal theory the punishment of *degredo* may have been exclusively for members of the nobility, in practice it was very clearly extended to all members of Portuguese society, including the clergy and commoners originally sentenced to the galleys.

15 Crimes not punished by exile were those of civil law and were usually settled by fines. Civil law is broadly defined as governing "the relations among members of the society in which they live, their rights, privileges, and obligations." Maria Chaves de Mello, *Dicionário Jurídico Português-Inglês* (Rio de Janeiro, 1987), p. 47. Examples of civil cases include: libel; breaking a contract; failing to pay for rent, goods or services rendered; fraud; and minor cases of assault. Existing civil proceedings can be seen in the *comarca* records of Évora (Arquivo Distrital de Évora, fundo cíveis, maço 1 [1729–1802]) and in several examples from the Goan High Court. The Goan example, undoubtedly working from a metropolitan model, established a schedule of fines from 20 to 40 *xerafins* for these civil infractions (Historical Archives of Goa, códices 2655, 2808, 2656, and 1193; a schedule for fines is shown in códice 1844).

16 The first reference encountered to this substitution dates from the reign of King Fernando (1367–1383) and was renewed in 1423. It stated that all sentences other than the death penalty could be satisfied through fines. See Eduardo Freire de Oliveira, *Elementos para*

insight into what authorities felt threatened the social order in early modern times. These crimes ranged from blasphemy and murder to committing an injury, kidnapping, rape, witchcraft, attacking jailers, and entering a convent with dishonorable intentions. These were the crimes labeled *serious* and were frequently exempted from general pardons.[17] Four crimes fell into the last category of absolutely unpardonable: heresy, treason, counterfeiting, and sodomy. At times, falsifying papers was included with this list while on other occasions it was omitted.[18] These four crimes were held above all others as especially threatening because they challenged the early modern Portuguese state at its theological, political, economic, and social foundations.[19]

The origins of exile as punishment in early modern Europe have their roots in aspects of Roman law common to much of the Mediterranean region. In the case of early modern Europe, it was not just Portugal but also France and England which made notable efforts in the use of the penalty of "transportation," the term used in much of the literature written in English.

The sentence of banishment, that is, sending someone away from his or her place of residence, was transformed into something these early modern states found more useful: transportation – a rational concept of forced colonization from the European homeland to one or more of its colonies. Specifically, transportation was a form of coerced colonization which, by commuting the original sentence, forced a criminal to reside in one of the colonies. However, one of the basic differences between banishment and transportation is that the latter requires colonies that are distant, strategic and undesirable (at least, in the popular perception) or, at the very least, outposts of a central authority, locales where the state wishes to re-enforce its often tenuous hold and which cannot

a história do município de Lisboa [*Elementos*], 17 vols. (Lisbon, 1882–1911), 1:259. "Sentences to Castro Marim and other places in the kingdom can be commuted into fines": Perreira e Sousa, p. 219.

[17] See, for example, the two general pardons for criminals in and within five leagues of Lisbon granted on 9 August 1687 (in honor of the entrance into the city of the queen) and on 30 August 1688 (in honor of the birth of a prince and repeated on 26 October 1689) in José Justino de Andrade e Silva, ed., *Collecção Chronologica da Legislação Portuguesa* [*CCLP*], 10 vols. (Lisbon, 1854–57).

[18] In 1672, counterfeiting was specifically included in this category. *CCLP*, 16 and 29 July 1672.

[19] These four crimes were considered especially dangerous by other early modern powers, as well. Sodomy was a capital offence in England: a person over fourteen could be hanged for this crime. In colonial New England, heresy was considered to be equally dangerous and was commonly punished with banishment: Roger Williams was banished from the jurisdiction of the Massachusetts court in 1635 because of "his new and dangerous opinions." See Edwin Powers, *Crime and Punishment in Early Massachusetts, 1620–1692: A Documentary History* (Boston, 1966), pp. 43, 117, 210, and 217. Treason and counterfeiting were two crimes singled out for especially severe corporal punishment in colonial North Carolina: see Donna J. Spindel, *Crime and Society in North Carolina, 1663–1776* (Baton Rouge, 1989), p. 125.

attract sufficient voluntary immigration. In short, transportation assumes the existence of an empire. This explains the presence of transportation in such powers as France and England and its absence from the Germanic lands of northern Europe.[20]

What makes these other European cases all the more intriguing is that they occurred well after the Portuguese had firmly established a penal exile system of their own. The Portuguese developed their system from a Roman model, very much in use in the Mediterranean in the fifteenth century, notably by Venice on Crete. In turn, this Portuguese system, which incorporated orphan girls, prostitutes, gypsies and other marginal figures as colonizers, supplied a blueprint for the other powers. In doing this, the Portuguese made an important transition in the overall development of penal exile as used by Europeans.

Criminals as Colonizers: Internal Exile ("coutos do reino")

During the early fourteenth century, the Portuguese Crown began to use a system of asylum cities (*coutos*) to populate border regions which had remained empty after the Christian reconquest of the Iberian peninsula from the forces of Islam. These same areas were also devastated during the wars with Castile during the second half of the fourteenth century. These (mostly) border towns were transformed into legal havens for criminals, other than those guilty of fraud or treason.[21] This system was started by King Dinis in 1308[22] and continued, with some changes, until the middle of the eighteenth century, with a brief pause from 1691 to 1692.[23]

---

[20] Banishment, often with corporal punishments included, was common in Germanic lands during early modern times. From these regions, criminals were sold to Italian city-states for galley service. In Frankfurt, 626 of 644 men and 363 of 373 women convicted in the local court between 1562 and 1696 were sentenced to one of nineteen combinations of exile and corporal punishment. Würzburg had ten such combinations: Richard van Dülmen, *Theatre of Horror: Crime and Punishment in Early Modern Germany* (Cambridge, 1990), p. 45. In sixteenth-century Florence, the shift from banishment to a minor form of transportation was underway: John K. Brackett, *Criminal Justice and Crime in Late Renaissance Florence, 1537–1609* (Cambridge, 1992), pp. 68–70. The question arises as to why the Dutch appear to have avoided the use of transportation. One answer is supplied by Pieter Spierenberg, *The Prison Experience: Disciplinary Institutions and their Inmates in Early Modern Europe* (New Brunswick NJ, 1991), who claims that the Dutch were early to use workhouses and prisons to intern criminals.

[21] Henrique de Gama Barros, *História da Administração Pública em Portugal nos Séculos XII a XV*, 5 vols. (Lisbon, 1947–54), 5:255–64.

[22] Asylum cities such as these have their roots in Visigothic as well as Roman law. See José Anastasio de Figueiredo, *Memorias de Litteratura Portugueza*, 8 vols. (Lisbon, 1792), 1:109–10.

[23] *CCLP*, 13 September 1691.

In spite of the need for people in an ever-expanding overseas empire after 1415, these internal *coutos* continued to exist and simply operated on a legal track parallel with imperial exile. Some of the more important sites are shown on Map 1 and include: Noudar (made a refuge in 1308), Sabugal (1369), Miranda do Douro, Freixo de Espada à Cinta,[24] Caminha (1406), Monforte do Rio Livre (1420), Segura (lit. "safe," 1421), Celorico de Basto (1441), Chaves (1454), Marvão (1483), and Sesimbra (1492).[25] Typically, a ceiling was placed on the number of criminals who could claim asylum in each locale. For example, only thirty individuals would be pardoned by moving to Celorico de Basto; fifty was the limit placed on Monforte de Rio Livre.[26] This form of pardon was specifically directed at male criminals, but females were also pardoned by moving to one of these towns – with the additional proviso that they could not be guilty of adultery. A further clause allowed male residents to leave the safety of their homes and transact business (within ten leagues) without fear of capture for three months of the year. These pardoned men could move freely around the kingdom, as long as they maintained their homes in asylum cities and traveled with letters of authorization issued by local judges.

Asylum could be, and was, withdrawn from any city once the Crown felt that its population had reached a satisfactory level or another city had a more pressing need for new residents. Mértola lost its status as a haven in 1535;[27] Alhandra (a small town near Lisbon) lost its asylum status in 1586.[28] By the end of the sixteenth century, internal exile became synonymous with Castro Martim, a village in the extreme south-east corner of the Algarve (Map 1). Any legal supervision was largely on paper, but those exiled internally were required to obtain certificates upon completion of their sentences.[29]

This system, along with some of its details, would be taken overseas and modified. In 1493, *degredados* (male criminals sentenced to exile) sent to São Tomé (Map 2) were allowed to return to Portugal for a limited period (not to exceed four months) to transact any business they might have. Their four months started with the required registration with a judge in Lisbon.[30] Three years later in 1496, *degredados* on São Tomé were given a virtual *carte blanche*

---

24 Both Miranda and Freixo de Espada à Cinta were recognized by King João I in 1406 as pre-existing asylums: Gama Barros, 5:260–61.
25 Ibid., 5:255–64.
26 Ibid., 5:263–64.
27 Joze Anastasio de Figueiredo, *Synopsis Chronologica de Subsídios Ainda o Mais Raros para a História e Estudo Critico da Legislação Portuguesa*, 2 vols. (Lisbon, 1740), 1:354, 19 May 1535.
28 Biblioteca da Ajuda, códice 44–XIII–52, ff. 127–8, *alvará* of 25 January 1586.
29 Manoel Lopes Ferreira, *Pratica Criminal Expedida na Forma da Praxe* (Lisbon, 1742), p. 230.
30 *Monumenta Missionaria Africana: Africa Occidental* [*MMA*], 15 vols. (Lisbon, 1952–1988), 1:152–53, doc. 36 (*alvará* of 9 February 1493).

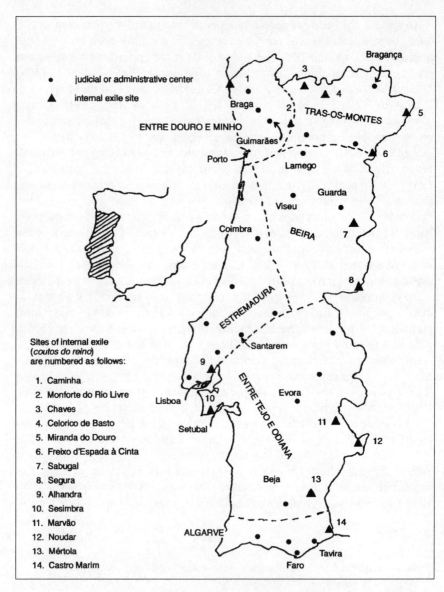

Map 1. Sites of Portuguese internal exile

to import goods from Portugal and to conduct slave raids in the Mina area.[31] Within twenty years, the right to leave the island was revoked. By 1560, any *degredado* found off the island of São Tomé had the length of his exile doubled.[32] Presumably, too many *degredados* were not returning to the island, and this aspect of the system was discarded.

Criminals as a Labor Source: The Galleys

As with so much of the legal basis of banishment and transportation, penal labor directed to the galleys had its origins in Roman law. The punishment of service in the galleys was an important aspect of legal and social control in early modern France, Spain,[33] and Portugal – as well as in other Mediterranean lands such as Malta and Venice. The development and use of oar-powered ships from the late Middle Ages until the seventeenth century in Mediterranean Europe required a massive input of rowers. None of these early modern powers was able to supply its manpower needs for galleys through the use of paid labor alone; over this period, the judicial system came to provide an alternative: criminal manpower.

Portuguese galleys were similar in design to those used by other Mediterranean powers and developed in Portugal by way of a Genoese connection dating from King Dinis.[34] A royal letter to the "city council" (*câmara*) of Lisbon in 1386 referred to a register kept of those men who could serve in the galleys.[35] The maintenance of this list would appear to have been an intermediate step in an overall transition to forced labor. Galleys were certainly in full use in Portugal by the end of the fourteenth century when King João I (1385–1433) leased ten to King Richard II of England (1307–1327) for his campaigns in the English Channel in 1389.[36]

"Sentencing to the galleys" is actually something of a misnomer, since work was not exclusively on such ships. Labor began on the galleys themselves and was extended to a variety of naval-related tasks. The seasonal nature of the work encouraged the state to adopt other activities for this otherwise idle labor

---

[31] The trading factory at São Jorge da Mina falls outside the patterns of colonization suggested here, since it was primarily a commercial enterprise and the number of Portuguese allowed to remain there was strictly controlled by Lisbon: see A. Teixeira da Mota, *Some Aspects of Portuguese Colonization and Sea Trade in West Africa in the Fifteenth and Sixteenth Centuries* (Bloomington IN, 1978), p. 10.

[32] Figueiredo, 2:51 (dated 1560).

[33] In the Spanish case, penal labor was being used on galleys during early modern times as early as 1428 in Aragón: Francisco-Filipe Olesa Muñido, *La organización naval de los estados mediterráneos y en especial España durante los siglos XVI y XVII*, 2 vols. (Madrid, 1968), 2:749.

[34] Eugénio Estanislau de Barros, *As Galés Portuguesas do Século XVI* (Lisbon, 1930), p. 8.

[35] *Elementos*, 1:284 (*carta régia* of 26 July 1424 [1386]).

[36] P. E. Russell, "Galés Portugueses ao Serviço de Ricardo II de Inglaterra (1385–89)," *Revista da Faculdade de Letras* 2nd. ser., 28(1953): 61–73.

force.[37] We know, for example, that galley prisoners made rope and filled sand bags for ballast.

The entire system can perhaps best be understood as one of state-directed labor by convicts. Sentences to the galleys were reserved for male commoners. Prisoners sentenced to the galleys were periodically conveyed to Lisbon in chain gangs, along with those destined to exile overseas. Such levies were not unique to Portugal; similar systems conducted criminals to the galleys in both Spain and France.[38] In the Portuguese case, after their arrival in Lisbon's Limoeiro jail, galley prisoners began their service when they were entrusted to the Master of the Galleys and his guards. The details of this process, as well as how criminals and "Moorish" slaves were to be treated and what papers were to accompany them, were stipulated in a set of guidelines (regimento) which was similar and complementary to the broader guidelines governing all degredados.

Time in the galleys was frequently the sentence for those convicted of bigamy or an unpardonable crime, in particular sodomy.[39] Each type of galley had a specific manpower requirement, depending on the number and length of its oars. Given that the number of ships and other tasks at hand was limited, the state would want a finite number of galley workers. Because of the problems of maintaining security and the expense of providing food and shelter for the men, accepting only the required number of men was in the state's own best interest. Whenever convenient or necessary, the Crown either commuted all sentences of colonial exile to the galleys or re-sentenced galley prisoners to imperial military service, depending on its needs at the moment. In other words, the galley system ran parallel to the exile system and alternatively provided emergency manpower or absorbed the most serious criminal element for the state's labor needs. For example, legislation in 1521 and 1551 temporarily directed courts to send all penal exiles to the galleys rather than overseas.[40] Providing sufficient labor for the galleys was a constant challenge to the

[37] Lopes Ferreira, p. 225: "If the degredado has been sentenced to the galleys, he should be held in jail during the period March to October because no boats leave at that time."

[38] The Spanish case is examined in Ruth Pike, Penal Servitude in Early Modern Spain (Madison, 1983), pp. 18–20. Penal servitude in France is the subject of Paul Bamford, Fighting Ships and Prisons: The Mediterranean Galleys of Louis XIV (Minneapolis, 1973). Even the Netherlands used a limited form of galley servitude under King Filipe II. Galleys patrolled canals acting as both mobile jails and workhouses, compare Spierenburg, pp. 259–60.

[39] See Luiz Mott, "Justiça e Misericórdia: a Inquisição portuguesa e a repressão ao nefando pecado da sodomia," Inquisição: Ensaios sobre Mentalidade, Heresias e Arte, ed. Anita Novinsky and Maria Luiza Tucci Carneiro (São Paulo, 1992), pp. 737–38, tables 5 and 6.

[40] For 1521, see Figueiredo, 1:250; for 1551, see Ordenações de D. Manuel I, Livro Morgado, 1551.

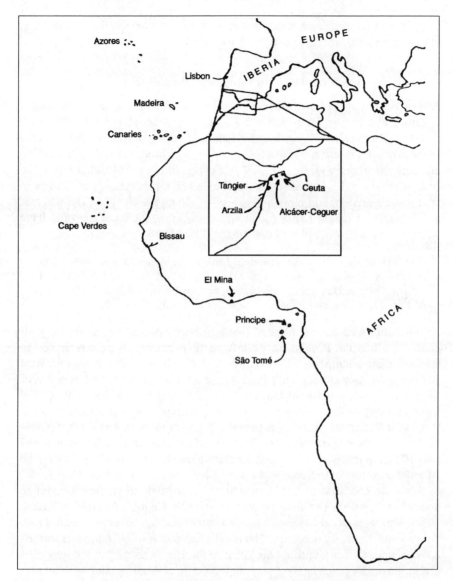

Map 2. Sites of Portuguese external exile in Africa

early modern Portuguese state. In the long run, it attempted to satisfy this requirement with criminals and, later, gypsies.[41]

Criminals as Soldiers: The North African "Presidios"

At the beginning of the fifteenth century, the Portuguese began to cast a covetous eye on the grain-rich cities along the coast of (present day) Morocco.[42] Cities such as Ceuta, Tangier, Salé, and Azamour were well-connected to the northern, interior, wheat-producing areas of Morocco and were termini, not only for trade in grain, but West African gold as well.[43] Ceuta fell to the Portuguese in 1415 (a date often used to mark the beginning of European overseas expansion) and remained part of the empire until 1640. The fact that it was a city of fabled riches (including wheat in abundance) can only have added to any religious spirit of conquest:

> The sack of the city [Ceuta] brought forth many riches in gold, silver, and expensive objects, because the city was the richest and most fertile in all Africa – where Damascus, Alexandria, and all Libya and many other parts of Europe, Africa, and Asia came together with valuable goods.[44]

What followed the conquest of Ceuta in North Africa was a type of shell game in which the Portuguese eagerly participated, but were guaranteed to lose. In their attempt to gain control over North African wheat and West African gold, they established a military presence at the perceived terminus of the trade – only to discover that the North Africans would then redirect this trade to a city under their control. All such entrepôts would shortly become targets for Portuguese military expansion. These *lugares de Africa* (lit. "places in Africa"), the *Algarve de além* (lit. "Algarve on the other side") developed into a chain of garrison forts which the Portuguese Crown maintained along the Atlantic coastline of extreme north-west Africa and are shown on Map 2.

After the conquest of Ceuta, an attempt was made to capture Tangier in 1437, but it failed. The next target was Alcácar Ceguir (Al-Qasr al-Sagir), which was captured in 1458 and remained under Portuguese control until 1550. Tangier and Arzila were occupied by the Portuguese in 1471. Tangier remained a Portuguese territory until it was given to the British as part of the dowry of Catherine of Bragança in 1662. The imperial role of Arzila (Asila) was smaller

---

41 As early as 1573, Gypsy men had been singled out as a likely labor source. Laws coupled galley service with their expulsion from Portugal, chiefly to Brazil. See Bill M. Donovan, "Changing Perceptions of Social Deviance: Gypsies in Early Modern Portugal and Brazil," *Journal of Social History* 26(1992): 34.

42 Andrew C. Hess, *The Forgotten Frontier* (Chicago, 1978).

43 For a complete discussion of these aspects, see Vitorino Magalhães Godinho, *História Económica e Social da Expansão Portuguesa* (Lisbon, 1947), pp. 76–97. The title of the work is misleading since it deals with Morocco exclusively.

44 Jeronimo de Mascarenhas, *História de la Cuidad de Ceuta* (Lisbon, 1915), p. 94.

and limited to the periods from 1471 to 1550 and 1577 to 1589. Azamour (Mulai Bu Saib) came under the Portuguese rule from 1513 to 1541. The capture of Mogador (Essauira, Portuguese from 1504 to 1510) and Santa Cruz do Cabo de Gué (Agadir, 1505–1541) were followed by that of Safim (Safi, 1508–1541) and Mazagão (El-Jadida, 1514–1769).[45]

The North African enclaves were eventually recognized as the imperial liabilities that they were: strong consumers of wheat and other goods, constantly in need of additional military personnel, yet producers of very little. They offered no control over the countryside around them and required constant expenses for the army to defend them from frequent attacks and blockades. This was formally recognized by King João III in 1542 when he withdrew from Safi and Azamour. The Portuguese also later abandoned Alcáçar-Ceguir (1549), and Arzila in (1550).

Of the cities on this list of presidios, Ceuta, Tangier, and Arzila were the larger ones under Portuguese control during the fifteenth century. Because of their varying manpower requirements, the Crown required flexibility in sentencing exiles to this region and in 1519 informed judges "not to sentence [degredados] to a specific place but, when the sentence is made, to make it to one of the places on the other side [of the Straits of Gibraltar]."[46] Many degredados escaped by persuading or bribing captains to issue premature certificates of completion. These garrisons were usually undermanned and were favored exile locations for males who had committed serious crimes throughout the fifteenth century. Each of these garrison cities under Portuguese rule has been the subject of study; unfortunately, neither degredados nor soldiers, in spite of their relative importance, are central subjects in these works.[47]

Supplying manpower is one problem; the use of exile locations is another. How quickly did these North African garrisons become incorporated in the judicial system as exile sites? The answer appears with the arrival of the first Portuguese soldiers. A general pardon was issued as early as 1415 for those criminals who had served in the army conquering Ceuta in that year and who would agree to remain there for brief periods of up to one year.[48] A similar pardon for military service in the assault on Tangier was issued in 1437.[49] Two years later, one Gomes Esteves had his ten years of exile to Setúbal reduced by half for serving in this battle.[50] The first pardon with a condition of required service in Ceuta appeared in 1439, only twenty-four years after its conquest.

---

[45] See Antonio Henrique de Oliveira Marques, *História de Portugal*, 2 vols. (Lisbon, 1978), 1:298–99.

[46] *Hum dos lugares d'além* [lit. "one of the places on the other side"], *alvará* dated 28 March 1519 in Figueiredo, 1:234.

[47] For a short bibliography of these, see Alfredo Pinheiro Marques, *Guia de História dos Descobrimentos e Expansão Portuguesa* (Lisbon, 1988), pp. 83–86.

[48] *DP*, 1:265–68.

[49] Ibid., 1:375–77.

[50] Pardon dated 26 April 1439, in *DCR, Vol. I (1415–1450)*.

During the period of 1415 to 1456, at least 455 criminals were exiled to Ceuta; the vast majority (383) were deported in the six years between 1450 and 1456.[51] In those same six years, only one criminal was sent to Tangier. These figures do not include the people already sentenced there, approximately 200 cases.

In the eleven years between 1481 and 1492, numerous criminals were sentenced to exile, some of whom served out their sentences while others avoided doing so through various means.[52] In the latter case, payment of a fine exempted the criminal from going overseas. The crimes committed ranged widely from murder to insulting a judge.[53]

Table 1 outlines the shifting of exile throughout the garrisons of North Aftica for most of the fifteenth century and demonstrates that exile to these outposts was quickly interwoven into a new fabric of exile, which blended the internal with the overseas.

Table 1. Shifting internal exile in North African presidios and the Atlantic islands, 1415–1456 and 1481–1492

Internal exile locations in Portugal are noted on Map 1 and consisted of Caminha, Monsaraz, Chaves, Miranda, Segura, Freixo de Espada à Cinta, Ouguela, Noudar, Marvão, Arronches, Lavre, Niza, Arraiolos, Sabugal, Mourão, Castro Marim, Mértola, Portimão, Milfontes, Monforte, Tavira, and Crato. North African presidios mentioned were Ceuta, Tangier, and Arzila.

Original exile in	Commuted to	No. of cases
Portugal	North Africa	11
North Africa	Portugal	56
	Elsewhere in North Africa	2
	São Miguel, Graciosa, or Madeira	4
	"One of the Islands"	1
	Cape Verde, Mina, or São Tomé	1
Cape Verde, Mina, or São Tomé	North Africa	5

Sources: Pedro de Azevedo, ed., *Documentos das Chancelarias Reais anteriores à 1531 relativos a Marrocos.* [*DCR*] *Vol. I (1415–1450) Vol. II (1450–1456)* (Lisbon, 1915–1934); António Baião, ed., *Documentos do Corpo Chronológico relativos a Marrocos (1488–1514)* (Coimbra, 1925); P. M. Laranjo Coelho, ed., *Documentos Inéditos de Marrocos: Chancelaria de D. João II* (Lisbon, 1943); and João Martins da Silva Marques, ed., *Descobrimentos portugueses: documentos para a sua história* [*DP*], 3 vols. (Lisbon, 1944–71).

51 *DCR, Vol. I and Vol. II (1450–1456)*.
52 The cities involved in exile and numbers of cases were as follows: Arzila, 113; Ceuta, 63; Tangier, 62; *Africa* or the *Algarve de Além*, 32; Alcácar-Ceguir, 11; and Safi, 1
53 Other crimes included were: attempted murder; escaping from prison; committing an

As in the case of all materials with criminal exiles in early modern times, we can occasionally see bits and pieces relating to them in much larger statements. For example, an author in the early eighteenth century writing on manpower shortages in the North African *presidios* noted that "In the time of King João III (1521–1557), in a battle in Safim, when it was surrounded by over 100,000 men, the captain-general was forced, because of the lack of manpower, to order that the women take up arms."[54] Not many Portuguese women, however, were exiled to these rough frontier towns. In fact, by the late sixteenth century, Portuguese women actually were not allowed to be exiled to these *presidios*. Instead of North Africa, they were to be sent to one of the internal asylum cities, Brazil, São Tomé, or Príncipe, according to the severity of the crime committed.[55] Nevertheless, more women were present than the documents might suggest. Several women with Portuguese names were present in Arzila in 1561, including one D. Isabel who was specifically mentioned as being Portuguese.[56] What is more, at Alcáçar-Ceguir, archaeological evidence indicates that females formed 28 percent of the almost two hundred graves examined from the Portuguese period. Few of these women, however, appear to have been over the age of forty.[57]

Criminals as Colonizers: The Atlantic Islands

At the same time as these North African adventures, or perhaps as a result of them, the Portuguese continued to press further down the west coast of Africa and explore the mid-Atlantic region. The islands of Porto Santo and Madeira were discovered in 1418–1419, and colonization began in 1425. The eastern and central Azores were discovered in 1427 (Flores and Corvo in the western Azores were not discovered until 1452), and colonization began in 1439. Both Madeira and the Azores were (relatively) quickly colonized after their initial discoveries and a similar future was envisioned for both island groups: they were to be granaries to grow and export wheat to the European homeland. In the case of Madeira, wheat was being grown (and exported to Portugal) by

injury or act of violence; disobedience, injury, or giving offense to authority; adultery; smuggling; allowing prisoners to escape; robbery; offenses to religion; blasphemy; sexual offenses; and bigamy. Sources as in Table 1.

54 Diogo Manuel Ayres de Azevedo, *Portugal Illustrado Pelo Sexo Feminino* (Lisbon, 1734), p. 117.

55 Biblioteca da Ajuda, 44–XIII–57, f. 110.

56 Biblioteca da Academia das Ciências de Lisboa, azul MSS 47: Bernardo Rodrigues, *Historia da Praça de Arzila, 1508–1561*, dated 1561.

57 Charles L. Redman and James L. Boone, "Qsar es-Seghir (Alcácer Ceguer): A fifteenth and sixteenth century Portuguese colony in North Africa," *Studia* 41–42(1979): 39–40. Women over forty formed only 5 percent of those whose ages could be determined.

1455 – only twenty-five years after colonization had begun.[58] However, when it was discovered that sugar would thrive on Madeira, wheat was abandoned for this much more valuable crop. By 1500, Madeira "had become the world's greatest producer of sugar . . . a prototype of that momentous and tragic social and economic system of sugar and slavery that was to be repeated, on a far larger scale in the West Indies and Brazil."[59]

In both the Azores and Madeira, Portuguese plans envisioned the use of criminals as the first colonizers. For example, in 1453, the Crown planned to populate the Island of São Miguel in the Azores with *degredados* and began to do so the next year.[60] Table 1 provides a few cases of exiles sent to Madeira during the first thirty years after its discovery and initial colonization. However, the fertility of both Madeira and the Azores made these island groups attractive and forced colonization was soon found to be unnecessary. Madeira was populated in the 1420s with farmers from lands "belonging to Prince Henry or to the Order of Christ, the majority coming from the Algarve."[61] The Azores were colonized later in the 1460s and 1470s and included families brought from Flanders.[62] In both cases, the use of *degredados* were first considered, but the islands were able to attract a sufficient number of free colonizers.[63]

Where, then, were *degredados* sentenced overseas during the fifteenth century, if not to the Azores or Madeira? Table 1 shows that both the *presidios* of North Africa and internal exile remained in use throughout this period. In addition, the islands of Cape Verde (discovered in 1460) were used as exile sites as early as six years after the first arrival of the Portuguese. A published collection of documents from this period shows fourteen exiles sentenced to the Cape Verde Islands from 1466–1513.[64] When the Portuguese first arrived, they considered the islands to be virtually uninhabitable. In the words of Orlando Ribeiro, "In such a land so unfavorable to agriculture, the type of colonization which was characteristic of the Azores and Madeira was not

---

[58] T. Bentley Duncan, *Atlantic Islands: Madeira, the Azores and the Cape Verdes in Seventeenth Century Commerce and Navigation* (Chicago, 1972), p. 10.

[59] Ibid., p. 11.

[60] For more discussion on this subject, see Verlinden, pp. 222–23. Verlinden cites as his source a document in *DP*, 2:344. See also *DP*, 1:517.

[61] Oliveira Marques, *História de Portugal*, 1:218. See also Maria de Lourdes de Freitas Ferraz, *A Ilha da Madeira sob o Domínio da Casa Senhorial do Infante D. Henrique e seus Descendentes* (Lisbon, 1986).

[62] Oliveira Marques, *História de Portugal*, 1:222–23. See also, Viriato Campos, *Sobre o Descobrimento e Povoamento dos Açores* (Lisbon, n.d.).

[63] On the early settlement of the Azores, see also Artur Teodoro de Matos, "Origem e reminiscências dos povoadores das ilhas atlânticas," *Actas do Congresso Internacional Bartolomeu Dias e a sua Época*, 3 vols. (Oporto, 1989), 3:241–52.

[64] *História Geral de Cabo Verde: Corpo Documental*, 2 vols. (Lisbon, 1988–1990).

possible."[65] In other words, *free* colonization could not occur, and the use of *degredados* had to be attempted. By 1515, however, after the early phase of Portuguese colonization, exile to the Cape Verdes became infrequent. Guiné (modern Guinea Bissau) was also used as an exile site during the first phases of Portuguese expansion. A recent study has outlined nineteen cases of penal exiles, guilty of a wide range of crimes, sent to Guiné between 1463 and 1500.[66]

On the other hand, it was neither Cape Verde nor Guiné, but instead the islands of São Tomé and Príncipe which rapidly became associated with criminal colonizers during the fifteenth century. São Tomé was discovered in 1471 or 1472. By the time of the publication of the *Ordenações Manuelinas* in the early sixteenth century, this island was identified as the ideal exile location for the most serious of criminals and would remain so until well into the nineteenth century.[67] The island was the destination of one of the more horrific deportations which took place in early modern Portugal: two thousand children under the age of eight were taken from their Jewish parents in Portugal in the 1490s, forcibly baptized and taken to São Tomé.[68]

Much of the continual problem in maintaining a stable European population base on São Tomé was undoubtedly caused by malaria, as in other tropical areas along coastal West and South Africa. Nevertheless, the Crown never ceased in

---

[65] Orlando Ribeiro, *Aspectos e Problems da Expansão Portuguesa* (Lisbon, 1962), p. 157. For a brief discussion of the very unfavorable conditions first faced by the Portuguese on the Cape Verde Islands, the cultivation of foodstuffs, and the beginnings of the slave trade from Guinea via these islands, see pp. 156–58. A. H. de Oliveira Marques has examined the early agriculture and other commerce begun by the Portuguese during the fifteenth and early sixteenth centuries in "Gaspar Frutuoso e a Colonização de Cabo Verde," in *Portugal Quinhentista (Ensaios)* (Lisbon, 1987), pp. 111–19. See also: António Brásio, "Descobrimento/ Povoamento/ Evangelização do Arquipélago de Cabo–Verde," *Studia* 10(1962): 49–97; Deirdre Meintel, *Race, Culture, and Portuguese Colonialism in Cabo Verde* (Syracuse NY, 1984), pp. 32–33; and Oscar Barata, *Cabo Verde, Guiné, São Tomé e Príncipe* (Lisbon, 1965), pp. 921–58; Teixeira da Mota, *Some Aspects*, pp. 7–11.

[66] Vítor Luís Pinto Gaspar da Conceição Rodrigues, "A Guiné nas cartas de perdão (1463–1500)," *Actas do Congresso Internacional Bartolomeu Dias e a sua época*, 5 vols. (Oporto, 1989), 3:397–412.

[67] For this reason, it is all the more odd that *degredados* and their role in colonization and commercial activities on São Tomé have been almost totally ignored.

[68] José Manuel Azevedo e Silva, "A mulher no povoamento e colonização de São Tomé," in *A Mulher na Sociedade Portuguesa: Visão Histórica e Perspectivas Actuais*, 2 vols. (Coimbra, 1986), 1:230. On São Tomé's early years, see also António Alves dos Santos Júnior, "O povoamento de S. Tomé," *Elementos de História da Ilha de São Tomé* (Lisbon, 1971), pp. 71–78. Of these 2,000 children, only 600 were reported alive sixteen years later: Santos Júnior, p. 74. See also Viana de Almeida, *Povoamento e Colonização da ilha de S. Tomé* (Lisbon, n.d.) and Almada Negreiros, *História Ethnográphica da Ilha de S. Tomé* (Lisbon, 1895).

its efforts to populate the island with *degredados*. It could be argued that São Tomé, with its slavery and sugar cultivation, was a model for what was to follow in Brazil. It could also be stressed that São Tomé was also another type of model: an early modern island penal colony with two distinct and parallel forms of forced labor. White, European criminal exiles conducted a slave trade and supervised black African slaves producing refined sugar on the island.[69] It was for this reason that Teixeira da Mota called the island a "human laboratory," the settlement of which was novel and quite different from Mediterranean-type colonization.[70]

The Crown certainly went out of its way to ensure that *degredados* sent to São Tomé would be made as comfortable as possible, under the circumstances. By 1506, the Crown counted around one thousand residents on the island, the majority of whom were exiles living from the slave trade. Each exile was to be given a male or female slave for his personal service; the cost would be paid by the state, from royal taxes.[71]

Early in the sixteenth century, the Crown required that anyone being sent to São Tomé should go for at least five years.[72] The nearby island of Príncipe was also used for exiles until it lost that status in 1549. After that date, all exiles who would have been sent to Príncipe were to be sent instead to Brazil.[73]

Another aspect of this mixture of internal Portuguese and North African-Atlantic Islands exile sites was its flexibility. The ratio of sentences in these distinct locales (one year overseas for two years of internal *degredo*) was apparently put into practice well before it became law in the *Ordenações of D. Manuel I*. For example, the practice was utilized in the case of Gil Eanes, who in 1451 had the site of his exile shifted from Ceuta (North Africa) to Ouguela (Portugal) and, at the same time, had the length of his sentence for murder doubled from three to six years.[74] Another case of a two-year sentence being doubled when shifted to Portugal occurred in 1452 when a convict was sent from Ceuta to Marvão.[75] In addition, the system was sufficiently lenient to allow someone such as Fernão Ribeiro, sentenced to three years exile in Ceuta, to have his site shifted to Freixo de Espada à Cinta in 1451. In this case, the

---

69 Compare Carlos Alberto Garcia, "A Ilha de S. Tomé como centro experimental do comportamento do Luso nos trópicos," *Studia* 19(1966): 209–21. See also Robert Garfield, *A History of São Tomé Island, 1470–1655: The Key to Guinea* (San Francisco, 1992).

70 Teixeira da Mota, *Some Aspects*, p. 11.

71 *MMA*, 4:33, doc. 11 (*alvará* of December 1506).

72 Figueiredo, 1:355–56 (19 June 1535).

73 Ibid., p. 408 (5 May 1549).

74 *DCR*, 2:18 (7 May 1451).

75 Ibid., 2:108 (22 February 1452). For an example of the reverse (sentence reduced by half for service abroad), see pp. 49–50 (9 September 1451).

length of the sentence was not doubled due to the convict's impoverished condition.[76] Poverty also allowed Constança Fernandes to have her exile shifted from Ceuta to Miranda.[77] In another case, João Freire had his exile shifted from Ceuta not due to poverty, but as a result of his occupation: he was a fisherman.[78]

Criminals as Cultural Intermediaries

The last of the four models under discussion in this essay is perhaps the most intriguing, and that is the use of criminals as cultural intermediaries in the process of maritime discovery. Unfortunately, it is also the area with the least solid documentation. Nevertheless, this systematic use of criminals by the Portuguese Crown was a direct outgrowth of the penal exile process.

In the Portuguese case, during the fifteenth century, those guilty of unpardonable crimes were taken on board departing ships. In an effort to ensure communication with the peoples they encountered, the Portuguese adopted a two-fold strategy of leaving these *degredados* along the African shore while they simultaneously captured a number of unsuspecting locals to take back to Portugal. In both cases, their objective was to ensure linguistic and cultural intermediaries for future trade. Portuguese criminals left on African shores became known as *lançados* or *tango-maos* and were a prominent feature of Afro-European interaction, especially in West Africa.[79]

Lançados left on the shores of West Africa were convicts usually guilty of serious crimes, such as murder. João Barreto, in his study of Portuguese West Africa, defined them as, "generally, people of little moral fiber who served as intermediaries between the indigenous people and merchants. They lived in native straw huts, allied with one or more indigenous women whose customs and lifestyle they easily adopted."

From the start, the Crown encouraged the policy of having *lançados* in this region to facilitate commerce. *Degredados* sailed on the voyages of both Vasco da Gama and Pedro Álvares Cabral. Da Gama took twelve with him and

---

76 Ibid., pp. 14–15 (12 February 1451).
77 Ibid., pp. 138–39 (27 November 1452).
78 Ibid., pp. 66–67 (10 April 1451).
79 See Charles R. Boxer, *The Portuguese Seaborne Empire, 1415–1825* (London, 1977), pp. 31–32. The process of collecting African peoples during the fifteenth century and bringing them to Portugal with this intention is outlined in Jeanne Hein, "Early Portuguese Communication with Africans on the Sea Route to India," *Terrae Incognitae* 25(1993): 41–52. Hein has collected her sources on this subject from the *Chronicle of Guinea* by Zurara and other accounts. The early use of *degredados* as intermediaries is the subject of Elkiss, pp. 44–53; but he overstates his case when he claims that this use of exiles *began* with da Gama's voyage of 1497. Activities of the Portuguese in West Africa, including *lançados* well before 1497, are central in Blake, *West Africa*.

probably left several in south-eastern Africa.[80] It became clear, however, that the Portuguese Crown was unable to utilize these "castaways" in its effort to keep these regions free of non-Portuguese commercial activities. Consequently, in 1518, the Crown reversed the policy of creating *lançados* and attempted to round them up.[81] According to Meintel, these *lançados* and their descendants developed into a distinctive group which regarded itself as both Portuguese and African and continued to play an important role as intermediaries in West Africa, notably in the spread of Cape Verde *crioulo* as the language of commerce.[82]

What quickly developed from this experiment? The state abandoned the policy of deliberately creating runaways and replaced it with the controlled, directed use of criminals as soldiers or as colonizers – as it had done previously in North Africa and in the colonization of Madeira and other islands. By 1498, exploration of the sea route to India was complete; people were now needed to provide logistical and other support for it. As a result, many were now settled in a wide variety of strategic locations between Lisbon and South Asia. This would explain why both male and female penal exiles, clearly labeled as such in the documents, begin to appear in Sofala (modern Mozambique) on the East African coast by 1506.[83]

Conclusion

Along with their obvious cultural traits such as language and religion, the Portuguese took their judicial system with them overseas and readily converted new territories into a pre-existing system of exile. Several aspects of this system were first applied to the Portuguese *presidios* of North Africa and the Atlantic islands during the late fifteenth and early sixteenth centuries; and for the next five hundred years, the use of exile would continue to define their global penal system.[84] By the end of the period under review in this essay, the Crown turned away from two of the models presented and concentrated on extracting labor or military service from criminals.

---

80 Elkiss, p. 46.
81 João Barreto, *História da Guiné, 1418–1918* (Lisbon, 1938), pp. 68–69, 75.
82 Meintel, pp. 33–35. See also Bentley Duncan, pp. 212–15, and António Carreira, "Aspectos da influência da cultura portuguesa na área comprendida entre o rio Senegal e o norte da Serra Leoa (Subsídios para o seu estudo)," *Boletim Cultural da Guiné Portuguesa* 19(1964): 373–416.
83 Payments and maintenance given to *degredado* soldiers in Sofala can be easily traced in *Documentos Sobre os Portugueses em Moçambique e na Africa Central, 1497–1840,* 9 vols. to date (Lisbon, 1962–). For the first reference, see 1:435, payment of one *mitical* (gold measure) made to the *degredada* Ines Roiz in February, 1506. Systematic payments to criminals appear throughout the remaining volumes of this series.
84 The last punishments of exile were only removed from the Portuguese legal code in 1954.

The entire early modern imperial *degredo* system became notable for ratios to equalize sentences between and among sites; payment of fines, often combined with internal exile to replace service overseas; and a relative leniency on the part of the Crown to grant pardons, especially in recognition of royal service. Furthermore, the Crown normally commuted sentences of capital punishment to military service or labor, to extract whatever utility it could from criminals. In this context, the nearly complete avoidance of the use of the death penalty is noteworthy.

Table 2 outlines the major shifts under discussion in this essay and shows the rapid incorporation of overseas locations into the judicial system.

Table 2. Overview of the shift in sentencing, 1400 and 1500

Type of crime (example)	Typical sentence/length c.1400	Typical sentence/length c.1500
minor (insulting an official)	banishment from town 6 months to one year	internal exile one year
serious (highway robbery)	internal exile two to five years	North Africa two to four years
unpardonable (treason)	galley service five to ten years	galley service or São Tomé five to ten years

All these aspects, shown here to be working at home, in North and West Africa, and in the Atlantic islands, contributed to a flexibility which made the penal system responsive to both individual desires and imperial needs. It was this flexibility of the system, developed in the fifteenth century, which primarily explains its longevity in the Portuguese world.

It is tempting to view this outline of crime and punishment in the early Portuguese Empire as unique or extraordinary. Neither adjective is really applicable. Rather, in closing, I would suggest that the Portuguese case is the norm for the use of criminals by the early modern state – at least for Latin Europe and Great Britain, which would follow the Portuguese example with their own penal exiles in the late seventeenth century. In something of a massive understatement, a Portuguese author at a conference on colonization and immigration in 1903, stated that "Penal exile is a traditional sentence among us."[85] Indeed, what separates the Portuguese use of exile as punishment, I believe, is its global application and remarkable longevity.

---

[85] Francisco Xavier de Silva Telles, *A Transportação Penal e a Colonização* (Lisbon, 1903), p. 9.

Non Potest Appellum Facere: Criminal Charges Women could not – but did – Bring in Thirteenth-Century English Royal Courts of Justice

PATRICIA R. ORR

When Juliana de Holeworth and Edelina, mother of Peter, brought appeals (private criminal charges)[1] against William Pech for the death of their sons, the justices dismissed the appeals, saying "a woman cannot make an appeal except for the death of her husband or rape done to herself" (*non potest appellum facere nisi de morte viri sui vel de rapo sibi facto*).[2] Glanvill[3] and *Bracton*[4]

---

[1] Appeals were not what the modern term connotes, an attempt to re-open a court case in a higher court. They were criminal charges brought by individuals against whom a crime had been committed or, in the case of homicide, who were connected with the victim in certain degrees of blood relationship, homage, or, as we shall see below, marriage. Appeals were useful in a time without a police force and in the earliest stages of the development of the grand jury, but considerable care was taken to see that they were not fraudulently and maliciously instituted to settle personal grudges. The process included steps to ensure that the evidence that a crime had occurred was seen when it was fresh. The victim was supposed to raise the hue and cry, that is, instigate community pursuit of the offender, if pursuit was possible. Then he or she had to make local officials aware of the offense and show them evidence that it had occurred (injuries, in the case of wounding); bring charges in the county court; and, often, pursue the charges in the eyre, the royal itinerant court, when it came into the area. The appellor, as the accuser was called, had to be careful to allege felony and make sure the charges were those that could be heard in the royal court. He or she found pledges to guarantee that some amount of money would be paid if the appeal was not prosecuted, or, if in poverty, "pledged his (or her) faith" to sue. In the latter case, a non-prosecuting appellor would be arrested and imprisoned. See Samuel E. Thorne, ed. and trans., *Bracton on the Laws and Customs of England*, 4 vols. (Cambridge MA/London, 1968–77), 2:336, 344–45, 406–7, 414–16, for some routine procedures for the appeal; Sir Frederick Pollock and Frederick William Maitland, *The History of English Law before the Time of Edward I*, 2 vols. (Cambridge, 1968), 2:605.

[2] Doris Mary Stenton, ed. and trans., *Pleas Before the King and his Justices [PKJ]*, Selden Society, 67, 68, 83, 84 (London, 1952–53, 1967), 2:730, 731.

[3] G. D. G. Hall, ed. and trans., *The Treatise on the Laws and Customs of England Commonly Called Glanvill* (Oxford, 1993), pp. 173–76.

agreed: no woman could bring an appeal to the royal courts of justice[5] for any crime other than the death of her husband or injury to herself. This limiting rule[6] was cited in legal authorities[7] and plea rolls alike,[8] often enough that at least one twentieth-century scholar accepted it as a rule of law.[9] Had the limiting rule been scrupulously observed, a woman who had suffered from a crime outside the rule, with no interested and eligible male to take up her cause and bring an appeal, might have been denied a hearing. In fact, the rule, though operative, was flouted widely enough to make the appeal available to women; in the majority of cases women's appeals were heard in spite of their sex, and were occasionally carried on regardless of objections from the appellee (the defendant). This paradox, though long apparent to some editors of the rolls,[10] has not been widely known, and has never been studied for answers to some of the perplexing questions it raises: why were women willing to bring appeals, and why did justices hear them, in the face of the limiting rule? Why was the rule enforced in some cases and ignored in others? Is there any identifiable pattern in the rule's application? The answers to these questions, though probably in some respects fated to remain obscure, reflect a complex situation in which women's initiative and determination brought them before justices whose adherence to the limiting rule vied with a real interest in seeing justice done. The result was that the appeals a woman could not bring were brought, heard, and adjudicated on their merits, usually without recourse to, and sometimes in defiance of, the rule and its restrictions.

A wealth of documentation in the legal treatises establishes the limiting rule as a commonplace in legal thinking. In its first recorded appearance in *Glanvill*,

---

4   *Bracton*, 2:419–20.
5   This could be the county court at one of its regular sessions; the eyre, the court that attended the king in his travels; or the permanent royal court at Westminster. See Robert C. Palmer, *The County Courts of Medieval England, 1150–1350* (Princeton NJ, 1982), pp. 3–23; Ralph V. Turner, *The King and his Courts: The Role of John and Henry III in the Administration of Justice, 1199–1240* (Ithaca NY, 1968), pp. 9–28.
6   Term used by C. A. F. Meekings in *The 1235 Surrey Eyre* [*1235 SE*] (Castle Arch, Guildford, 1979), p. 123; *Crown Pleas of the Wiltshire Eyre, 1249* [*CPWE*] (Gateshead-on-Tyne, 1961), p. 88.
7   See, for example, Francis Morgan Nichols, ed., *Britton: the French Text Carefully Revised with an English Translation, Introduction and Notes* (Oxford, 1845) pp. xvi–xvii, 114; Andrew Horne, ed. and trans., *The Mirror of Justices* [*Mirror*] (Washington DC, 1903), p. 181; J. M. Kaye, ed. and trans., *Placita Corone or La Corone Pledee Devant Justices* [*PC*], Selden Society Supplementary Series, 4 (London, 1966), p. 9.
8   For the limiting rule cited in court see, *inter alia*, Frederick William Maitland, ed., *Select Pleas of the Crown, A.D. 1200–1225* [*SPC*], Selden Society, 1 (London, 1888), p. 32; Alan Harding, ed. and trans., *The Roll of the Shropshire Eyre of 1256* [*RSE*], Selden Society, 96 (London, 1981), 123; Doris M. Stenton, ed., *The Earliest Lincolnshire Assize Rolls, A.D. 1202–1209* [*ELAR*] (Lincoln, 1926), p. 855; *PKJ*, 2:730, 731.
9   *ELAR*, p. xxiii.
10 *CPWE*, p. 78; *PC*, p. xxx.

probably written between 1187 and 1189 by a learned and experienced jurist,[11] it gives the impression of being an accepted part of criminal law: "Moreover, it must be understood that in this suit [of homicide] a woman is to be heard in accusing someone of the murder of her husband if she can give testimony from having seen it . . . and generally the woman is heard in accusing someone of inflicting injury on her body" (*Preterea sciendum quod in hoc placito* (homicide) *mulier auditur accusans aliquem de morte uiri sui si de uisu loquatur . . . et generaliter admissum est quod mulier auditur accusans aliquem de iniuria corpori suo inflicta*).[12] Magna Carta refers indirectly to the rule.[13] *Bracton*, written and revised from as early as the 1220s and completed probably by 1257, gives a brief statement of the rule and a writ for a woman appealing for the death of her husband.[14] *Britton*, from the reign of Edward I, gives a treatment of the rule that is similar in essentials, as do its contemporary authorities, *Fleta*, the idiosyncratic *Mirror of Justices* and, in a fuller treatment, the late thirteenth-century treatise *Placita Corone*.[15] Even Coke discusses the rule, in connection with Magna Carta.[16] This continuity indicates that there was a basis in the minds of jurists for the rule, and the court records bear this out in the above-mentioned appeal brought by Juliana de Holeworth and Edelina, mother of Peter, as well as others.[17]

The statements of the rule are ambiguous about the conceptual reasons for barring most appeals by women, but the practice is generally taken to be the result of a woman's incapacity to fight the judicial duel. Male appellors had to offer battle as a means of proof, and the possible risk to the appellor's life and body was a way to discourage the bringing of frivolous or malicious appeals against enemies.[18] No source expressly forbids women from engaging in trial by battle, but there is no example of an English woman undertaking it; and the thirteenth-century *Placita Corone* states that appeals by women are among those in which a man must defend himself by a jury.[19] Probably custom

---

11 If not by Rannulf Glanvill, justiciar 1175–1179, then perhaps Hubert Walter or Geoffrey fitz Peter, also justiciars, *Glanvill*, p. xxxi; for a recent discussion of the question of authorship see Ralph V. Turner, "Who was the Author of Glanvill? Reflections on the Education of Henry II's Common Lawyers," in Ralph V. Turner, *Judges, Administrators and the Common Law in Angevin England* (London, 1994), pp. 71–118.

12 *Glanvill*, pp. 174–75.

13 J. C. Holt, *Magna Carta* (Cambridge, 1992), pp. 466–67.

14 *Bracton*, 2:419–20.

15 *Britton*, p. 114; H. G. Richardson and G. O. Sayles, ed. and trans., *Fleta*, Selden Society, 72, 79 (London, 1955–72), 2:88–89; *Mirror*, p. 181; *PC*, p. 9.

16 Sir Edward Coke, *The Second Part of the Institutes of the Lawes of England* [*Institutes*], 2 vols. (New York, 1979), 1:68–69.

17 See *PKJ*, 2:730–31; Sir Francis Palgrave, ed., *Rotuli Curiae Regis: Rolls and Records of the Court Held before the King's Justiciars or Justices* [*RCR*], 2 vols. (London, 1835), 1:57–58; *1235 SE*, p. 123; *ELAR*, p. 690.

18 See, for example, *PC*, p. xxx; *CPWE*, p. 88.

19 *PC*, p. 9.

reserved the duel to males, though practice in Germany allowed women to do battle under restricted conditions.[20] Meekings states that not having to offer battle gave women a procedural advantage, and there seems to be some assumption that women would be likely to bring false appeals as a form of harassment.[21] Present-day commentators consider this assumption to be linked to a fear that women would bring false appeals at the instigation of men who wanted to harass the accused without offering battle themselves,[22] and *Bracton*'s statement that the appeals *per quod alicui lex apparens debeat adiudicari* should be kept to a minimum may refer to the same concern.[23] If successful, the ploy resulted in considerable inconvenience, expense, and even danger for the defendant, who might have been sent to the ordeal before its abolition in 1215, and who faced the exigencies of trial and possible conviction at any date. Furthermore, offenses against a woman would normally be the business of her husband, father, guardian, or some male relative who could offer to fight the duel.

Given such thinking, it may be wondered why women were allowed to make any appeals. The reasons are not easy to find, but probably have to do with the idea in English law that an appeal lies with the one most nearly affected by the offense, who has "an interest enabling him to appeal."[24] The treatises are generally silent on the matter; only *Glanvill* alleges that a wife had an appeal because she and her husband were one flesh, and she was appealing for an injury to herself.[25] More practical reasons also suggest themselves. A woman who had suddenly lost her husband might be under threat herself, and might lack any near male relatives to take up the legal gauntlet for her. Giving her an appeal would provide a way to attain her security and achieve justice. Perhaps a recognition of the effect that the death of a husband has on the wife's interest and the total disruption of her life caused by his death is part of the psychological background for allowing her the appeal. Likewise, young women with little

---

[20] *Fleta*, p. 83; Henry Charles Lea, *The Duel and the Oath*, ed. Edward Peters, additional documents trans. Arthur C. Howland (Philadelphia, 1974), pp. 152–54; in one curious case a man claimed, in a formula often used as an offer of a champion to do battle in civil cases (use of champions was forbidden in criminal cases), that his mother was prepared to offer proof, *Curia Regis Rolls . . . Preserved in the Public Record Office* [*CRR*], 17 vols. (London, 1922–1991), 2:207.

[21] *CPWE*, p. 80.

[22] *CPWE*, p. 80; *PC*, p. xxix; William Sharp McKechnie, *Magna Carta: A Commentary on the Great Charter of King John* (New York, 1960), p. 453.

[23] *Bracton*, 2:419; the translation reads "there are no more than two by which one ought to be put to battle or the grand assize," though neither of these forms of trial is expressed in the text. Thorne later declared his intention to revise the translation of passages he had translated so freely as to go beyond the wording of the text, 3:v.

[24] *Bracton*, 2:413, see also p. 399: *Et quo casu oportet eum docere quod sua intersit appellare, quia alias appellum non habebit, non magis quam de morte alicuius extraneae personae.*

[25] *Glanvill*, p. 174; see *PC*, p. xxix, for lawyers' comments, similar in intent, from the next century; *Bracton* is silent on the question.

or no male protection might be preferred targets for the crime of rape, and need their own appeal. Thus a woman might appeal only on account of the offenses that touched her most nearly: injury to her body or loss of a husband who was in theory the flesh of her flesh and in practical terms her protector.

Some ambiguity remains about the conditions under which she might make even those appeals. For example, it is not clear what constituted an appealable injury to a woman's body. *Glanvill* says a woman may appeal for "injury done to her body, as is explained below" (*de iniuria corpore suo inflicta, sicut inferius dicetur*), but his later discussion speaks only of rape, the most frequently reported injury done to women.[26] *Bracton* states that she may appeal for "an injury done to her person" and, later, "a forcible harm done to her body, as for rape." *Fleta* uses the wording: *de raptu et violencia corpori suo illata*, thus apparently allowing women appeals for violence other than the crime of rape.[27] The allusions focus on rape, but do not necessarily rule out appeals for other types of personal injury. On the rare occasions when the rule is spelled out in the court rolls, it seems to restrict women's injury appeals to rape,[28] and at least one present-day commentator assumes that it does.[29] It is not at all clear that a woman might appeal for other sorts of wounds; perhaps such a possibility was not anticipated.

Between the time of *Bracton* and *Glanvill* appeals on account of death of a husband came to be further restricted; the female appellor was constrained to say that her husband had died "in her arms."[30] Three possible reasons have been put forward for this. Her courage may have been involved; one source has her trying to shield him from the attacker with her own body.[31] Coke had an idea that she was expressing some kind of seisin of her husband.[32] Kaye, commenting on this, concedes that there could be some "primitive idea that only if a woman had actual 'seisin' of her husband, so to speak, could she be heard in preference to the nearest male heir." A third reason is the requirement that an appellor must actually have witnessed the crime; in the case of a woman appellor, this is intensified to become a requirement for close physical proximity to her husband, the victim.[33] That close proximity would guarantee that the woman in question had seen the crime and its perpetrators and could legitimately bring an appeal, an idea supported by *Glanvill* and by a case preserved

---

[26] *Glanvill*, pp. 174–75; Patricia Orr, "English Women at Law: Actions in the King's Courts of Justice, 1194–1222" (Ph.D. diss., Rice University, 1989), pp. 152, 209.

[27] *Bracton*, 2:353, 419; *Fleta*, p. 88.

[28] *PKJ*, 2:730, 731; and see *PC*, p. xxxi; *CPWE*, p. 88.

[29] *CPWE*, pp. 88–90.

[30] *Bracton*, 2:353; *PC*, p. 28.

[31] *PC*, p. 5; Kaye finds evidence that later lawyers supported this view, *PC*, p. xxix.

[32] In the land law, possession secure enough to support an action at law if ejected, Pollock and Maitland, 2:29–80; Coke, p. 2; *Institutes*, 1:68.

[33] *Bracton*, 2:398.

in *Bracton's Note Book*.[34] Kaye asserts that the words clearly were meant to be taken literally, that the woman could bring an appeal only if her husband had in fact been killed in her arms.[35] If this was so, she was to be held to a far more stringent standard than male appellors, who had only to allege sight and hearing.

A picture is built up, then, of a rule that restricted women from most appeals, and gave them narrower limits than males even in one of those that was permitted. In this picture, a female victim of a crime outside the "limiting rule" who had not been made the subject of a presentment[36] and who had no husband or near male relative willing to pursue an appeal for her would have been at a severe disadvantage. The picture dissolves, however, on reading the court records. Far more frequently than not, the rule was disregarded, a phenomenon which leads some to assert that women had wide latitude in bringing appeals. The rule was "but rarely invoked as an exception[37] by an appellee or promulgated by the justices in quashing an appeal."[38] In practice, there was no limit on who might bring an appeal; at no time did the court dismiss an appeal out of hand on the grounds that it had been brought by a woman.

In cases in which the appellee had fled, the female appellor was allowed to carry her suit to the point of outlawing the absconding appellee, just as a male appellor could.[39] In a typical case, Alice, mother of Margery, lodged an appeal against two men who had killed her daughter and then had fled. The pair were outlawed at Alice's suit.[40] The "limiting rule" was never invoked. This may have been for procedural reasons; flight brings the presumption of guilt, so the appellor was permitted to continue with the process of outlawry.[41] In one case the court declared that the defendant, who had escaped from custody and then

---

34 *Glanvill*, p. 174: *Preterea sciendum quod in hoc placito mulier auditur accusans aliquem de morte viri sui si de visu loquatur*; Frederick William Maitland, ed., *Bracton's Note Book* (London, 1887), 3:1600: . . . *sicut illa quae interfuit et hoc videt, ita quod eum tenuit inter brachia sua.*

35 *PC*, p. xxix.

36 *Glanvill*, p. 171; *Bracton*, 2:329; Pollock and Maitland, 2:642–43.

37 An objection to the legality of an appeal that, if sustained, results in the appeal being quashed, or, to use another term, abated, Pollock and Maitland, 2:611–20.

38 *CPWE*, p. 88.

39 See, for example, *PKJ*, 2:260, 686, 738; 3:686, 714; Doris Mary Stenton, ed., *Rolls of the Justices in Eyre . . . for Yorkshire in 3 Henry III (1218–19)* [*RJEYH3*], Selden Society, 56 (London, 1934), 531.

40 Doris Mary Stenton, ed., *Rolls of the Justices in Eyre . . . for Gloucestershire, Warwickshire, and Staffordshire, 1221, 1222* [*RJEGWS*], Selden Society, 59 (London, 1940), 734, 924, 948, 970.

41 The appellee was to be summoned to answer the appellor's charges at four consecutive meetings of the county court; if he did not appear he was to be outlawed at the fifth: *[q]ui si infra tempus illud non venerit pro ex lege tenebitur, cum pricipi non obediat neque legi, at extunc utlagabitur sicut ipse qui est extra legem, Bracton*, 2:352; outlawry put a man outside the protection of the law; women were said to be waived, to be waifs under no man's protection, Pollock and Maitland, 1:482; 2:580–82.

fled, had convicted himself by his action and was to be treated as a convict if found.[42] The *Placita Corone* concurs with this, saying that if a woman appeals against a man for such offenses as robbery, wounding, the murder of her husband in her arms, that of her father, mother, brother, sister, or any other near relation, or rape, and the accused refuses to appear in court or to find pledges that he will do so, then he is to be outlawed because his contumacy indicates his guilt.[43]

The question of whether women could appeal on account of bodily injuries other than rape is not specifically addressed in the rolls or treatises, but the appeal seems to have been tacitly allowed. There were fewer appeals on account of wounding than for rape, but the wounds women suffered could be quite serious. Gunilda, who brought an appeal of wounding against Gilbert de Hamet, had been beaten and trampled. Bela, widow of Roger, had been beaten and wounded by four men. Edith of St. Teath had been so severely beaten that the jurors said sixteen bones had been extracted from her head. In all these cases, the male defendants were convicted. Women's appeals on account of wounding were never challenged, by justices or defendants, despite the focus on rape as the injury on account of which women could appeal.[44]

Women's appeals on account of the death of someone other than a husband, though clearly prohibited by the limiting rule, were more likely to be heard on their own merits than rejected out of hand. If the appellee had fled, as shown above, proceeding for outlawry usually followed, and in such cases, there was never any objection against the appellor.[45] If the appellee was present in court and the appellor had died or did not prosecute, the royal justices could choose whether or not to continue the case.[46] Cases occasionally lapsed with no further action,[47] but at least as often they were carried on, either by asking the jurors their opinion of the appellee's guilt, or by directing the appellee to find pledges that he would return to court, if summoned, when the justices were next in the area.[48] If appellor and appellee were both present, the appeal usually proceeded

---

42 *CRR*, 268.

43 *PC*, pp. 9, 29.

44 *PKJ*, 2:323, 382; *CRR*, 6:270; see Orr, "English Women" pp. 209–13 for a discussion of women's wounding appeals in the early thirteenth century.

45 See *RJEGWS*, 734, 804, 948, 970; PRO, JUST 1/800, m. 3; F. W. Maitland, ed., *Pleas of the Crown for the County of Gloucester . . . 1221 [PCCG]* (London, 1884), 15.

46 According to *Bracton*, 2:355, no proceedings to outlawry could take place without suit unless the royal justices so commanded.

47 Doris Mary Stenton, ed., *The Earliest Northamptonshire Assize Rolls, A.D. 1202 and 1203 [ENAR]* (London, 1930), 87, 88, 95; *RJEGWS*, 924, in which one of three accused men fled but was not outlawed, another had fled to a church and abjured the realm, and another was present and was acquitted.

48 Jurors did not suspect the appellee because the "victim" died a natural death ten years before, *ENAR*, 72; jurors did not suspect the appellee so he was quit (acquitted), *RJEGWS*, 92; appellee to be under pledges, *PKJ*, 2:749,750; four men were outlawed at appellor's suit and the fifth denied the crime and was not suspected, so he was quit.

without reference to the limiting rule, its result depending on the circumstances of the case. Some appeals were adjudged false: in one case the "victim" had died of natural causes; in another the defendant produced the alleged victim, alive and well. The appellor in the latter case, who had to be summoned to get her into court, denied she had ever made the appeal.[49]

Edith de Motton, a servant, appealed against two men for beating her employer and killing his wife. One of the accused died in jail, and at the time of the trial, Edith could not be certain that the other was the person who had come by night and committed the crimes. The jurors did not suspect him, and he was acquitted.[50] In another case, the jurors said the alleged victim had not been slain, but had been ill a long time and had finally died from that illness. Nevertheless, the four appellees had to pay a fine of 40 marks because they were not present at the opening day of the proceedings.[51] This is an unusually hefty sum for a relatively minor transgression; perhaps the judges suspected them of being more culpable than the jurors had declared and wanted to administer a sharp warning to forestall further wrongs.

Eva, wife of Walter de Motcumbe, accused three men of coming to her house at night, maiming her husband and child, and killing a serving woman.[52] Since they were suspected by the twelve knights of the neighborhood and by the men of the four nearest villages, they were directed to undergo the ordeal of water.[53] In none of these cases[53a] did anyone, justices or defendants, raise the limiting rule to disqualify the appeal, though it would seem to be in the defendant's interest to end an appeal as quickly as possible if a way to do so were available.

The limiting rule was fully and definitively stated in very few homicide cases. Three of these were quashed by the application of the rule, but with attendant circumstances which were enough to disqualify the appeal or render it useless to pursue. The justices invoked the limiting rule in the case of Juliana de Holeworth and Edelina, mother of Peter, who accused William Pech of sending his sons Roger, Henry, and Hugo to kill the women's sons. But in both of these cases, the law had already dealt with the actual perpetrators as far as it

---

M. T. Clanchy, ed., *The Roll and Writ File of the Berkshire Eyre, 1248* [*RWFBE*], Selden Society, 90 (London, 1973), 810.

[49] *CRR*, 6:52; *PCCG*, 482.

[50] *PKJ*, 2:735.

[51] *CPWE*, p. 374.

[52] Her appeal could be heard, even though she was a married woman whose husband did not participate in the appeal, because the courts allowed a woman to begin her husband's appeal of wounding or mayhem if he were still recovering from the wound, probably because she would have the appeal if he died, and perhaps as an extension of *Bracton's* statement, 2:353, 407 that a kinsman or friend may begin a wounded man's appeal, but on his recovery such appeals cease and he must sue, if he will, for himself. Her appeal about the killing of the serving woman was, of course, not allowed under the rule.

[53] *PKJ*, 2:734.

[53a] *RJEGWS*, 750; *CPWE*, p. 172; *CRR*, 7:26–7; *PKJ*, 2:336, 738.

could. Two of the slayers had already been outlawed for the killing and another was a clerk whose case would have to be heard in the ecclesiastical courts. The women were accusing a man whom they thought had planned and directed the killings.[54] In the case of Hawis, daughter of Thurston and wife of Robert Franctenant, lodged a complaint against two men for killing her father and then wounding her. Her husband did not enter into the appeal and the justices declared it null on the grounds that "a woman cannot make an appeal against anyone even for the death of her husbands or for her own rape" (*femina non habet appellum versus aliquem nisi de morte uiri sue uel de rapo*). In the end, the appellees were acquitted and Robert was amerced for his wife's appeal.[55]

In another case, the defendant stated the rule. Maud, daughter of Godfrey, appealed against Adam de Tid for having sent Richard the outlaw to kill her father. She claimed that as Richard had stabbed Godfrey she heard him say, "Take this for Adam de Tid." She also alleged that William de Tid, Adam's brother, was with Richard during the murder. Adam challenged the appeal on the basis of the limiting rule.[56] The case breaks off abruptly with no conclusion, and there is none recorded elsewhere in the rolls. It is remarkable that two of the cases in which the limiting rule was fully stated contained factors that at least rendered the appeal questionable, and one has no recorded conclusion. These cases are the only homicide cases so treated in these sources.[57]

Robbery appeals were seldom challenged in these rolls. As with any set of appeals, brought by male or female, they met with varying fates. Some were not prosecuted. Of these some were allowed to lapse,[58] but others were carried forward another step at the court's initiative: putting the appellees under pledges till the justices next came into the neighborhood, amercing an absent defendant, or asking the jurors for a verdict before considering the case ended.[59] For example, the action of Alice, widow of Harold, and her son against eight men had no conclusion in the rolls but was held over for a later session. It was supposedly to go before a jury of twelve knights who had no allegiance to either side. The outcome was not recorded, but it is instructive that the court was willing to go to such lengths for an appeal that was denied Alice without the limiting rule even being mentioned.[60]

---

54 *PKJ*, 2:730–31.
55 *ELAR*, 690.
56 Adam offered ten marks for a jury verdict on whether a related appeal, brought by a male, was brought because of malice; presumably Maud's appeal and another of wounding brought by messengers of two wounded men arising from the same incident would await that verdict, *RCR*, 1:57–58.
57 *CPWE*, p. 88.
58 PRO, JUST 1/613, m. 3d; *ELAR*, 721; *CPWE*, p. 561.
59 *ELAR*, 994; *PKJ*, 2:732; *RJEGWS*, 757, the appellee was acquitted.
60 The legal position of Alice's son's appeal was assailable since he had associated himself with his mother in making it, but no one, defendants or justices, chose to raise the rule, *CRR*, 6:237.

A handful of women appellors preferred to reach a settlement. In one case, this took place despite the defendant's invocation of the limiting rule. Agnes of Glaston withdrew her appeal in which she had charged Walt Tautre of stealing two shifts from her garden at night. The jurors stated that Agnes and Walter had come to an agreement to settle the appeal. The court ruled that she was to be taken into custody for having withdrawn from the appeal; Walter was to suffer the same fate for having avoided justice by coming to an agreement with her.[61] Sibilla, daughter of Engelard, appealed against Ralph of Saunford for coming to her house, breaking down the doors, and carrying off her chattels. The excitement of these events had led her to miscarry. She also withdrew her appeal. This was allowed by the justices as was the settlement she made with Ralph which obliged him to pay her the value of the chattels, as appraised by independent authorities.[62] Christina, widow of John Clerk, lodged an appeal against Robert, son of Hugh, saying that he had come to her house at night, ejected her, and abducted her son and married him to his (Robert's) daughter without Christina's consent. Robert put forward a barrage of exceptions. He first denied everything. He then said he was a clerk and thus should be tried in an ecclesiastical court. He then recounted a completely different version of the events, saying that the son of Christina's late husband had arranged the marriage and she had consented to it.[63] Finally, he claimed Christina's appeal was invalid because it was made by a woman. The court listened to none of this and allowed the case to proceed. In the end, Robert settled with Christina, agreeing to restore to her some of the chattels he had withheld from her, some of the land her husband had given her long before their marriage and her dower (that portion of a husband's lands that a widow was supposed to enjoy during her lifetime).[64]

Some cases proceeded in a straightforward way, just as they would have if the appellor had been male. Leticia de Clixby accused Hugo Shakespeare of coming to her mother's house, where he tied up Leticia and her mother, and proceeded to rob them. The jurors suspected Hugo of this crime and the court sent him to the ordeal of water. He was "cleared" by the ordeal, but paid 2 marks for permission to stay in the area and not to adjure the realm.[65] Agnes, daughter of Edric and Hawis of Abeston, charged two men, both servants, with robbery and burglary. One of the men was a servant of Hawis's late husband. The two defendants, denying everything, submitted to a jury trial. Both were

---

[61] A concord was allowed if the justices gave their permission; it was a form of contempt of court if it was arrived at without permission, *CPWE*, p. 550.

[62] *PKJ*, 3:690.

[63] Almost certainly Christina's stepson.

[64] *CRR*, 7:187–88; the dower lands would revert to her late husband's heir after her death, see Pollock and Maitland, 2:420–28.

[65] A clerk who was appealed along with Hugh was handed over to the ecclesiastical courts, *ELAR*, 855.

convicted and hanged.[66] In a remarkable case, Lucia de Morestowe's appeal of robbery proceeded to a monetary award, though it was far less than the amount she had originally claimed. She accused three adolescents of robbing her of 20 shillings, 4 pence and a cloak worth half a mark. Only one defendant appeared in court, and he denied all the charges. The judge turned to the jury for the facts. They told him that Lucia was a prostitute and had been entertaining a client in a field when three boys had taunted her until she ran away, leaving her cloak behind. The boys took the cloak and pledged it for two gallons of wine. The judges decreed that the one defendant who had appeared in court was to give her the 3 pence which the wine normally cost. With this money, she could redeem her cloak, probably a necessity in her business.[67]

An action brought by Edith de Wacheford, however, was quashed, but in the end she got a judgment that was more than anyone bargained for. The case has its comic dimension at first. It was about the "appropriation" of three of Edith's pigs by William Netebech. She had put the pigs in a forest under the care of some foresters, expecting to retrieve them and pay later for their pannage. But William claimed the pigs before she returned for them. She took her case to the local court, and then things started to escalate. Her son, probably to support her, put in his own complaint about the pigs, offering to prove his charge by battle. William denied that the pigs had ever belonged to Edith, and the court ruled that Richard and William would have to do battle over the possession of the pigs. At this point, alarmed by the turn of events, Edith complained to the royal court that a false judgment had been made. The royal justices ordered that the record of the case be brought to them. The constable conveyed it there, along with numerous men of the court who could bear witness to the accuracy of the record. Everyone agreed that the case had proceeded as described. The justices ruled that the appeal was invalid on two counts: Edith, as a woman, could not lodge a complaint against William in regard to her belongings; and Richard could not fight William over the possession of the pigs because they had never belonged to him. Therefore, the local court had given a false judgment in allowing the duel to be sworn. It was thus amerced, and the appeal declared null. The court then turned to the jurors to find out what had really happened in the matter of the pigs. The many witnesses stated under oath that the pigs had been Edith's all along. The justices ruled that she was to get her pigs back. They hanged William.[68]

Several women tried to enhance their chances of success by combining forbidden appeals, such as those of robbery, with the charge of wounding. For example, Eva de Babinton filed a complaint against Richard Frend, claiming that he had killed her son and wounded her in the breast. Richard denied her accusation, but the knights of the county said that they suspected him as the

66 CPWE, p. 497.
67 PKJ, 2:399.
68 CRR, 15:905; BNB, 2:824.

result of his past record which included theft of sheep and flight from justice after the death of Eva's son. Consequently, Richard was directed to undergo the ordeal of water.[69] Another woman accused four men and a woman of beating and robbing her. She did not prosecute her appeal, but the jurors, asked by the court, said one of the men had beaten the victim at the command of the accused woman. Eventually, the court acquitted the other three men, but directed the male defendant and the woman to pay the substantial sum of 100 shillings to make fine, that is, to pay a sum to the Crown to have the case concluded.[70] One woman's appeal concerning robbery and a brutal beating was quashed because it had not been made correctly. In this case, the defendant did not mention the limiting rule. Another woman accused a man of having stolen her pigs (once again there were three of them) and, in the process, of giving her a one-inch wound on the head. However, her case was thrown out. She had appealed without her husband, but that was not the problem. The defendant said her pigs had got into his field and when he had tried to round them up, she attacked him with her staff. In the process of struggling over the staff, she had hit herself in the head with it. The jury agreed with the defendant.[71] The story sounds a little contrived, but if true, her own negligence, followed by an assault on the defendant, constituted a poor basis for an appeal.

Occasionally, women turned to more sophisticated strategies. Agnes de Torlee had her vassal appeal in her stead, while, at the same time, alleging the robbery of his own goods. The defendant challenged the suit, saying that it was brought in order to delay a civil action between the parties. However, given the circumstances, he could not challenge it under the limiting rule.[72] Gunnilda, wife of Osbert de Luton, chose to use what was known as a plaint, an all-purpose suit that could be brought without writ under certain circumstances and did not have the rigid restrictions of an appeal in order to get her grievance heard.[73] Gunnilda settled her plaint which concerned beating, robbery, and imprisonment, even though her husband had not appeared in the case with her.[74] Sibilla de Burtone, wife of Peter Russell, brought a plaint against Samuel de Burtone, her former brother-in-law, and three other men concerning a robbery and the forcible eviction which had taken place while she was a widow before her re-marriage to Peter. Peter now joined her in bringing the charges and offered to prove them as the court might consider, a formula for the offer of battle. The defendants, after denying the charges, gave their versions of the

[69] This case was heard in 1201, *PKJ*, 2:742.

[70] *RWFBE*, 816, 1034; JUST 1/54 m 12.

[71] *CPWE*, p. 169.

[72] *CRR*, 1:347–48.

[73] See H. G. Richardson and G. O. Sayles, ed., *Select Cases of Procedure without Writ under Henry III* [*SCP*], Selden Society, 60 (London, 1941) pp. xiii, xxii and *passim*.

[74] *CRR*, 4:295–96; and see Katrina de Hundlaneside, who wanted her plaint of robbery to be heard with the civil pleas because it also concerned her lands and the disputed custody of an heir, *PCCG*, 260.

events according to which Sibilla had ejected Samuel from land that was rightfully his. They further declared that Peter could not speak "of his own sight and hearing" about the incident and they also raised the limiting rule. Samuel refused to submit to a jury, but the court overruled him. The jury declared for Sibilla, and the case ended with a settlement.[75] A plaint was a viable alternative for a woman whose husband lacked the ability, interest, or qualifications to enter effectively into an appeal with her.

The quashing of an appeal did not necessarily end a case. For example, in two appeals of 1249, defendants were convicted even though the appeals were declared null. Both appeals were brought by one woman against different groups of defendants; both were quashed, even though the woman's lord was one of the defendants, because the correct appeals process had not been carried out. Despite this, the court turned to the jury to determine the truth and, as a result, the defendants were convicted and compelled to make a large fine, in one case the enormous sum of 100 marks.[76]

In a time when it was very difficult to bring any appeal to a successful conclusion,[77] the record of women pursuing appeals which were officially prohibited was surprisingly good. Forbidden appeals were heard, judged on their merits, and acted on, even in instances in which the defendant invoked the limiting rule or the court quashed the appeal. If a clue to this high success rate is to be found, it may be found in an appeal that was allowed to women: the appeal for the death of a husband. Though seemingly hemmed in by restrictions, the appeal was used freely and the restrictions were often overlooked, and the court sometimes took extra steps to override the circumstances which normally would halt the process. *Bracton* requires that the appeal must state specifically that the husband's death took place "in her [the wife's] arms" (*in brachia sua*). The version of the appeal found in *Placita Corone* sets out a long list of conditions which had to be met: the wife had to have clearly seen and heard the offense, the husband had to die *in brachia sua* and, as soon as she was sure he was dead, she had to go without delay to rouse the neighborhood and alert the proper authorities.[78] Despite the existence of these requirements, the records show that the court was not bent on enforcing them. The term "in her arms" may have been a formality, and even sight and hearing of the crime was not rigidly required. Furthermore, the court was willing to go out of its way to pursue these supposedly illegal appeals, following them up even when the widow failed to prosecute or when her appeal had been quashed, and, in at least one case, following up an appeal that never had been made.

The court was more than usually diligent in following up a widow's suit

---

[75] *PCCG*, 100.
[76] *CPWE*, pp. 44–45.
[77] *ELAR*, lix.
[78] *Bracton*, 2:419; *PC*, p. 28.

against an absent defendant, whether the widow prosecuted her appeal or not.[79] A defendant who did not appear in court or answer a widow's charges when she was in court to press them was almost invariably outlawed.[80] *Bracton* declares that a prior appeal, even if discontinued, raised a presumption of guilt sufficient to direct the county court to continue the process of outlawry, but in cases other than a widow's appeal about the death of her husband, the court was often lax.[81] Sometimes no action was taken beyond collecting a monetary penalty from the pledges of the absconding defendant. Sometimes no action whatever was taken.[82]

On the other hand, when a widow appealed about the death of her husband, the court more often than not continued the process of outlawry even after the widow had allowed her suit to lapse.[83] The court also paid more than the customary attention to a widow's suit when the defendant claimed to be a cleric. When Robert the clerk was accused by Swanild, widow of Hugh, he claimed to have been ordained by the archbishop of Canterbury. Furthermore, the bishop's official supported his claim. Ordinarily, this would have been enough to move the case to the bishop's court. In this instance, however, the justices refused to surrender Robert until letters from the archbishop attesting his ordination could be presented to the court.[84]

The court also followed up cases in which a widow had let her prosecution lapse, and the defendant was present to deny the charges. In such cases, the widow was usually amerced for her failure to prosecute, but the accused seldom got off scot-free. In one instance, the court acquitted two accused men because their accuser, Alice, widow of Thomas, withdrew from her suit.[85] In most cases, however, the justices took further steps. One possibility was for the court to put the defendants under pledges, persons who produce them for further court proceedings or pay a financial penalty.[86] Alternatively, the court might ask the jurors if they suspected the defendants of having committed the crime. Even if the jurors did not suspect him, acquittal was not automatic. The court might decide to release the defendants under pledges in case someone

---

79 *PKJ*, 2:260, 738; 3:686, 714; *RJEYH3*, 531.
80 See for example *CPWE*, pp. 92, 115, 151, 194, 355, 685; *RWFBE*, pp. 815, 858; *RSEGWS*, 733, 737, 793, 794, 803, 1278.
81 Patricia Orr, "Men's Theory and Women's Reality: Rape Prosecutions in the English Royal Courts of Justice, 1194–1222," in *The Rusted Hauberk: Feudal Ideals of Order and their Decline*, ed. Liam O. Purdon and Cindy L. Vitto (Gainsville,1994), pp. 121–59.
82 A tithing, or frankpledge, was a neighborhood group to which all males over the age of twelve were supposed to belong and which was supposed to produce any accused members in court to answer the accusations against them, *Bracton*, pp. 351, 355, 359, 362, 374; Pollock and Maitland, 2:529.
83 *RJEGWS*, 955; appellor had died, *RWFBE*, p. 975.
84 *PKJ*, 2:740.
85 Ibid., 2:298.
86 Ibid., 2:745, 747.

else might file a complaint against them.[87] On the other hand, if the jury declared them suspects, they would be imprisoned until their cases could be disposed of or they could be released on bond.[88]

The most remarkable example of following up a widow's appeal after she had let it lapse was a scandalous case that reached the ears of the king, the appeal brought by Christina, widow of Geoffrey de Suttone. Christina accused six members of the Basset family, apparently brothers, of killing her husband. She did not prosecute, but one of the Bassets, named Robert, appeared and submitted to a jury trial to decide his guilt or innocence. The jurors, the coroners and all the men of the county court unanimously held that Christina had already pressed her suit at two sessions of the county court following her husband's death, after which she had reached a settlement establishing peace between the two families. By its terms, Robert's son Walter[89] had married the daughter of the slain man, Geoffrey. Robert had also given a generous measure of land to Geoffrey's surviving family. It is remarkable that two men, Walter Hunder and his son, had fled after the crime. Walter was directed to leave the country by King John himself and his son was beheaded. Christina had to pay 40 shillings to requite her part in the illicit settlement of the case, even while asserting that she had been able to pursue the case any further. Despite this, the judges pursued the cases, perhaps because Geoffrey, the slain man, had accused Robert and his brothers before he had passed away. The jury stated that all the brothers had been members of Robert's household, that they had accompanied him to the "ale" or drinking party where the killing had taken place, and had returned home with him after the deed. All of this clearly indicated their complicity. But the court focused its attention on Robert. The jurors said they knew full well that Robert was guilty, because he had given his land to make peace, Robert was sentenced to be hanged.[89a]

In another case, the judicial machinery followed up an appeal that had never been made. Emma, widow of Reginald the clerk, did not make an appeal about her husband's death at any time, either during the three days her husband lay dying or after his death. After some time, a sergeant of her local district came to ask her if she wanted to bring an appeal against anyone. She, however, was terrified and did not dare do so. She told him privately the names of the five men whom she thought might have done it, and the court was going to pursue the case without her participation.[90]

When a widow persevered with her appeal, her case received its full share of attention, but an appeal with little apparent merit would be quashed. Edith, widow of Jacob the merchant, accused Ketel of Warwick of killing her hus-

---

[87] Acquitted, ibid., 2:298; released to pledges, PRO, Just 1/800, m. 2; *PKJ*, 4:3457.

[88] Imprisoned, *PKJ*, 2:250,747; paid 4 marks to be released to pledges, *ELAR*, 872.

[89] Not the Walter who had abjured the realm, below.

[89a] *PCCG*, 101; *RJEYH3*, 529

[90] *CRR*, 6:341–42.

band. Ketel denied the charge and pointed out that another man, William Maynard, had already fled to a church, confessed the crime, and adjured the realm after Edith had accused him. For her part, Edith had not accused Ketel at the time of the offense but had only brought her charges at a later meeting of the county court. The accused gave 5 marks for a jury verdict. The jurors ruled that Ketel was not guilty. He had had no dealings with Jacob except on one occasion when he had ordered Jacob to post a bond because of a fight between Jacob and William Maynard, the man who had eventually killed him. Another widow appealed solely on the basis of rumor. A third appealed the wife and daughter of a man outlawed for her husband's murder, declaring they had incited him to the act. When questioned she admitted that the two women had not been at the scene of the killing nor had she ever seen or heard them inciting the killer.[91] All three of these relatively weak appeals were quashed.

For other widows, however, the court was likely to proceed with the case regardless of its technical deficiencies or questions about process. One man accused by a widow was attested in the county court to have been captured in flight. The hundred, a local court, sentenced that he clear himself by the ordeal of water.[92] Another woman's questionable appeal was put before the justiciar himself. The defendant claimed that the widow had previously accused him in the court of Geoffrey Fitz Peter and had withdrawn from her appeal. The whole county court testified she was jailed for refusing to sue and had to pay one mark, twice the usual amount for this transgression. Despite this, the court did not quash her appeal, preferring to consult Geoffrey Fitz Peter before doing anything else.[93]

Agnes, widow of Robert de Bosco, had a new husband who would not join in her appeal and so it was quashed. Nevertheless, the court wanted to take the case further. The defendant refused to "put himself on the jury," in the terminology of the time. The year was 1221 and the ordeal had recently been abolished. The jury was evolving to take its place, but there still was some perplexity as to what to do when a man refused a jury trial. In this case, the court took an aggressive approach and asked the jurors and twenty-four other knights chosen for the purpose for their opinion. They all said he was guilty, and he was hanged.[94]

A widow's inability "to see or hear the crime" did not necessarily end her appeal. The court took an equally aggressive approach in the case of Maud, widow of Walter, whose inability to see or hear the crime did not end her appeal. She got her information by going to the fields where the crime had

---

91 *RJEGWS*, 832; *ELAR*, 763b, 834.
92 *PKJ*, 2:620; a man was sent to the ordeal after he denied a widow's accusation of the killing of her husband but was suspected by the whole county court, PRO, JUST 1/799, m. 2d.
93 *ELAR*, 922.
94 *RJEGWS*, no. 728.

taken place and asking some children and other people what had happened. There is no indication that these people had witnessed the killing, but her appeal was not quashed. Nevertheless, the court in the area where the husband was killed took up the case.[95] Denise, widow of Anthony, could not claim to have seen the crime and, as a result, her appeal was quashed. Here, too, the court proceeded to ask the jurors about the defendant. Since the jurors and the men of the court suspected him, he was required to face the ordeal of water.[96] Gunnilda, widow of Robert the Franklin, did not see the men who killed her husband because the night was dark and the attackers had beaten her so badly she could not see. Nevertheless, she suspected Henry the cooper, her husband's longtime enemy who was already being held by the justices on a charge of theft. Although Henry refused to undergo a jury trial, the coroners, the jurors and the four townships argued that he was guilty of these and other offenses. Since this case also arose in 1221 after the abolition of ordeal, the court directed the defendant only to find a pledge for the relatively large sum of 60 shillings, but also fifteen other pledges who would personally guarantee that he would be available if summoned for trial.[97]

A widow who made her appeal correctly was very likely to be successful with it. If it had no basis, the defendant would be acquitted, as in any other appeal. The cases of two women who brought appeals when their husbands had died of natural causes bear this out.[98] On the other hand, those women who brought reasonable appeals could count on the court to take them seriously. In one case, the king ordered a woman's appeal held over until he could return from the Continent and hear it himself.[99] In two other cases, defendants were hanged in a time when hangings were unusual.[100]

The court gave further special treatment by overlooking, in a time when it was difficult to bring any appeal to completion, those very conditions that would normally invalidate it. For one thing, it overlooked complications brought about by the remarriage of a widow. A married woman was not supposed to sue alone; her husband was supposed to sue along with her or in her place. If he was not interested in her appeal, she was not to be heard. A remarried widow appealing on account of the death of her previous husband, therefore, faced a dilemma. If she sued without her present husband, her case might be invalidated for that reason. On the other hand, if he joined her in her suit, it was highly unlikely that he could allege "sight or hearing" in any

---

95 *ENAR*, 714.
96 *PKJ*, 2:265.
97 Presumably if Henry could not find this large number of pledges he could remain in prison indefinitely, *PCCG*, 414.
98 One had been beaten by the defendant, but had not died until a year after the assault, *PKJ*, 4:3457; *PCCG*, 343.
99 *CRR*, 4:225.
100 *CPWE*, pp. 168, 312.

convincing way. In either case, she would be unable to complete the appeal. The court cut through this tangle by either ignoring inconvenient circumstances and going on with the appeal or quashing it and following up with the court's own investigation. Another restriction – that the husband must have died in his wife's arms for her to accuse his slayer – was for all practical purposes an empty one. It is mentioned in one appeal;[101] however, no defendant ever tried to argue that a widow's appeal was invalid because her husband did not die in her arms. In fact, as we have seen, appeals sometimes continued, even when the widow had not seen the killing of her husband, despite the basic requirement that men and women alike must have seen and heard the crime.[102] Certainly, the system went to lengths seen in no other cases in the rolls when it disrupted the settlement in the Basset case, and hanged Robert Basset and sought out Emma, widow of Reginald, about the appeal she was too terrified to make.

Emma's case embodies a possible reason why the court might do so much for widows. Emma's fear of retaliation, were she to make an appeal, was the reason for her silence, and the system's desire for justice in her case was the reason for seeking her out. A widow was particularly vulnerable. The sudden and violent loss of her husband and protector could easily become a threat to her. The perception of widows as persons defenseless against powerful and violent men and the desire to extend to them the protection of the law, even at the expense of the principle that restricted women's appeal, is a likely reason for the courts' actions.

One way to test this supposition is to examine the cases and see if there is a pattern in their treatment. The appeals that were quashed do have a common characteristic. Edith, widow of Jacob, was accusing one man after another had already confessed to the crime. The other two whose appeals were quashed were appealing about instigating a crime, not committing it, or on the basis of bare rumor.[103] On the other hand, substantive appeals were pursued by the court despite technical disqualifications. The Bassets had killed Christina's husband and the justices went out of their way first to uncover the crime and then to execute one of the perpetrators in a period when hangings were relatively rare. For her part, Christina disavowed any connection with the settlement. She may have wanted to avoid penalties for withdrawing from her appeal; she may have agreed unwillingly out of fear of the violent Bassets. Certainly, fear kept Emma, widow of Reginald, from making her appeal. The court found it worthwhile to follow up the appeal of Agnes, widow of Robert de Bosco, even after quashing it because of her remarriage. Maud, widow of Walter, may be the only person mentioned in this article whose appeal went forward, even though she had obtained her information from children and strangers. In her case, the court was willing to continue the process due to her obvious effort to

---

101 Given as part of the appeal in *PKJ*, 2:11; *Bracton*, p. 419; *PC*, p. 5.
102 *ENAR*, 714; *PKJ*, 2:265; *PCCG*, 414.
103 *RJEGWS*, 832; *ELAR*, 763B, 834.

find the truth. Gunnilda, widow of Robert the Franklin, beaten too badly to see her husband's murderers, had the court's full support. All of these examples show that a medieval English court was willing to bend over backwards to aid a widow to act on appeals she had made in good faith.[104]

Appeals that violated the limiting rule followed a similar pattern. *Bona fide* appeals of this sort were allowed and were pursued by the court. The maimed husband and child and slain servant woman of Eva, wife of Walter de Motcombe, the beating and robbery of Leticia de Clixby, and even the three pigs of Edith de Wacheford or the cloak of Lucia de Morestowe were as important to the court as to the women themselves.[105] The few cases that were quashed on the grounds of the limiting rule were much less compelling. Juliana's and Edelina's pursuit of the supposed instigator of their sons' murders may have seemed gratuitous, once the slayers had been dealt with.[106]

Two questions, inextricably linked, remain to be answered: why was the limiting rule so often ignored in practice, and why was it retained and cited if so little used? One possible reason that inevitably springs to mind is that the courts "bent" the rule for women of high status, and kept it in force for those of lower classes. This contention, however, is not readily supported from the rolls. For one thing, the social status of most women in the court records is not easily identified. For another, even in cases which proceeded, thus leaving us some information, women of many social ranks were represented.

Another possible reason is a change on societal and judicial conditions since the limiting rule was first instituted. According to one line of reason, it was framed to eliminate one class of frivolous or malicious appeals. Meekings proposes:

> Since a woman could not offer battle she had a procedural advantage and since she had a procedural advantage there must have been at times a strong temptation to an ill-disposed man to persuade a woman, say the daughter of a tenant, to bring an appeal against his enemy in the hope of encompassing his ruin or at least exposing him to much trouble yet without any risk to himself or his agent.[107]

In the thirteenth century, however, the judicial duel was seldom seen. F. W. Maitland avers that it had fallen out of favor with the justices, who seemed to have "delighted in crushing appeals" that might have led to a duel. On the

---

104 Christina, widow of Godfrey de Suttone, *PCCG*, 101; Emma, widow of Reginald the clerk, *CRR*, 6:341–42; Agnes, widow of Robert de Bosco, *RJEGWS*, 728; Maud, widow of Walter, *ENAR*, 714; Gunnilda, widow of Robert Franklin, *PCCG*, 414.

105 *PKJ*, 2:399, 734; *ELAR*, 855; *CRR*, 15:905.

106 *PKJ*, 2:730–31.

107 *CPWE*, p. 88, and see *1235 SE*, p. 123; *PC*, p. xxix; Harding, speaking of rape, an appeal reserved at that time to women alone, says that women were coerced or persuaded to bring appeals because trials *super patriam* might be substituted for battle in such cases, *RSE*, p. xli.

have "delighted in crushing appeals" that might have led to a duel. On the other hand, Michael Clanchy finds that it was coming to be the exclusive province of approvers, confessed criminals who tried to save themselves by in turn accusing their accomplices and defeating them in battle.[108] Few other defendants ever faced battle.[109] Moreover, legal machinery was in place to end malicious appeals: the exception *odio et atia*, which claimed that the appellor was lodging a complaint, not for true cause, but from hate and malice. The exception called for a jury to declare the truth of the matter.

Given these circumstances, it is surprising that the limiting rule was so long maintained. The inertia of judicial conservatism is probably a partial explanation. The rule reflects a mind set, which assumes that trial by battle is an integral part of judicial procedure. Inertia alone, however, would hardly support the limiting rule's long career as an element of court records and treatises. It must have had some practical use in court, besides its stated, and unfulfilled, purpose. Its very existence may have had some deterrent value in keeping forbidden appeals out of the courts.

In its mundane operation within the judicial arena, the simultaneous affirming and setting aside of the limiting rule permitted a useful reciprocity between the courts and women, with perceived advantages to both. The rule provided the justices a useful tool to dismiss out of hand weak appeals of little substance, thus perhaps deterring similar motions from even coming into court. Conversely, if an appeal had substance, they could overlook the rule and investigate the case. The court's practice of setting aside the rule gave women, who were left without male protection of their interests, but who had sufficient initiative to make an appeal, the opportunity to gain attention for their complaints and to find justice in English courts. Even if the justices sometimes affirmed the theoretical rule: "Non potest appellum facere . . .," the truth was often quite different. In reality, women could and did bring the prohibited appeals, and, more often than not, brought them successfully.

[108] *SPC*, 24; R. F. Hunnisett and J. B. Post, eds., *Medieval Legal Records Edited in Memory of C. A. F. Meekings* (London, 1978), p. 29.
[109] Orr, "English Women," p. 170.

PART FOUR

Crime and Punishment

War, Women and Crime in the Northern English Border Lands in the Later Middle Ages[1]

CYNTHIA J. NEVILLE

At a session of gaol delivery held in the northern English town of Carlisle in the winter of 1331, two women appeared before the justices of assize to answer charges of theft. Eda, the wife of John Valleson of Houghton in the Forest, indicted in the sheriff's tourn, was accused of stealing two geese from her neighbor, Thomas, son of Michael, a haul worth altogether 4 pence. She denied committing the offense, but the jurors returned a guilty verdict.[2] On the same day,[3] the justices heard that Mariota of Galloway had been taken in possession of stolen goods that included a surcoat, a coat of blue cloth, two kerchiefs, two ells of white cloth and a blanket, allegedly stolen from Christina of Petterel Wraw. The jurors of Allerdale returned a guilty verdict against Mariota, too.[4] But whereas Eda was remitted to Carlisle gaol to serve a brief term as punishment for her offense, Mariota was sentenced to hang, and was probably dead by the time the justices had departed the town. Eda's offense, probably motivated by hunger and poverty was, in the minds of jurors and justices, excusable; the Scotswoman Mariota's was not.

The motives and actions of medieval jurors, who were so crucial a component of the English machinery of criminal justice, have been the subject of a great deal of interest among historians for some years now. More particularly,

[1] The author wishes to acknowledge the assistance of the Social Sciences and Humanities Research Council of Canada in the preparation of this work.
[2] PRO, JUST 3/214/4, m. 43d. Unless otherwise stated all references are to documents in the Public Record Office.
[3] The brief duration of medieval trials, in which upwards of fifty individuals might be processed in a single day, is discussed in R. B. Pugh, "The Duration of Criminal Trials in Medieval England," in *Law, Litigants and the Legal Profession*, ed. E. W. Ives and A. H. Manchester (London, 1983), pp. 104–10, and, more recently, in E. Powell, "Jury Trial at Gaol Delivery in the Late Middle Ages: The Midland Circuit, 1400–1429," in *Twelve Good Men and True: The Criminal Trial Jury in England, 1200–1800*, ed. J. S. Cockburn and T. A. Green (Princeton, 1988), pp. 52, 82, 98–99. See also M. Gollancz, "The System of Gaol Delivery as Illustrated in the Extant Gaol Delivery Rolls of the Fifteenth Century" (M.A. thesis, University of London, 1936), pp. 140–42.
[4] PRO, JUST 3/214/4, m. 32.

scholars have traced a relationship between patterns of indictment and guilty verdicts, on the one hand, and, on the other, the social attitudes reflected in the jurors' punitive strategies.[5] The question of the place of women in criminal activity has also begun to be examined in recent years. Some very good work has been done on the seventeenth and eighteenth centuries by John Beattie,[6] but for the medieval period much of the current history of women and crime is the work of Barbara Hanawalt.[7] She painstakingly investigated some 15,000 felonies in a wide range of English counties for the period 1300–1348.[8] From these numbers, she extrapolated statistics concerning women's involvement in different types of offenses, the seasonal variations of these misdeeds, the sorts of goods women stole, the weapons they used, the rates of acquittal, the guilty verdicts and, not least, the sociological motivations underlying the behavior of female felons.

This paper does not attempt anything on the scale of Hanawalt's study. It seeks, rather, to test some of her findings against source materials that originated in a single judicial circuit – the northern – over a period of some 150 years. More specifically, it examines the incidence of criminal activities among

5   See especially T. A. Green, "Societal Concepts of Criminal Liability for Homicide in Medieval England," *Speculum* 47(1972): 669–74. These arguments are substantially revised and expressed more forcefully still in idem, *Verdict According to Conscience* (Chicago, 1985), pp. 28–102. Some of Green's conclusions with respect to the behavior of medieval juries have, however, been challenged by legal scholars. See, for example, J. B. Post, "Jury Lists and Juries in the Late Fourteenth Century," in *Twelve Good Men and True*, pp. 72–77, and Powell, pp. 78–97.

6   J. M. Beattie, "The Criminality of Women in Eighteenth-Century England," *Journal of Social History* 8(1974–75): 80–116, and, more recently, idem, *Crime and the Courts in England, 1660–1800* (Princeton NJ, 1986), pp. 97, 105–6, 113–24, 237–43. For the sixteenth century, see C. Z. Wiener, "Sex Roles and Crime in Late Elizabethan Hertfordshire," *Journal of Social History* 8(1974–75): 38–46. A recent collection of essays examines several different aspects of women's experience in the criminal courts of early modern England: J. Kermode and G. Walker, eds., *Women, Crime and the Courts in Early Modern England* (Chapel Hill NC, 1994).

7   B. A. Hanawalt, "The Female Felon in Fourteenth-Century England," *Viator* 5(1974): 253–68; idem, *Crime and Conflict in English Communities, 1300–1348* (Cambridge MA, 1979), pp. 111–12, 115–25, 192–95, 263–64; idem, "Women Before the Law: Females as Felons and Prey in Fourteenth-Century England," in *Women and the Law: A Social Historical Perspective*, ed. D. K. Weisberg, 2 vols. (Cambridge MA, 1982), 1:165–95. The field is also explored, to a lesser extent, in K. E. Garay, " 'No Peace Nor Love in England?' An Examination of Crime and Punishment in the English Counties, 1388–1409" (Ph.D. diss., University of Toronto, 1977), pp. 253–67, 349–51, 370–71; idem, "Women and Crime in Later Medieval England," *Florilegium* 1(1979): 87–109; J. M. Bennett, *Women in the Medieval English Countryside: Gender and Household in Brigstock before the Plague* (New York, 1987), pp. 38–41, 191; and H. M. Jewell, "Women at the Courts of the Manor of Wakefield, 1348–1350," *Northern History* 26(1990): 64–66.

8   The figures and their sources are discussed in Hanawalt, "Women Before the Law," 1:167.

women whose lives were arguably more stressful and precarious than those of most medieval Englishwomen. Here I shall argue that the very sociological factors that historians have shown to be so profound an influence on jury attitudes were themselves shaped, sharpened and sometimes altered altogether by economic and social circumstances such as war and want. These conditions characterized the late medieval border lands of the north of England.

The source materials used here are the rolls of gaol delivery generated by the work of the itinerant justices of assize as they traveled around the kingdom on their judicial circuits;[9] they are supplemented with the records of the King's Bench, from the periods when that court was temporarily moved to York.[10] Durham gaol delivery rolls survive in far fewer numbers than those of the other English counties. In large part, their patchier preservation is a consequence of the bishops' independence from the Crown and the normal mechanics of common law justice. The period under examination is the entire span for which these records remain extant, 1300 to 1460. The geographical focus, however, is the most crucial of the many factors that influenced the production of these records and the everyday lives of the people to whom they relate: it is the border counties of Lancashire, Cumberland, Westmorland, Northumberland and Durham. The total number of felony cases examined from these counties amounts to just over four thousand; when the Yorkshire records are included, that figure expands rather dramatically to almost three times the number.[11] Yorkshire, however, is referred to only in passing in this paper although its situation exposed it on occasion to the depredations of the king's enemies (notably in the second decade of the fourteenth century), it was never a frontier to the same extent as were the most northerly shires.

The history of the late medieval northern border lands in the fourteenth and fifteenth centuries is the history of a society deeply affected by war. From 1296 down to the early sixteenth century, war was endemic. Though open conflict was frequently suspended by periods of truce, raids and counter raids continued unabated throughout these years. Indeed, during the fourteenth century, it is not unreasonable to suggest that many of the king's northern subjects could expect at some point in their lives to experience at first hand the tribulations of an attack. Chronicles, petitions to Parliament, estate documents, and ecclesiastical rent rolls in particular, provide vivid testimony of the devastating effects of depredations committed by the Scottish enemy.[12] To a people whose economy

---

9   Classified in the PRO as JUST 3.

10 Classified in the PRO as KB 27. The King's Bench sat in York in 1318–23, 1327–28, 1332–37, 1340, 1343–44, 1348–49, 1362 and 1392.

11 Hanawalt's Yorkshire figures for the period 1300–1348 are reviewed in *Crime and Conflict*, p. 13. For the present survey all the surviving Yorkshire rolls were examined, including those that record gaol deliveries of the archbishop's liberties of St. Mary, St. Leonard, St. Peter, Beverley, Ripon and Knaresborough.

12 The literature on this topic is vast. See, for example, J. Scammell, "Robert I and the North of England," *EHR* 73(1958): 385–403; J. F. Willard, "The Scotch Raids and the

was largely pastoral, the ever present threat of losing cattle and sheep in Scottish raids lent a precariousness and uncertainty to life which other regions in England did not suffer. As a result, the jurors who were called to bear witness either for or against their fellows brought with them to the sessions of assize a host of sentiment with respect to criminal activity in their midst. It has been shown elsewhere that these men worked consciously and deliberately both to indict and, more seriously, to convict northerners who colluded in crime with the Scots.[13] The argument here is that, to a great extent, the experience engendered by the constant threat of deprivation is reflected, too, in their treatment of women accused of committing a range of felonious offenses.

The pattern of prosecution of females in the gaol delivery rolls of the border counties is instructive: about one woman appeared in court for every fifteen men. This is a considerably smaller ratio than that proposed by Hanawalt for the first half of the fourteenth century, but it is significantly higher than has been suggested elsewhere.[14] There are immense problems inherent in depending solely on gaol delivery rolls as accurate and complete records of criminal activity.[15] Even so, these figures suggest that, as elsewhere in England, women

Fourteenth-Century Taxation of Northern England," *University of Colorado Studies* 5(1907–1908): 237–42; K. M. Longley, "The Scottish Incursions of 1327: A Glimpse of the Aftermath (Wigton Church Accounts, 1328–9)," *Transactions of the Cumberland and Westmorland Antiquarian and Archaeological Society* new ser. 83(1983): 63–72; G. W. S. Barrow, "The Aftermath of War: Scotland and England in the Late Thirteenth and Early Fourteenth Centuries," *TRHS* 5th ser. 28(1978): 103–25; E. Miller, *War in the North: The Anglo-Scottish Wars of the Middle Ages* (Hull, 1960); I. Kershaw, "A Note on the Scots in the West Riding, 1318–1319," *Northern History* 17(1981): 231–39; A. J. L. Winchester, *Landscape and Society in Medieval Cumbria* (Edinburgh, 1987), pp. 44–47; J. A. Tuck, "War and Society in the Medieval North," *Northern History* 21(1985): 33–52; F. Musgrove, *The North of England: A History from Roman Times to the Present* (Oxford, 1990), pp. 126–29, 147–54; E. Miller, ed., *1348–1500*, vol. 3 of *The Agrarian History of England and Wales* (Cambridge, 1991), pp. 34–52.

13 C. J. Neville, "The Law of Treason in the English Border Counties in the Later Middle Ages," *Law and History Review* 9(1991): 1–30.

14 Hanawalt proposes a ratio of female indictments between 1:9 and 1:10, while Garay finds a ratio of 1:25. Bernard McLane suggests a ratio of between 3:10 and 4:10 in Lincolnshire. See Hanawalt, "The Female Felon," 254; idem, "Women Before the Law," 1:174; Garay, p. 89; B. L. McLane, "The Royal Courts and the Problem of Disorder in Lincolnshire, 1290–1341" (Ph.D. diss., University of Rochester, 1979), p. 96. Hanawalt and Garay, however, take into account only women brought to trial by formal indictment or appeal; their figures do not include women who were presented on suspicion of felony alone, against whom no formal accusations were laid. For the importance of neighborhood suspicion in the medieval English trial, see below, pp. 168–69, and Post, pp. 75–77.

15 B. L. McLane, "Juror Attitudes toward Local Disorder: The Evidence of the 1327 Lincolnshire Trailbaston Proceedings," in *Verdict According to Conscience*, pp. 50–51; J. S. Cockburn, "Early Modern Assize Records as Historical Evidence," *Journal of the Society of Archivists* 5(1974): 215–31; T. F. T. Plucknett, "A Commentary on the Indictments," in *Proceedings Before the Justices of the Peace in the Fourteenth and Fifteenth Centuries*, ed. B. H. Putnam (London, 1938), p. clix.

were not generally perceived by juries of presentment as deserving the same rigors of justice as were males. The options for otherwise pursuing and punishing their transgressions were numerous. Women might, for example, be charged with the lesser offense of trespass, and so be dealt with in a venue other than gaol delivery.[16] Moreover, at the village level there existed myriad ways of imposing sanction on nuisance makers, including village courts, traditional charivari ceremonies, and ecclesiastical tribunals.[17] Formal presentment before the awesome figure of a justice of assize was reserved only for those whose misdeeds were considered most disruptive or reprehensible and most deserving of punishment, and it is in this light that the figures for accused women in the northern counties should be interpreted. The numbers are telling: over a period of 160 years fewer than three hundred women appeared before the justices of gaol delivery in the border counties.

Of greater interest – and surely of a more trustworthy nature – are the sorts of offenses which women were accused of committing and the verdicts handed down with respect to their crimes. As elsewhere in England, theft of one sort or another predominated as the main item of business in the courts. Larceny accounted for almost 60 percent of the charges brought against women; burglary, an offense which combined theft with damage to property and one often committed under cover of night, made up another 15.5 percent. Robbery occurred only rarely,[18] a fact that may reflect, in indirect fashion, the tendency of northern travelers to move about the roads of the border region well-armed against potential Scottish enemies.

Studies of the types of goods stolen by thieves have suggested that the value of stolen items mattered less to medieval trial juries than did the circumstances under which they were carried off.[19] Cecilia, daughter of Christina Barre, was indicted and committed to trial for breaking into the abbot of Coxton's grange in Lancashire, even though she did not succeed in carrying anything away. But she was said to be "a common thief of geese, capons and hens." Although she was found not guilty, the justices permitted her to leave the sessions only after she had produced six manucaptors, who undertook to guarantee her good behavior.[20] Other editorial additions to the normally terse wording of indict-

---

16 McLane, "Juror Attitudes," pp. 38–39; B. A. Hanawalt, "Community Conflict and Social Control: Crime and Justice in the Ramsey Abbey Villages," *Medieval Studies* 39(1977): 404, 418; Bennett, *Women*, pp. 38–42.

17 See, for example, Jewell, 64–66; Bennett, *Women*, pp. 21–22. The effective use of church courts as venues for imposing communal sanction has yet to be evaluated by medievalists, but the subject has been extensively explored by historians of the early modern period, and their findings may, with due caution, be applied to the fourteenth and fifteenth centuries. See K. Wrightson and D. Levine, *Poverty and Piety in an English Village: Terling 1525–1700* (New York, 1979), pp. 110–41, and M. Ingram, *Church Courts, Sex and Marriage in England, 1570–1640* (Cambridge, 1987).

18 Only three allegations of robbery were made.

19 McLane, "Juror Attitudes," p. 51.

20 PRO, JUST 3/135, m. 6d (Lancashire, gaol delivery of 13 August 1345).

ments for larceny and burglary speak equally clearly to the reputation of women brought to trial for offenses that were not otherwise remarkable, either for their violence or the reward of their haul. Christina, the wife of William Florenson of Cumberland, for example, was "a common thief of geese and hens, and of wheat sheaves in the Autumn."[21] The disapproval of the community is even more evident in the presentment of women simply on suspicion of having committed felony, who were then required to appear before the justices without formal indictment or appeal. The circumstances under which these women were taken are not revealed in the brief wording of the record,[22] but ill fame may be inferred from entries such as the following, found in the gaoler's calendar for the delivery of Newcastle town gaol in 1441: "Maria Douse of Newcastle, spinster, was indicted because she is a common receiver of felons and thieves, and also because she is suspected of committing felonies both by day and by night."[23] No royal justice, least of all Thomas Fulthorp, who presided over these particular sessions, would submit such a vague charge to the full rigors of a trial, given the rigid rules governing the drafting of indictments which existed in the fifteenth century. Maria was released on his instructions and her name does not appear on the roll of that delivery.[24]

The women who were presented before the justices on suspicion of felony were alleged to have stolen goods of a particular sort: animals such as oxen, sheep and horses, which they probably intended to sell on local black markets (more particularly to the neighboring Scots) in order to supplement their family incomes, coined money, but also, very often, grain stuffs or barnyard fowl that were worth so little that they can only have been taken for purposes of consumption. The deprivation evinced by some of these thefts is striking.

On occasion, allegations of criminal activity on the part of both men and women can be attributed clearly to moments of particular tension in the political life of the border lands. In the Yorkshire rolls for the year 1320, for example, three men were indicted before the bailiff of Richmond for the theft of extraordinarily large numbers of animals and grain stuffs. These offenses

---

21 PRO, JUST 3/135, m. 9d (Carlisle, gaol delivery of 6 March 1344). In Yorkshire a woman known as Matilda the Strumpet was indicted for the theft of a ewe "and for other thefts." The second charge was unusually vague, but the woman's reputation is unambiguously revealed in her nickname. JUST 3/75, m. 7. Juliana of Hexham and Cecilia of Wetherby and their two male accomplices, of County Durham, were said in 1331 to be "common thieves, who regularly go from fair to fair stealing cloth and divers other things." Muniments of the Dean and Chapter, Durham Cathedral [DCD] Misc. Ch. 2640, m. 2d.

22 See, for example, PRO, JUST 3/169, m. 7 (Westmorland); JUST 3/211, m. 38 (Cumberland); JUST 3/208, m. 37d, JUST 3/211, m. 34d (Northumberland and Newcastle town gaols).

23 PRO, JUST 3/54/22, m. 5.

24 A. Luders et al., ed., *Statutes of the Realm*, 12 vols. (London, 1810–28), 2:171, 1 Hen V, st. 1, c. 5 (Statute of Additional Information). Two other women were similarly released from prison on this occasion; they, too, had been taken on suspicion of felony alone.

they were said to have disguised as depredations committed by enemy raiders "when the Scots were in those parts."[25] The Scots had, in fact, descended on Richmond in the summer of 1316.[26] Their raids did not merely furnish people with the opportunity to take advantage of disturbed local conditions in order to engage in criminal activities; they must also have provided strong incentives to those who had been deprived of their goods to replace animals and foodstuffs that had been carried off, and crops that had been burned. The dangerous threat posed by the Scots is vividly attested in the judicial records of the late Middle Ages. The northern gaol delivery rolls of the years 1315 to 1320 record a sudden flurry of indictments in which both men and women were accused of being "common spies for the Scots."[27] Ismania, wife of a man who bore the untimely name of John Scot, and her daughter Maud were indicted and gaoled "on suspicion of being common spies in England and enemies of the king on behalf of the Scots."[28] They were acquitted, but not until they had been required to submit to a jury trial for an offense that was not, strictly speaking, recognized at common law.

The inhabitants of the northernmost counties that were the more frequent targets of the Scots were intolerant of those in their midst who consorted with the enemy in order to turn profits for themselves. The rolls of Northumberland, Cumberland and Westmorland for the late medieval period abound in references to persons accused of this sort of activity, and conviction rates for such offenders were markedly higher than for people found guilty of committing common law felonies.[29] Women were not frequently the targets of these sorts of accusations. But when suspicions concerning their relations with known enemies began to mount, their neighbors did not hesitate to threaten them with the full rigors of the law, and to lay indictments against them with a view to making manifest communal mistrust. Emma Bewe of Newcastle was the target of this sort of suspicion. Two separate indictments were laid against her in the months leading up to her formal arraignment before justices of gaol delivery in the late summer of 1363. One of the charges alleged that, some twenty-three

25 PRO, JUST 3/75, m. 34.
26 The violence of the Scottish assault is vividly described by the Lanercost chronicler, whose own house experienced numerous attacks. See H. Maxwell, ed., *The Chronicle of Lanercost, 1272–1346* (Glasgow, 1913), p. 216. The border lands suffered further raids in 1317, 1318 and 1319. See H. T. Riley, ed., *Ypodigma Neustriae, a Thome Walsingham, quondam monacho monasterii S. Albani, conscriptum* (London, 1876), p. 252; H. T. Riley, ed., *Thomae Walsingham, quondam monachi S. Albani, historia anglicana*, 2 vols. (London, 1863–64), 1:155–56; E. M. Thompson, ed., *Adae Murimuth continuatio chronicarum. Robertus de Avesbury de gestis mirabilibus regis Edwardi Tertii* (London: 1889), p. 30; E. A. Bond, ed., *Chronica monasterii de Melsa, a fundatione usque ad annum 1396, auctore Thom de Burton, abbate*, 3 vols. (London, 1866–68), 2:333.
27 PRO, JUST 3/75, mm. 8d, 32, 34; JUST 3/76, mm. 31, 36; KB 27 236, m. 11 (Rex); KB 27/239, m. 87.
28 PRO, JUST 3/75, m. 8d.
29 Neville, pp. 13, 17.

years earlier, she had received John and Richard Wood, "traitors against the king," who had seized Robert de Isle and carried him off to Scotland, and there put him to ransom, "knowing of the said treason and sharing in the said ransom."[30] Emma's other alleged offenses were also of long standing,[31] and although she was never charged with doing anything other than receiving fugitive thieves, her reputation was apparently cause enough for her to be accused of committing what was by this time the most serious of offenses, treason.[32] Emma was able to avoid harsh punishment, but only because the persons named as principals in one indictment had died before she was arraigned and, in the case of the other indictment, the principal had refused to plead and had been committed to starvation in Newcastle gaol.

The 1380s witnessed a period of extreme tension in the border lands: in 1380, and again in 1383, the Scots descended in large numbers deep into Cumberland and Westmorland, and as far as Wark in Northumberland, leaving in their wake a terrible train of destruction and waste.[33] On the former occasion King Richard II's council forbade the warden of the marches to retaliate, hoping that diplomatic negotiations might settle matters with the enemy. A truce was duly concluded in 1381,[34] but was almost immediately broken, and by early 1384 formal war was again declared when John of Gaunt led a substantial English force into Scotland.[35] Relations with Scotland remained strained for the remainder of the decade, and it was not until 1389 that a lasting truce was achieved when the Scots were included in the Anglo-French treaty of peace.[36]

In the border lands the northerners settled down once again to a brief period of relatively undisturbed conditions. But they began, now, to look to those of their fellows whose activities had contributed to, or aggravated the ravages caused by, the Scots. The gaol deliveries of 1390 held in both Carlisle and Newcastle saw the trial of several individuals accused of consorting with the enemy, or of taking advantage of the troubled years of the 1380s to profit by

[30] PRO, JUST 3/145, m. 33.

[31] Two other incidents involving the reception of known thieves were said to have occurred in 1338 and 1358.

[32] Neville, pp. 7–8.

[33] *Chron. Walsingham*, 1:437–38, 446–47; 2:105; E. M. Thompson, ed., *Chronicon Angliae ab anno domini 1328 usque ad annum 1388, auctore monacho quodam Sancti Albani* (London 1874), pp. 269–70, 357; J. R. Lumby, ed., *Chronicon Henrici Knighton vel Cnithon monachi Leycestrensis*, 2 vols. (London, 1895), 2:203; C. Babington and J. R. Lumby, eds., *Polychronicon Ranulphi Higden monachi Cestrensis*, 9 vols. (London, 1865–66), 9:27; V. H. Galbraith, ed., *The Anonimalle Chronicle 1333 to 1381* (Manchester, 1970), p. 156.

[34] *Chron. Walsingham*, 2:41.

[35] *Chron. Angliae*, p. 358; *Chron. Walsingham*, 2:111–12.

[36] T. Rymer, ed., *Foedera, conventiones, litterae, etc.*, 10 vols. (The Hague, 1739–45), III. 4:39–42.

their attacks,[37] people whom their neighbors wished to see subjected to the onus of trial and the threat of severe punishment. Among them was Alice Emson of Holm in Cumberland. At sessions convened in August, 1390, the justices heard that she allegedly fired a signal "known as a beacon" when a force of Cumberland men set sail for Galloway preliminary to Gaunt's invasion of Scotland. She did so, it was said, in order to forewarn the king's enemies of their coming, "so that the Scots were prepared to resist their malice." The details included in the indictment are unusually fulsome; among other things, they note specifically that the fleet had been launched in retaliation for the depredations recently committed by the enemy. In fact, Alice's actions constituted no mere felony, but the much graver offense of treason.[38]

The Cumberland jurors returned a verdict of guilt against Alice Emson. At the prompting of the justices, however, they revealed that she had been born in the allegiance of the king of Scotland, and that she had never sworn allegiance either to the English Crown or its official representative in the north, the warden of the march. They claimed that for several years she had been living in the English marches, and that she had an English husband (now deceased), and English daughters. The jurors were prepared to overlook Alice's alien status at common law, as they had done with respect to another woman from Galloway on another occasion, sixty years before.[39] But Justices John Markham and Hugh Huls were compelled to observe the law, and they clearly considered the woman beyond the jurisdiction of their court. Alice Emson was remitted to the custody of the sheriff "until [the justices are] advised as to the judgment they should pass." She appeared once again before them when they next sat at Penrith the following year, when she was returned once more to gaol, and again the year after that. Finally, in 1392, her indictment was "carefully examined," as were the jurors' claims. Their findings with respect to her personal history were found to be accurate, and, in view of her alien status, the justices had no choice but to release her *sine die* (that is, with no obligation to return to a common law court to answer the charge). It is not known what ultimately happened to Alice Emson, though if she was wise she set about purchasing letters of denization or protection. Her accusers were denied the opportunity to see her subjected to the gruesome death of a convicted traitor, but must nevertheless have derived some satisfaction in the knowledge that she had languished in the dank gaol of Carlisle castle for more than two years.[40]

---

[37] PRO, JUST 3/176, mm. 20d, 21, 21d, 28.

[38] PRO, JUST 3/176, m. 28.

[39] See above, p. 163, and text at n. 2.

[40] Jurors' attitudes towards custodial imprisonment as a sanction against individuals whom a community considered deserving of some form of punishment are discussed in R. B. Pugh, *Imprisonment in Medieval England* (Cambridge, 1968), p. 388; J. G. Bellamy, *Crime and Public Order in England in the Later Middle Ages* (London, 1973), pp. 164–65; J. H. Langbein, "The Historical Origins of the Sanction of Imprisonment for Serious Crime," *Journal of Legal Studies* 5(1976): 38; and R. W. Ireland, "Theory and

The late 1420s witnessed another significant rise in indictments alleging collusion with the Scots. These were heard before justices of assize in Newcastle, and coincided with reports of the enemy's presence in the country.[41] The general unease felt in the town probably explains the curious and unusual indictment laid against two local men and a woman, who were taken and imprisoned "as persons suspected of the felony of theft, and because they are notorious night prowlers and slayers of vagabonds, doing no good."[42] The formal charge notes, however, that "nothing more specific is said against them." Not surprisingly, the suspects claimed that their indictment was insufficient in law, because it failed to accuse them of any particular felony. The justices agreed, and the three were released *sine die*.

The widespread expectation of acquittal for most felons at the stage of formal trial encouraged juries of presentment to make careful use of pretrial incarceration and the inconvenience of indictment itself as means of punishing trouble-makers in their midst. But even within the rigid rules that governed the return of a verdict of guilt at trial, there was room for maneuver and manipulation. Of particular interest here are the several occasions on which northern jurors convicted women of larceny, but then "found" that the goods they had stolen were valued at less than the 12 pence required to raise theft from mere trespass to the level of a felony. Historians familiar with the assize rolls of late medieval and early modern England have long been aware that rates of acquittal in the king's itinerant courts were always and everywhere high,[43] and the evidence of the northern records of the fourteenth and fifteenth centuries is consistent with their findings. Verdicts of guilt were handed down in only 6 per cent of the cases. Almost all the women represented by this figure committed some form of theft; either simple larceny or larceny combined with burglary. But only six were eventually hanged as felons. A few successfully claimed that they were pregnant and were remitted to gaol, whence they disappear. The others, however, were spared their lives because the trial juries purposefully devalued the goods they had stolen. Agnes de Wraton, for example, who appeared before justices of gaol delivery at Appleby in 1344, was acquitted of stealing 8 shillings of coined money from Agnes de Gaskill, but was found guilty of having taken a robe worth 10 pence from the same woman on the same

---

Practice within the Medieval English Prison," *American Journal of Legal History* 31(1987): 65.

41 PRO, JUST 3/199, mm. 17, 17d, 18, 18d, 20, 20d. The unstable political conditions of these years are reviewed in R. Griffiths, *The Reign of Henry VI* (Berkeley, 1981), pp. 155–57.

42 PRO, JUST 3/199, m. 20d.

43 See, for example, Hanawalt, *Crime and Conflict*, pp. 56–61; Green, *Verdict According to Conscience*, pp. 32, 59; Powell, pp. 100–105; McLane, "Juror Attitudes," pp. 56–62. For a discussion of the acquittal rates of women, see Hanawalt, "The Female Felon," p. 266, and Garay, p. 387.

occasion.[44] Two Cumberland women, said to be notorious in their respective neighborhoods as common thieves of barnyard fowl and wheat sheaves, and convicted for particular incidents of theft, were likewise spared the noose when the jurors specified that the value of their plunder was 3 pence and 4 pence respectively.[45] On at least one occasion another Cumberland jury demonstrated considerable ingenuity in its verdict that a man and woman had, indeed, stolen two bushels of wheat, but that they had carried off only one each, and that each bushel was worth no more than 10 pence. On the more serious charge that the couple on another occasion stole 40 shillings worth of goods in a burglary, the jury returned a verdict of acquittal.[46] The jurors stated clearly that the culprits should not be sentenced to hang "because of the smallness of the theft."

The relative rarity of this sort of jury behavior in the rolls that survive from the border counties does not obscure the crucial fact that juries could, and did, exercise a subtle but effective mitigation of the law of felony when they did not believe that suspects deserved to be hanged for their misdeeds. When the evidence of the Yorkshire rolls is taken into account, the incidence of this kind of jury behavior increases dramatically.

More interesting still, the Yorkshire trials show that in indictments in which both men and women were named as suspects, jurors not infrequently returned verdicts of guilt against the former, but acquitted the latter.[47] In the case of children, especially, juries were quite capable of tempering severity with compassion. At the delivery of York held in the spring of 1310, the jurors found that John, son of Agnes of Weldon, had stolen eight wheat sheaves, but, "because he does not deserve to forfeit life and limb for the theft," he was returned to prison for a brief period of incarceration.[48] When John de Butter-camb was found guilty of having stolen a horse, he too was remitted to gaol. He appeared a second time before the justices, now aged thirteen, to answer the charge afresh, but was acquitted "because the deed was done while he was under age."[49] Both jurors and justices clearly entertained some doubt about a child's ability to commit a felonious offense, and both felt that John's time in prison had been sufficient and condign punishment.

Circumstances of great poverty, then, as well as considerations of age, might

[44] PRO, JUST 3/135, m. 13.

[45] PRO, JUST 3/135, m. 9d.

[46] PRO, JUST 3/165A, m. 3. See also the trial of Juliana of Hexham and Cecilia of Wetherby and their male accomplices, noted above at n. 21. The jurors returned that all four were guilty of stealing items that were found in their possession, but noted carefully that "the value of said goods [8 pence] does not amount to the sum for which, by law, they should be hanged." DCD, Misc. Ch. 2640, m. 2d.

[47] See, for example, PRO, JUST 3/211, m. 1d (delivery of Yorkshire gaol, August 4, 1439), when William Watson was convicted on a charge of stealing seven cows, and sentenced to hang. His alleged accomplice, Johanna Gibson, was acquitted. See also KB 27/334, m. 43 (Rex); KB 27/322, m. 37 (Rex).

[48] PRO, JUST 3/74/3, m. 12.

[49] PRO, JUST 3/75, m. 37.

influence a jury's decision to bring down on suspects the severe penalties of death and forfeiture. So, too, were mitigating factors found in even the most serious of felonies, that of homicide.[50] But juries did not resort solely to recasting the events leading up to a violent affray so as to return verdicts of pardonable homicide. On occasion, they also made use of the plea of insanity to help explain unusual and tragic incidents of violence. Thus, at the delivery of Appleby gaol in September, 1342, the jurors found that Alice, daughter of John, killed her little son while she was in a state of madness, and that her actions had been those of an insane woman.[51] As occurred in these cases elsewhere in medieval England,[52] Alice was remitted to gaol "to await the king's grace."

The common law penalties of hanging and forfeiture of lands and goods were reserved for those who were perceived to have transgressed villages *mores* once too often, for those whose offenses were considered of the gravest sort, or for those who persisted in anti-social behavior even after repeated attempts by village communities to sanction them. As noted above, in the northern border lands verdicts of guilt were most often returned against women who had committed some form of theft. These women carried off a wide variety of goods, ranging from coined money, to ells of rough cloth, to animals. For the most part, they committed their crimes alone. But, as has been noted with respect to patterns of conviction elsewhere in England, there is a noticeable link between offenses that were brought to trial by means of appeal and the likelihood of conviction.[53] Moreover, persons caught with mainour – that is in possession of stolen goods – were more likely than not to be sentenced to death, unless they were able to disavow those goods.

Finally, jurors tended to lose patience with repeat offenders. One woman was given the death penalty when a Cumberland jury found her guilty of committing burglary and of stealing foodstuffs on four separate occasions in the span of a single month;[54] and this in a winter already made lean by the recent ravages of Scots and the heavy expense incurred in purchasing from them a respite from further depredations.[55] Her alleged accomplice on one of these occasions, a man, was acquitted. In Yorkshire, which was profoundly impoverished by Scottish raids in the years 1315 and 1316,[56] verdicts of guilt

---

50 Green, *Verdict*, passim.

51 PRO, JUST 3/135, m. 17d. See also KB 27/335, m. 17d and, by contrast, KB 27/355, m. 48d (Rex).

52 The fate of persons against whom verdicts of insanity were returned is discussed briefly in Hanawalt, *Crime and Conflict*, pp. 145–46, 149–50.

53 Powell, pp. 104–5. The link was earlier noted in Bellamy, pp. 125–31.

54 PRO, JUST 3/135, m. 3.

55 *Anonimalle Chron.*, p. 24; *Chron. Lanercost*, p. 322. A truce with the enemy was purchased for 300 marks, "so that within the boundaries of [the bishopric of Carlisle] and the surrounding countryside the Scots would refrain from burning or wasting vills, castles or hamlets, or from otherwise inflicting any other harm or hardship on them."

56 PRO, JUST 3/75, mm. 7, 9d, 26, 26d, 29, 30.

were returned against no fewer than seven women involved in the theft of animals and foodstuffs from neighbors who had already lost a great deal to the Scots, and who, moreover, were suffering the ravages of the Great Famine. Another surge in such convictions occurred in 1360 and 1361, when the north of England was visited by another wave of plague and food again ran short.[57]

While historians have long been familiar with the functions that medieval juries were required to perform at common law, they are beginning now to understand more fully how they actually exercised the judicial authority vested in them. In their capacities both as agents of arraignment and as participants in trials, juries made careful and deliberate use of the latitude inherent in their office to impose sanctions on women suspected of committing felonious offenses. That latitude was very broad, indeed: it ranged from the mere threat of indictment to forfeiture of a convicted woman's chattels and her life. Northern jurors were drawn from the same ranks as their fellows elsewhere in England, the lower levels of the gentry, who very often performed official duties in the region as tax collectors, coroners, escheators and the like.[58] They indicted and convicted women for the same sorts of reasons as jurors did elsewhere, reasons which historians are also now beginning to understand more clearly.[59] But as the inhabitants of a politically unstable and an impoverished region, these men were also profoundly influenced by the constant threat of devastation and deprivation represented by the proximity of a ferocious enemy. The unique experience of the late medieval northern border lands can be traced in the treatment that jurors meted out to women who were singled out by local opinion for aggravating already stressful conditions of life. The history of medieval jurors' attitudes towards their fellows, male and female, is one that is yet in the process of being written. But if an accurate history of such an ephemeral topic as human sentiment is, indeed, possible, it is one that must take into account the role of local conditions in shaping community experience.

---

[57] *Anonimalle Chron.*, p. 50; R. Lomas, "The Black Death in County Durham," *Journal of Medieval History* 15(1989): 137.

[58] The social and economic backgrounds of jurors are discussed in McLane, "Juror Attitudes," pp. 41–43; Post, p. 68; and Powell, pp. 88–97.

[59] For a review of recent scholarship on the role of jurors, see J. B. Post, "The Justice of Criminal Justice in Late-Fourteenth-Century Britain," *Criminal Justice History* 7(1986): 33–49.

PART FIVE

A Medieval Mystery

The Wreck of the *White Ship*:
A Mass Murder Revealed?

VICTORIA CHANDLER

"It was a dark and stormy night"[1] – well, it was dark – on 25 November 1120, when William, son of King Henry I of England (1100–1135), driven by the titanic pride of the young and the rich, coerced the captain of the *White Ship* to take it and its two to three hundred passengers and a drunken crew across the Channel from Barfleur, with the result that all were lost except for one who "escaped to bring you the news."[2] The story fits beautifully into the genre of shipwreck literature, with its morality tale about the evils of pride and excessive alcohol, its sole survivor, the grieving families, the mutability of life, even for kings. However, an examination of those who were known to have died on the *White Ship* suggests another genre, that of the murder mystery.[3] The story is

---

1   Research on this paper has been assisted by grants from the Georgia College Faculty
    Research and Development Committees. John Le Patourel, *The Norman Empire* (Ox-
    ford, 1976), p. 177, stated that most sources agreed that the night the *White Ship* sailed
    was calm.
2   Job 1: 15, 16, 17, 19 (RSV). Herman Melville, *Moby-Dick, or The Whale*, epilogue, had
    Ishmael use the translation, "And I only am escaped alone to tell thee." Orderic Vitalis,
    The Ecclesiastical History [OV], ed. and trans. Marjorie Chibnall, 6 vols. (Oxford,
    1969–80), 6:298, identified the survivor as Berold, a butcher from Rouen; see discussion
    in note 2. The main contemporary accounts of the shipwreck were OV, 6:294–306, who
    gave the number of about three hundred; Simeon of Durham, *Symeonis monachi opera
    omnia*, ed. Thomas Arnold, 2 vols., RS, 75 (London, 1882–85), 2:258–59, who gave the
    number two hundred; William of Malmesbury, *Willelmi Malmesbiriensis monachi de
    gestis regum Anglorum*, ed. William Stubbs, 2 vols., RS, 90–91 (London, 1887–89),
    2:496–98; *EHD*, 2:321–23; Henry of Huntingdon, *Henrici Huntendunensis historia
    Anglorum*, ed. Thomas Arnold, RS, 74 (London, 1879), pp. 242–43; Florence of
    Worcester, *Florentii Wigorniensis monachi chronicon ex chronicis*, ed. Benjamin
    Thorpe, 2 vols. (London, 1848–49), 2:74. On the subject of royal Channel crossings, see
    Le Patourel, pp. 163–72, 176–77, and Richard H. F. Lindemann, "Channel Crossings by
    English Royalty: 1066–1216" (Ph.D. diss., University of Virginia, 1981) especially pp.
    50–55 on the *White Ship*. A recent work on the classical sea-story motifs available to
    medieval chroniclers is Pamela Lee Thimmes, *Studies in the Biblical Sea-Storm Type-
    Scene: Convention and Invention* (San Francisco, 1992).
3   Ken Follett used the idea of the wreck as a murder scheme as a subplot in his book on
    the politics of cathedral building, *Pillars of the Earth* (London, 1989).

complete with suspects who had motives and opportunity, some with alibis and possible accomplices, and a good detective-reporter, the chronicler Orderic Vitalis. Was the wreck really an accident, or was the ship somehow directed toward the rock that tore it apart? This paper will examine the main suspects and their motives and suggest a possible mass-murderer who, along with an accomplice, arranged the whole thing.

William the Atheling, the only son of Henry I and Queen Matilda, must have felt very pleased with his life as he surveyed the crowds of family members, barons, household officers, soldiers and other courtiers waiting to embark for England from the port of Barfleur. Since birth he had been pampered and indulged by the doting king and had become notorious for his luxurious living.[4] His introduction into public life had begun early and had been stately and unhurried. In a life blotted only by the death of his mother two years before, William must have felt that he was favored by God. Here again, as he prepared to leave Normandy, he was very much getting his own way, receiving permission to sail on the *White Ship*, the best among the many ships gathered to transport the court to England. He had also surrounded himself with an ambient company of young and glittering nobles who shared with him the inclination to celebrate.[5]

The Atheling's comfort with having the Anglo-Norman world at his feet had begun probably as early as the first half of 1115, when King Henry arranged for the chief men of Normandy to do homage to the young boy, then aged about eleven.[6] Back in England on 6 September, William made his debut as a witness to one of his father's acts in council at Westminster, and appeared with him and with Queen Matilda at several subsequent occasions through the next spring.[7] In the same year, William received the homage and allegiance of the English.[8]

With his son safely received as overlord by the barons of both of his main territories, King Henry returned to Normandy in April 1116, on a military and diplomatic exercise that would keep him there for four-and-a-half years.[9] Back

---

4   Henry of Huntingdon, pp. 304–5. For an evaluation of William's character at this age, see Charlotte A. Newman, *The Anglo-Norman Nobility: The Second Generation* (Philadelphia, 1988), pp. 55–58.

5   All contemporary chroniclers emphasized the high rank of the passengers. By the time Roger of Wendover was writing in the early thirteenth century, the luxurious lives of those lost were interpreted as deviance and thus enabled Roger to consider the wreck as a kind of punishment. John A. Giles, ed., *Flowers of History*, 2 vols. (1849; repr. New York, 1968), 1:473.

6   *ASC*, s.a. 1115; Henry of Huntingdon, p. 239; Simeon of Durham, 2:258, confusing two events.

7   Calendared in Charles Johnson and H. A. Cronne, eds., *Regesta Regum Anglo-Normannorum, 1100–1135* [*RRAN*], 4 vols. (Oxford, 1956), 2: nos. 1091, 1092, 1098a, 1102, 1108 (a charter of Matilda's), 1131.

8   Florence of Worcester, 2:69.

9   William Farrer, *An Outline Itinerary of Henry I* (Oxford, 1920), nos. 371–406; *RRAN*, p. xxx.

home in England, William was able to stretch his wings a little at a time. He started issuing royal orders – mainly instructions to sheriffs – as early as the year of his father's departure and no later than 1118.[10] Although Queen Matilda may have been his main supervisor during this time, William's governor or tutor was Othuer fitz Count, the illegitimate son of Hugh of Avranches, Earl of Chester.[11] Othuer was also custodian of the Tower of London and was authorized to authenticate the king's orders.[12] His place in the Atheling's life must have increased in importance after the near-contemporaneous deaths of Queen Matilda and Robert, Count of Meulan, one of Henry's most trusted advisers.[13]

The year 1119 was the most important in the prince's life. He was called to Normandy to join his father and to marry Matilda, daughter of Fulk V, count of Anjou. The wedding took place in June at Lisieux.[14] About the same time he reached a kind of pinnacle when he was named "king-designate" (*rex designatus*), and was able to make his own monastic donations.[15] Henry, victorious in his recent wars on the Continent, was able to enforce this decision on King Louis VI (1108–1137), who was compelled to receive William's homage for Normandy.[16] William tarried in the duchy with his father until the decision was made to return to England in November, 1120.

The king's party had arrived in Barfleur by 21 November, where he met in council with some of his chief men.[17] A fleet had begun to assemble, and by

10 *RRAN*, nos. 1189–92, 1201–2, the last of which may be dated as early as 1115.
11 Othuer's career is discussed in detail in C. Warren Hollister, "The Misfortunes of the Mandevilles," *History* 58(1973): 18–28, esp. 21–24. For the role of royal tutor see Ralph V. Turner, "The Children of Anglo-Norman Royalty and their Upbringing," *Medieval Prosopography* 11:2(1990): 17–52, esp. pp. 26–27 for Othuer.
12 *RRAN*, nos. 1174–76, and the comments in Marjorie Chibnall, *The Empress Matilda: Queen Consort, Queen Mother and Lady of the English* (Oxford, 1992), p. 37.
13 Matilda died 1 May; *ASC*, s.a. 1118. Robert died 5 June; David Crouch, *The Beaumont Twins: The Roots and Branches of Power in the Twelfth Century* (Cambridge, 1986), pp. 3, 216–17; Sally N. Vaughn, *Anselm of Bec and Robert of Meulan: The Innocence of the Dove and the Wisdom of the Serpent* (Berkeley, 1987), pp. 359–61.
14 *ASC*, s.a. 1119; OV, 6:224; C. Warren Hollister, "War and Diplomacy in the Anglo-Norman World: The Reign of Henry I," *Anglo-Norman Studies* 5(1983): 72–87, esp. p. 82; Le Patourel, p. 187.
15 *Rex designatus*, in *Cartularium monasterii Sancti Johannis Baptiste de Colcestria*, ed. S. A. Moore, 2 vols. (London, 1897), 1:4–10, calendared in *RRAN*, no. 1223. A *notitia* of his and Henry's gifts to St. Maurice, Angers, is in *Cartulaire Noir de la Cathédrale d'Angers*, ed. C. Urseau (Paris, 1908), p. 168, no. 91, calendared in *RRAN*, no. 1204a. William also verified Henry's gifts to Tiron, with Othuer as a witness: Lucien Merlet, ed., *Cartulaire de l'abbaye de la Ste-Trinité de Tiron*, 2 vols. (Chartres, 1882–5), 1:41, calendared in *RRAN*, no. 1223.
16 Le Patourel, pp. 82, 187. The event was used in a dating clause in a charter in the Préaux cartulary Archives départementales de l'Eure, MS H 711, f. 119; abstracted in *Calendar of Documents Preserved in France, 918–1206*, ed. J. H. Round (London, 1899), no. 332, where Round gave the date as 1119.
17 William Dugdale, *Monasticon Anglicanum*, ed. John Caley et al., 6 vols. in 8 pts. (London: 1817–30), 6, pt. 2:1075, calendared in *RRAN*, no. 1233.

the end of the day on 25 November the wind became right for England.[18] Before setting sail, Henry had to deal with a great number of requests which he settled in a diplomatic and successful manner. One request came from a ship's captain, Thomas, the grandson of Airard, who had carried William of Normandy to conquer England in 1066, thereby winning for himself a small fief in Berkshire.[19] Thomas had brought his sleek new vessel, the *White Ship*, to Barfleur in response to the royal summons. He now offered it to the king, hoping for a reward similar to that which his grandfather had won. Although Henry had already committed himself to using another ship, he was able to take advantage of Thomas's offer on behalf of the newly-married crown prince.[20]

It suited William well to have the choicest ship in the fleet at his disposal. The chance to sail without the king's supervision must also have appealed to the young nobles who clustered around William and fell immediately into a celebratory mood. The sailors in Thomas's employ, who must have readily recognized the Atheling's inexperience, arrogance, impatience for adulthood, and wealth, played up to him, asking for wine.[21] Drink was immediately forthcoming, and both sailors and passengers began to indulge to extremes. Among the passengers were a handful whose decision to sail with William was much to be expected – his young relatives. Leading this group was his half-brother Richard, who had fought for Henry in numerous Norman encounters, including the definitive battle of Brémule, and who had recently become betrothed to Amicia, daughter of Ralph of Gael.[22] Also on board was William's half-sister Matilda, the wife of Rotrou III, count of Perche; two cousins (Stephen, count of Mortain, and his sister Matilda, countess of Chester) as well as a noble named Thierry, or Dietrich, who was a kinsman of the Emperor Henry V. The countess of Chester's 27-year-old husband, Earl Richard, was also present. Long a favorite of King Henry, who had enjoyed special royal protection since his father, Earl Hugh, had died in 1101, Richard was a regular

---

18 Lindemann, p. 62, gives Portsmouth; Le Patourel, p. 175, gives Southampton. On Barfleur as a port during the era in question, see John Le Patourel, "Le gouvernement d'Henri II Plantagenêt et la mer de la Manche," in *Recueil d'Études offert en hommage au Doyen Michel de Boüard*, 2 vols. (Caen, 1982), 2:323–33; Lucien Musset, "Les ports en Normandie du XIe au XIIIe siècle: esquisse d'histoire institutionnelle," in *Autour du pouvoir ducal normand, Xe–XIIe siècles*, ed. Lucien Musset, Jean-Marie Bouvris, and Jean-Marie Maillefer, Cahier des Annales de Normandie, 17 (Caen, 1985), pp. 113–28, esp. p. 120; and a popular history by Bernard Leblond, *Naufragés sous Barfleur* (Coutances, 1969), esp. pp. 15–22.

19 OV, 6:296. On Stephen see John A. Giles, ed., *Scriptores rerum gestarum Willelmi Conquestoris* (London, 1845), pp. 21, 211; *Domesday Book, Liber censualis vocatus Domesday-Book*, 2 vols. (London, 1783) Berkshire, 1 63c. It is possible that the "Stephen the Steersman" who had a house in Southampton of King William was the same man: idem., Hampshire 1:52b.

20 William of Malmesbury, 2:496–97.

21 OV, 6:296.

22 Ibid., 6:216, 220, 228, 236–38, 246–48.

member of the royal court and was presumably William's close friend.[23] The Atheling's female relatives were not the only noble women on board. There were as many as sixteen others.[24] Some may have come over for the prince's wedding; others may have been visiting husbands who were too long overseas.[25] Still others may have been making their first trip across the Channel.

If Henry entertained concerns about letting William travel on a different ship or about the inebriated state of the crew, he must have taken comfort in the knowledge that some of the men whom he ordered[26] to sail with William were reliable soldiers and government officials. The devoted Othuer was present, as were the chamberlain Rabel of Tancarville,[27] William Bigod, a royal steward,[28] and Gisulf, the royal scribe.[29] Barons who had proven themselves as soldiers in the wars in Normandy, including Gilbert of Exmes and Ralph the Red of Pont-Échanfray, were also along.[30] Even servants of God were on the passenger manifest: Bishop William of Coutances, the king's chaplain; Geoffrey, archdeacon of Hereford, and at least two monks from the abbey of Tiron.[31]

Conspicuously absent from the collection of glittering young nobles seeking passage on the *White Ship* were William's new wife, Matilda, and the pair known to later writers as the Beaumont twins – Waleran II, count of Meulan, and Robert II, earl of Leicester, the oldest sons of the recently-deceased Robert, count of Meulan. Contemporary chroniclers did not comment on Matilda's

---

23 Richard was at court as early as 1113, *RRAN*, no. 1014, and witnessed a charter with William by 1115. Ibid., nos. 1091, 1102, by which time he was married to Matilda: Richard C. Christie, ed., *Annales Cestriensis*, Record Society of Lancashire and Cheshire, 14 (Manchester, 1887), p. 18. For Richard's life see George E. Cokayne, *The Complete Peerage of England, Scotland, Ireland, Great Britain and the United Kingdom* [*CP*], ed. Vicary Gibbs et al., 13 vols. (London, 1910–59), 3:165–66, and his charters in Geoffrey Barraclough, *The Charters of the Anglo-Norman Earls of Chester*, Record Society of Lancashire and Cheshire, 126 (Manchester, 1988), pp. 12–19.

24 OV, 6:304.

25 Ibid., 2:218–20, reports an example of what could happen when husbands and wives were too long separated by the Channel.

26 Ibid., 6:296, said that many barons embarked with Henry's son "at the king's command."

27 *CP*, 10:53–54, app. F; Judith A. Green, *The Government of England under Henry I* (Cambridge, 1986), p. 275; John Le Patourel, *Normandy and England, 1066–1144* (Reading, 1971), pp. 37–38.

28 *CP*, 9:579; Green, pp. 235–36; I. J. Sanders, *English Baronies: A Study of their Origin and Descent, 1086–1327* (Oxford, 1960), p. 47.

29 *RRAN*, nos. 1363–64; J. H. Round, "Bernard the King's Scribe," *EHR* 14(1899): 417–30, esp. 418, 422–23.

30 OV, 6:41, no. 9; Crouch, pp. 107–11; Green, pp. 24–25, 149.

31 OV, 6:296; for the monks, 6:300; Florence of Worcester, 2:74. There is reason for the monks' presence there. Several abbeys of the Tironian reform had been founded in England in the decade before 1120: David Knowles and R. Neville Hadcock, *Medieval Religious Houses: England and Wales* (London, 1972), pp. 106–7. Also, William had recently issued a charter confirming his father's gifts to that house: *Cartulaire de Tiron*, 1:41.

absence, but her behavior after the events of that day suggests a possible explanation. The new bride may have been no more than twelve years old at the time of the wedding.[32] If the prince was more concerned with starting the next generation of kings, or perhaps with impressing his male associates, than he was with letting the young countess grow up a little, then it is possible that she preferred not to be in close quarters with William and his drunken friends and chose instead the safety of the king's ship.[33] In any case, while in England after the wreck and even after she returned to Anjou, she refused to go back on the marriage market, opting instead for the tranquility of the abbey of Fontevrault, of which she eventually became abbess.[34]

The absence of the Beaumonts from the *White Ship* can be explained in part by known facts but also allows room for conjecture. William must have known the twins, or at least known of their existence, for most of his life. Given the shortage of multiple births among the Anglo-Norman nobility, the Beaumonts must have been something of a curiosity, not the least because of the implications of their twinhood in an era working toward primogeniture.[35] Since their father, Count Robert, was frequently at court, William may have spent time playing with them as children, and could very well have found himself not being the center of attention when the twins were around.[36] After the death of their father, when they were about fourteen, they fell under King Henry's direct custodianship. They were with the king at Gisors in November 1119, showing off their education at a disputation with visiting cardinals.[37] The next year, probably as the treaties ending the war in Normandy were being concluded, the twins' minority was formally declared ended and each was allowed to assume his full titles and lands.[38]

Not to put too fine an edge on the issue, one may suspect that there was no love lost between William and the Beaumonts. For a young man who had been given almost every luxury his heart could desire from the earliest age, there could have been few things more grating than the existence of two adolescents

[32] OV, 6:330, although see also 6:302. William of Malmesbury said that she was "scarcely of marriageable age": 2:497–98.

[33] For a contemporary example of the traumatic effects of marrying too young, see Guibert of Nogent's description of his parents' marriage in John F. Benton, ed., *Self and Society in Medieval France: The Memoirs of Abbot Guibert of Nogent* (New York, 1970), pp. 63–68.

[34] OV, 6:330; Simeon of Durham, 2:267; William of Malmesbury, 2:498.

[35] Of all the cases of inheritance studied by Emily Zack Tabuteau in her immensely thorough article, "The Role of Law in the Succession to Normandy and England: 1087," *The Haskins Society Journal* 3(1991): 141–69, the Beaumonts are the only case of twins mentioned. Having studied so far about four thousand individuals from the Anglo-Norman period for a biographical dictionary, I have not to my recollection encountered any other multiple births among the Anglo-Norman nobility.

[36] Crouch, p. 7; Turner, pp. 26–27.

[37] William of Malmesbury, 2:482.

[38] Crouch, p. 7.

who, although younger than he, had three things which he did not: physical uniqueness, an attention-getting intelligence and an independent inheritance. However little their scholarship might have meant once they had adult responsibilities,[39] their possession of it could have been an aggravation to the Atheling, whose character was never described as studious and intellectual. What is more, despite the fact that his inheritance would some day be far greater than theirs, it had not yet materialized as theirs had. All together, it must have suited William very well that Robert, who had been at Barfleur since 21 November, had decided to sail with the king instead of joining his own company and that Waleran was apparently in Meulan taking care of local religious business at the time.[40]

Whatever the combination of circumstances, the *White Ship's* passenger list was now set. After the king's ship had departed and the wine consumption on shore had increased, the Atheling's company began to crowd aboard, joining the oarsmen and marines already in place. Once on the splendid vessel, some of them conceived of the plan of overtaking the king's vessel, which had already set sail. Captain Thomas, suffering from a susceptibility to flattery and to alcohol, agreed to the challenge. Before departure, however, several of the more judicious travelers, including the monks from Tiron, and at least one young nobleman, the royal cousin Stephen of Mortain, who might already have overindulged to the point of illness, disembarked.[41] Perhaps, in all the confusion, there was one man trapped aboard as a reluctant passenger – Berold, the butcher from Rouen, described as a rustic whose very presence among the high-born was an insult.[42] He might have come to Barfleur with the court as a food supplier and could have stayed to collect debts.[43] The rambunctious barons would have doubtless found it great fun to give the defenseless tradesman a free vacation across the Channel. However he came to be there, his presence was providential.

Having disdained the religious amenities usually attendant upon a ship's departure, the revelers set out into a dark night on a sea that was noteworthy for its calm. After the ship had maneuvered away from the dock and the fifty oarsmen had built up speed for several hundred yards, the vessel's progress was

---

[39] Ibid.; as Crouch put it, "the king had only a limited use for ornaments."

[40] *RRAN*, no. 1233, for Robert's name on the royal witness list. Crouch, pp. 8, 13; E. Houth, ed., *Recueil des chartes de Saint-Nicaise de Meulan* (Paris, 1924), pp. 4–5, for the re-dedication of the priory of St. Nicaise.

[41] OV, 6:296–98, 306.

[42] Orderic gives the name (OV, 6:298, 300), describing him as "the poorest of all"; see Chibnall's note, p. 298, n. 2. William of Malmesbury, 2:497, and Eadmer, *Historia novorum in Anglia*, ed. Martin Rule, RS, 81 (London, 1884), p. 289, called him a rustic (*agrestis, rusticus*); Florence of Worcester, 2:74, said the *rusticus* was "not worthy of being named."

[43] Simeon of Durham, 2:259; Wace, *Le Roman de Rou*, ed. Anthony J. Holden (Paris, 1970), lines 10190–10202.

violently and terminally impeded by impact with the granite outcropping now called Quilleboeuf, which was obscured by the still waters.[44] However much the crew tried to dislodge the ship from its port-side trap, it would not budge, and the water began to claim the lives of some who had fallen overboard and others who were caught inside the wreck. Finally a skiff was launched to take the Atheling to safety, but he ordered it returned in response to the cries of his half-sister, Countess Matilda of Perche. Once in range of the ship, the skiff was capsized by the desperate swimmers and all those aboard were lost.[45] As the sea continued to take its toll, two men clung to parts of the spar, waiting for rescue. The young soldier Geoffrey, the son of Gilbert of Laigle, slipped below the surface, but Berold the butcher, aided perhaps by the buoyancy and insulation provided by his rams' skin overgarment or by the extra layer of fat that accumulates on those who are well-fed and under-exercised, held on until morning, when he was rescued by fishermen.[46] Once he had recovered, the fortunate rustic told the tale that spread shock and sorrow throughout Normandy and England.

About a hundred miles south-east of Barfleur as the crow flies, the inhabitants of the abbey of St. Evroul must have heard the news within a few days. There were good reasons for the monks there to want as much information as possible about the disaster. Among the monks at the house at the time was Arnulf, or Arnold, of Tilleul, brother of Robert of Rhuddlan and uncle of William, one of the victims.[47] Other casualties included two brothers from the family of Grandmesnil, which had long been important to the abbey, as well as three other residents of the area – Hugh, son of William of Moulins-la-Marche, and Engenulf and Geoffrey, sons of Gilbert of Laigle.[48] The event was duly recorded in the annals of St. Evroul, a source that would be available to the Anglo-Norman monk Orderic Vitalis, who was shortly to commence writing a massive history of the nations of both England and Normandy.[49] The event,

---

[44] The figure for the oarsmen is from Simeon of Durham, 2:259. Details on the location of the wreck are from Le Patourel, *Norman Empire*, pp. 177–78.

[45] William of Malmesbury, 2:497.

[46] OV, 6:298–300.

[47] For Arnulf of Tilleul, see OV, 3:118, 226; 4:142; 6:322, 340 and n. 2. Robert and Arnulf's brother Roger was also a monk at St. Evroul: OV, 4:136, but I have not been able to determine whether or not he was living in 1120.

[48] For the abbey's relationship with the Grandmesnil family, see OV, vols. 2 and 3, passim, and Marjorie Chibnall, "Ecclesiastical Patronage and the Growth of Feudal Estates at the Time of the Norman Conquest," *Annales de Normandie* 8(1958): 103–118, esp. pp. 103–109. The victims were Ivo, son of Ivo of Grandmesnil, and a brother, OV, 6:18, 304. Vaughn, p. 361, gives the other brother's name as Hugh; Orderic gave no name. On the other families see OV, 1:86, 212; 3:132, and elsewhere; Emily Zack Tabuteau, "The Family of Moulins-la-Marche in the Eleventh Century," *Medieval Prosopography* 13:1(1992): 29–65.

[49] For the annals, see the edition of Orderic by Auguste Le Prévost, 5 vols. (Paris, 1838–55), 5:160. On Orderic, see Marjorie Chibnall, *The World of Orderic Vitalis* (Oxford, 1985).

coupled with the reactions of his community, had a profound effect on Orderic. When writing about the wreck years later, he not only composed a very full account, but also emphasized that he could give a truthful report because "the black deep swallowed none of my kindred."[50] It is this chronicler's lengthy tale which is crucial to sorting out the disaster as a possible mass murder.

In the classic manner of the murder mystery, the seeker of truth must pursue motive, means and opportunity. The one motivation that most of the likely suspects had in common was greed – for land, offices, power. Indeed, the list of people who profited by shifts in inheritance after the wreck is an impressive one, topped by Stephen, count of Mortain, the nephew and ultimate successor of Henry I, recently favored by the king with added lands and titles.[51]

Next is Robert II, earl of Leicester, who profited by the death of Richard, the illegitimate son of King Henry. Within a short time (probably in 1121), Robert married Richard's former fiancé, Amicia, daughter of Ralph of Gael, and became lord of the honor of Breteuil.[52] It was also useful to him that two brothers of the Grandmesnil family were drowned, since that meant two fewer people who might challenge his right to hold the lands which his father had acquired from Ivo of Grandmesnil in 1102.[53]

The most immediate beneficiary of the wreck was Ranulf Meschin, lord of Carlisle and Cumberland, *vicomte* of the Bessin, who acquired the earldom of Chester when Earl Richard died without an heir.[54] Although he surrendered some of his northern properties before being given the massive earldom, he gained tremendously in the bargain and became one of the masters of the midlands.

Two of Henry's other favorite officials gained from the disaster, although not so spectacularly or immediately. After a few years, Henry allowed William of Pont de l'Arche to marry Constance, heiress of the drowned chamberlain, Robert Mauduit.[55] William went on to become one of the king's most influen-

---

50 OV, 6:307.
51 R. H. C. Davis, *King Stephen, 1135–1154* (New York, 1990), p. 7. For other biographical notices of Stephen see H. A. Cronne, *The Reign of Stephen, 1135–54: Anarchy in England* (London, 1970); John T. Appleby, *The Troubled Reign of King Stephen* (New York, 1970), and Leslie Stephen and Sidney Lee, eds., *The Dictionary of National Biography* [*DNB*], 22 vols. (London, 1908–9), 18:1038–43.
52 On Robert of Leicester, see *DNB*, 2:66–67; *CP*, 6:452; 7:527–30. On Breteuil, see OV, 6:294; *CP*, 11:107, app. D. The marriage probably took place in 1121; Crouch, p. 14.
53 OV, 6:18–20; Crouch, pp. 90–91 and n. 140; Vaughn, pp. 238, 361; Levi Fox, "The Honour and Earldom of Leicester: Origins and Descent, 1066–1399," *EHR* 54(1939): 385–402; George W. Watson, "The Ancient Earls of Leicester," *The Genealogist* n.s. 10(1894): 1–16.
54 On Ranulf see *DNB*, 16:727–29; *CP*, 2:492; 3:116; Sanders, p. 32; David C. Douglas, "The Rise of Normandy," *Proceedings of the British Academy* 33(1947): 103–30, esp. p. 116.
55 Emma Mason, "The Mauduits and their Chamberlainship of the Exchequer," *Bulletin of the Institute of Historical Research* [*BIHR*], 49(1976): 1–23, esp. 2–3; idem, "The

tial servants. The king also granted custodianship over Geoffrey Ridel's son, Robert, to Richard Basset, who eventually married Geoffrey's daughter, Matilda, and obtained the Ridel inheritance when young Robert did not live to adulthood.[56]

Beyond these were numerous lesser beneficiaries. For example, Bernard, the king's scribe, acquired the lands of his colleague Gisulf; Hugh Bigod succeeded to his brother William's lands and, by 1123, to his stewardship; Walter of Salisbury's daughter, Hawise, eventually married Rotrou, count of Perche, whose wife Matilda, the king's illegitimate daughter, had drowned.[57] In addition to the names we know are the names we do not know, those whose fortunes shifted after the loss of a relative or a rival, but whose anonymity at the hands of the chroniclers must of necessity eliminate them from our list of suspects.

This preliminary examination of suspects concentrates on the motive of ambition. Unfortunately, there is insufficient information supplied by contemporary observers to allow for examination of other well-known motives for murder such as intense hatred, jealousy or lust. Were the Beaumont twins, already in possession of their inheritances, relentlessly tormented by the pampered but relatively powerless Prince William and his half-brother Richard, so much so that they decided to dispatch them to a watery grave? Did Count Rotrou of Perche have his eye on a better mate than a king's natural daughter? Since it is not possible to know these things, it will be more useful to refine the list of suspects on the basis of means and opportunity.

King, the Chamberlain and Southwick Priory," *BIHR* 53(1980): 1–10; Green, pp. 267–69; Le Patourel, *Normandy and England*, pp. 36–37; Davis, pp. 16–17, 73.

56 On Geoffrey Ridel, see *DNB*, 16:1160–61. On Richard Basset, idem, 1:1305–86; Green, pp. 231–33; William T. Reedy, "The First Two Bassets of Weldon," *Northamptonshire Past and Present* 4(1966–72): 241–45, 295–98, and idem, "Were Ralph and Richard Basset Really Chief Justiciars of England in the Reign of Henry I?" *The Twelfth Century*, *Acta* 2(1975): 74–103; *Basset Charters, c.1120 to 1250*, ed. William T. Reedy, Pipe Roll Society, vol. 88, new series, 50 (London, 1995). Henry I's charter settling Geoffrey Ridel's affairs is abstracted in *RRAN*, no. 1389; it is discussed and printed in F. M. Stenton, *The First Century of English Feudalism* (Oxford, 1961), pp. 34–36, 259–60, no 4, and translated on p. 35 and in *EHD*, p 998, no. 245. Richard also received the estates of Robert of Buci, the barony of Great Weldon, Northamptonshire; Sanders, p. 49. It is unknown how the Buci lands became available; one cannot help but wonder if he was one of the unnamed hundreds who died on the *White Ship*.

57 Round, "Bernard the King's Scribe"; Richard W. Southern, "The Place of Henry I in English History," *Proceedings of the British Academy* 47(1962): 127–70; idem, *Medieval Humanism and Other Studies* (New York, 1970), pp. 206–33, esp. pp. 225–27; Green, p. 235. For the Bigods see *CP*, 9:579–86; *DNB*, 2:484–86; *RRAN*, no. 1391 (where Hugh occurs as a steward, succeeding his brother); Green, pp. 235–36. For the marriage of Walter of Salisbury's daughter to Count Rotrou, see *CP*, 11:113, app. D. On Rotrou, see Oeillet des Murs, *Histoire des comtes du Perche de la famille des Rotrou de 943 à 1231* (1856; repr. Geneva, 1976). Kathleen Thompson is currently working on a doctoral thesis on the counts of Perche at the University of Sheffield.

Any discussion of means must address only one question: was it possible for anyone to cause the *White Ship* to strike the rock that sank it? Given the circumstances described by Orderic, plus what is known about ship design, the answer is yes. For one thing, the geographical setting was such that not much effort would be required to misdirect the ship. The rock was on the path to the English ports and was probably hard to see, if, in fact, it was not entirely under water, at the time the ship set out. For another thing, both the captain and the steersman were reported among the intoxicated. It would be an easy matter to distract the steersman and re-set the rudder. Further, assuming that the *White Ship* was like other ships of the time, the steering would be on the right ("steer board") side. Since the rock was on the port side at the time of the crash, it might not have been visible to even the soberest of sailors. It is, therefore, possible that a determined man with a minimum of knowledge could have set the vessel off course. However, even the most determined saboteur would want to make his escape. This could have been done by resorting to a skiff after the work was done. Since one chronicler reported the presence of one small boat on the *White Ship* – the one in which the prince initially departed – there could have been at least one more, given its large passenger capacity. A person with prior knowledge that disaster was on the way might have made good use of a dinghy, bobbing unobtrusively away from a catastrophe in the making.

Although motive could be attributed to any person whose situation advanced after the wreck, the method for causing it could only be used by someone on the scene. Thus, for the final determination of the murderer, it is necessary to examine opportunity: who was in a position to know who would be on the *White Ship* and that it would set sail in dangerous waters at a dangerous time, and who was in a position to do something about it?

Once again, Stephen, count of Mortain, rises to the top of the list. He was actually on the *White Ship* and was one of the handful who disembarked before it sailed, either from a disdain for the rambunctious behavior of the drunken passengers and crew or because of a bad case of diarrhea.[58] Two of the other prime suspects, Robert of Leicester and Ranulf Meschin, were in Barfleur on the fateful day and apparently sailed earlier with the fleet accompanying the king.[59] Thus, they knew who was left behind; however, was either one able to manipulate the situation on the shore before his own departure?

Before answering that question, it will be necessary to determine the intended victim or victims of the crime, and it is here suggested that William Atheling was *not* the target of the murderer, and consequently, Count Stephen was not the perpetrator. Stephen's main motive for killing the prince would have been a desire to move to the top of the line of succession. Numerous factors make it unlikely that Stephen could have hoped to win the throne after

---

[58] OV, 6:296 (to avoid the large and rowdy crowd), p. 306 (diarrhea).
[59] *RRAN*, no. 1233; Crouch, pp. 8, 13.

William's death. First among these was the fact that Henry I had proved himself to be prodigiously prolific in his production of children, and it seemed likely that he would have been able to provide England and Normandy with a male heir by the wife he had taken shortly before the shipwreck.[60] Also to be considered were the existence of Henry's daughter, the as yet childless Empress Matilda; of William Clito, an older nephew of Henry's whom many would give precedence over Stephen in the eventuality of the king's death without a son; of Stephen's older brother Theobald, count of Blois, and even of Henry's oldest natural son, Robert of Caen, who received the earldom of Gloucester soon after young William's death.[61] If William was not the primary target and Stephen is exonerated, who then *was* meant to sleep with the fishes?

A common thread connects several of the victims, a thread not immediately apparent without a study of their family ties. Matilda, daughter of Stephen, Count of Blois, and sister of Stephen of Mortain, was the wife of the previously mentioned victim, Richard, earl of Chester.[62] Othuer fitz Count, mentioned above as the prince's tutor, was an extremely favored individual in Henry's court. He was also the illegitimate son of Earl Hugh of Chester, thus a half-brother of Earl Richard. Geoffrey Ridel, a royal justice, was married to Geva, the illegitimate daughter of the same Earl Hugh.[63] Geoffrey and Engenulf Laigle were grand-nephews of Hugh. These brothers had been serving in the king's household troops, and Henry had even considered giving them their father Gilbert's English inheritance until their older brother Richer had rebelled in an attempt to attain that inheritance and had actually received it after being reconciled with Henry.[64] William, son of the great hero Robert of

---

[60] Chibnall, *Empress*, p. 37. Henry married Adeliza of Louvain before 2 February 1121: Henry of Huntingdon 243; *ASC*, s.a. 1121.

[61] Chibnall, *Empress*, p. 51; Sandy Burton Hicks, "The Impact of William Clito upon the Continental Policies of Henry I of England," *Viator* 10(1979): 1–21; OV, 6:368–70; C. W. David, *Robert Curthose, Duke of Normandy* (Cambridge MA, 1920), pp. 184–86; Robert B. Patterson, *Earldom of Gloucester Charters* (Oxford, 1973), p. 3, n. 3; J. H. Round, *Geoffrey de Mandeville* (London, 1892), pp. 420–36; *CP*, 5:683–86; *CP*, 11:106, app. D; *DNB*, 16:1242–44. Specific discussion on the succession crisis caused by William Atheling's death is in Davis, *King Stephen*, pp. 6–17; Chibnall, *Empress*, pp. 50–68; C. Warren Hollister, "The Anglo-Norman Succession Debate of 1126: Prelude to Stephen's Anarchy," *Journal of Medieval History* 1(1975): 19–41; Le Patourel, *Norman Empire*, pp. 187–90; Jane Martindale, "Succession and Politics in the Romance-speaking World, c.1000–1140," in *England and Her Neighbors, 1066–1453: Essays in Honour of Pierre Chaplais*, ed. Michael Jones and Malcolm Vale (London, 1989), pp. 19–41, esp. pp. 19–23; Karl Leyser, "The Anglo-Norman Succession, 1120–1125," *Anglo-Norman Studies* 13(1990): 225–41.

[62] OV, 6:304; *CP*, 3:165.

[63] On Geva, see William Farrer, *Honors and Knights' Fees*, 3 vols. (London, 1923–5), 2:269; Dugdale, 4:105; Christopher J. Holdsworth, ed., *Rufford Charters*, 4 vols., Thoroton Society Record Series, 29, 30, 32, 35 (Derry, Nottingham, 1972–81), 1:52; as well as references in n. 57, above.

[64] OV, 6:188, 250; Newman, p. 119.

CONNECTIONS OF CASUALTIES ON THE *WHITE SHIP* TO EARL HUGH OF CHESTER

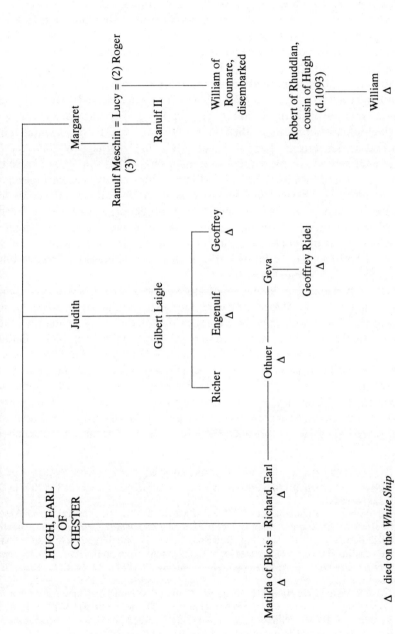

Δ   died on the *White Ship*

Rhuddlan, was going to England to receive his father's English estates. Robert of Rhuddlan was a cousin of Hugh of Chester.[65] After the wreck of the *White Ship*, then, not only was Earl Richard dead without an heir, but also gone were several relatives to whom all or parts of the Chester inheritance might have been given. The only likely heir left was the aforementioned nephew of Earl Hugh, Ranulf Meschin. However, if Ranulf left Barfleur with the king, how could he have arranged the "accident"?

Ranulf would have needed a co-conspirator on shore and he had a good one. Among those who, like Stephen of Mortain, disembarked before the ship sailed, was William of Roumare, son of Roger fitz Gerald and Lucy of Bolingbroke. After his father died during William's childhood, his mother had married as her third husband – Ranulf Meschin.[66] Perhaps William and his stepfather saw which passengers were boarding which ships that November day and realized they had a once-in-a-lifetime opportunity, a chance to acquire the earldom of Chester and, as a bonus, to confuse the royal succession, creating a situation for the future in which the holder of such a massive lordship could be a kingmaker. William, then in his mid-twenties, could look to a future in which he would control his mother's Lincolnshire-based barony, and his younger half-brother, the future Earl Ranulf II, would dominate large swathes of English and Norman territory.

This tidy package of an excess of motive and a sufficiency of opportunity needs only one element to make it complete, an agent on board who could have arranged for the rowers to be drunk and easily misdirected. The identity of this accomplice is provided, with extreme subtlety, by the chronicler Orderic Vitalis. Among those on his list of victims was William of Pirou, who was in fact alive until at least 1123.[67] How could Orderic have made such a mistake? Or was it a mistake? Could he have been trying to draw his readers' attention to Pirou? Was Pirou on board the ship when it set sail and found a way to leave it without detection? There is no evidence to suggest a motive for this man who had served King Henry to want to eliminate the heir or any of the others on

---

65 OV, 6:305 and 304, n. 2. On Robert of Rhuddlan, see OV, 4:112–13, 136–38, 140–42, 144–46; and Chibnall's suggested revision of his date of death from 1088 to 1093 in OV, 4:xxxiv–xxxviii.

66 For William of Roumare, see *CP*, 7:667–70; Fred A. Cazel Jr., "Norman and Wessex Charters of the Roumare Family," in *A Medieval Miscellany for Doris Mary Stenton*, ed. P. Barnes and C. F. Slade, Pipe Roll Society, n.s. 74, 36(1960): 77–88. A selection of the vast literature on the Countess Lucy includes John Brownbill, *CP*, 7:743–46, app. J; John H. Round, "Countess Lucy," *The Academy* 32(1887): 39; R. E. G. Kirk, "The Countess Lucy – Singular or Plural?" *The Genealogist* n.s. 5(1889): 60–75, 131–55, 163–73; Victoria Chandler, "Intimations of Authority: Notes on Three Anglo-Norman Countesses," *Indiana Social Studies Quarterly* 31, no. 1(1978): 5–17, esp. 8–10; Sanders, pp. 17–18. William Farrer mistakenly included her honor of Bolingbroke as part of the honor of Chester in vol. 2 of *Honors and Knights' Fees*.

67 *RRAN*, no. 1395. Green, p. 170, accepts Orderic's report of his death, with no explanation for the three royal charters for which he occurred as a witness after 1120.

board. However, there are two items of circumstantial evidence worth noting. When Ranulf Meschin appeared on a royal witness list as Earl of Chester for the first time, on about 7 January 1121, the list also included William of Pirou.[68] The two appeared as royal witnesses again in 1123, about 15 April.[69] William's last appearance was on the way to Normandy from Portsmouth, in early June, 1123. After this, he vanishes from history.[70] Did he vanish into the Channel after his role was discovered or suspected? Had he become careless in his words, making him dangerous to Ranulf and William of Roumare? Did his fellow steward and witness to that same Portsmouth charter, Hugh Bigod, come to believe that Pirou had been responsible for the death of his brother and take his opportunity for revenge while they were on the Channel? If Orderic knew, he was too circumspect to put anything in writing – except a survivor's name on the list of those drowned. He had over twenty years from the time of the event to go back and strike William of Pirou's name from the list of those lost,[71] but he never made the correction.

And so the crime was committed, and the conspirators could sit back and wait for their rewards. Ranulf Meschin was made Earl of Chester almost immediately, but there was a catch. He had to pay an enormous relief, which he must have expected, but he was also apparently required to surrender not only some of his own English lands but also some of the lands of the honor of Bolingbroke which William of Roumare had hoped to possess.[72] This was too much for William – to have taken such a great risk and apparently have succeeded, only to see his own part of the prize snatched from his grasp. He responded by fomenting rebellion, taking his fury out on the Normans around Neufmarché, and was not reconciled with the king until 1128, after suffering an illness which led him to get religion, and (coincidentally?) after the death of his potential overlord in Normandy, William Clito, that continental thorn in Henry's side.[73] As the years passed, however, William must have come to see that the effort to get Chester for his half-brother was worth the trouble. He eventually was named Earl of Cambridge, then of Lincoln, and he and Ranulf II became a formidable team during the civil wars under King Stephen (1135–1154).[74]

[68] *RRAN*, no. 1243.

[69] Ibid., no. 1391.

[70] Printed in *Ancient Charters, Royal and Private, prior to A.D. 1200*, ed. J. H. Round, Pipe Roll Society, 10 (London, 1888), no. 10, calendared in *RRAN*, no. 1395.

[71] Orderic was writing his history until 1141. OV, 6:xix. Although Chibnall notes that he was working on this section in 1138–1139, he mentions in the *White Ship* passage, 6:300, that Berold the butcher told his tale for another twenty years of his life, indicating that Orderic might indeed have come back to this section later on.

[72] *CP*, 3:166; Le Patourel, *Norman Empire*, p. 192.

[73] OV, 6:332–34, 380.

[74] J. H. Round, "King Stephen and the Earl of Chester," *EHR* 10(1895): 87–91; R. H. C. Davis, "King Stephen and the Earl of Chester Revised," *EHR* 75(1960): 654–60; and idem, *King Stephen*, passim, and pp. 161–65; Graeme White, "King Stephen, Duke

King Stephen? This reminds us of the other prime suspects. At the time of Henry's death in 1135, with William Clito gone, Stephen of Mortain was able to become king, over the claims of Henry's daughter Matilda, to whom the barons had been persuaded by Henry to swear allegiance, and in preference to his older brother Count Theobald (never, apparently, a serious candidate).[75] And what of Robert II, earl of Leicester? As mentioned before, he did marry Amicia, daughter of Ralph of Gael, the young woman formerly affianced to Richard the son of King Henry, and, with her, acquired the lordship of Breteuil. The Grandmesnil lands were not separated from the Leicester holdings. Further, he and his brother Waleran, count of Meulan, developed, like the Chester-Roumare brothers, an important partnership during the civil wars, in which they showed that uncanny ability of twins to mind different parts of the store at the same time.[76] The unrest in England seemed to suit them as well as it did Ranulf II and William.

How wonderfully convenient it is that the twelfth century has provided us with the very model of the modern murder mystery, even down to the final conclusion that the butler did it. Actually it was the steward, but there is no need to quibble. Probably the most intriguing aspect of the study is that, with the exception of a couple of points of conjecture and interpretation, the whole story is true.

Henry and Ranulf de Gernons, Earl of Chester," *EHR* 91(1976): 555–65; Henry A. Cronne, "Ranulf de Gernons, Earl of Chester, 1129–53," *TRHS* 4th ser. 20(1937): 103–34; Chibnall, *Empress*, pp. 105–13.

[75] Chibnall, *Empress*, pp. 51–52, 66; Davis, *King Stephen*, pp. 14–15.

[76] George H. White, "The Career of Waleran, Count of Meulan and Earl of Worcester (1104–66)," *TRHS* 4th ser. 17(1934): 19–48; Edmund King, "King Stephen and the Anglo-Norman Aristocracy," *History* 59(1974): 180–94, esp. 187–88; Davis, *King Stephen*, pp. 154–56; Crouch, pp. 96–98.

SELECT BIBLIOGRAPHY

Primary Sources

Ancient Charters, Royal and Private, prior to A.D. 1200, ed. J. H. Round. Pipe Roll Society, 10. London 1888.

Anglo-Saxon Chronicle, ed. Dorothy Whitelock, with David C. Douglas and Susie I. Tucker. London, 1961.

Anglo-Saxon Poetry, ed. and trans. Robert K. Gordon. 1927. Repr. London, 1982.

Anglo-Saxon Prose, ed. and trans. Michael Swanton. London, 1975.

Anglo-Saxon Wills, ed. and trans. Dorothy Whitelock. Cambridge, 1930.

Barrientos, Lope. *Refundición de la Cronica del Halconero*. Madrid, 1947.

Bede, *Ecclesiastical History of the English People*, ed. and trans. Bertram Colgrave and R. A. B. Mynors. Oxford, 1969.

Binué, Eulalia Rodón. *El lenguaje técnico del feudalismo en el siglo XI en Cataluña*. Barcelona, 1957.

Bracton on the Laws and Customs of England, ed. and trans. Samuel E. Thorne, 4 vols. Cambridge, Mass., and London, 1968–77.

Bracton's Note Book, ed. Frederick William Maitland. London, 1887.

Britton: The French Text Carefully Revised with an English Translation, Introduction and Notes, ed. Francis Morgan Nichols. Oxford, 1845.

Carillo de Huette, Pedro. *Cronica del Halconero de Juan II*. Madrid, 1946.

Carreter, Fernando Lázaro. *"Lazarillo de Tormes" en la Picaresca*. Barcelona, 1972.

The Charters of the Anglo-Norman Earls of Chester, ed. Geoffrey Barraclough. Record Society of Lancashire and Cheshire, 126. Manchester, 1988.

Collecção Chronologica da Legislação Portuguesa, ed. José Justino de Andrade e Silva, 10 vols. Lisbon, 1854–57.

Colección de los Cortes de los Antiguos Reinos de Aragón y de Valencia y del Principado de Cataluña, ed. Fidel Fita y Colomé and Bienvenido Oliver y Estreller, 27 vols. Madrid, 1896–1922.

Colección de fueros municipales y cartas pueblas de las reinos de Castilla, León, Corona de Aragon y Navarra, ed. Tomás Muñoz y Romero. Madrid, 1847.

Complete Peerage of England, Scotland, Ireland, Great Britain and the United Kingdom, ed. Vicary Gibbs et al., 13 vols. London, 1910–59.

Constitucions y Altres Drets de Catalunya Compilats en Vertut del Capitol de Cort lxxx II de las Corts per la S. C. Y. R. Senyor del Rey Don Philip IV, Nostre Senyor Celebradas en la Ciutat de Barcelona. Barcelona, 1704.

Coronel, Diego Gutierrez. *Historia Genealogica de la Casa de Mendoza*, ed. Angel Gonzalez Palencia. Cuenca, 1946.

Crónica de Alvaro de Luna. Madrid, 1940.

Crónica Latina de los Reyes de Castilla, ed. Maria Desamparados Cabanes Pecourt. Valencia, 1964.

Crown Pleas of the Wiltshire Eyre, 1249, ed. C. A. F. Meekings, Wiltshire Archaeological and Natural History Society, Records Branch. Gateshead On Tyne, 1961.

Curia Regis Rolls . . . Preserved in the Public Record Office. 17 vols. London, 1922–91.

D'Alessandri, Vicentio. *A Narrative of Italian Travels in Persia*, trans. Charles Gray, Hakluyt Society, ser. 1, 49. London, 1873.

Desclot, Bernat. *Chronicle of the Reign of King Pedro III of Aragon*, trans. F. L. Critchlow, 2 vols. Princeton, 1928.

Descobrimentos e Expansão Portugues, ed. Joao Martins da Silva Marques. Lisbon, 1988.

The Dictionary of National Biography, ed. Leslie Stephen and Sidney Lee, 22 vols. London, 1908–9.

La Documentación Pontificia hasta Inocencio III, 965–1216, MHV, 1. Rome, 1955.

Documentos das Chancelarias Reais . . . Vol. I and Vol. II (1450–1456), ed. Pedro de Azevedo. Lisbon, 1915–34.

Documentos de Jaime I de Aragón, ed. Ambrosio Huici Miranda and Maria Desamparados Cabanes Pecourt, 4 vols. Valencia, 1976–82.

Documentos Sobre os Portugueses em Moçambique e na Africa Central, 1497–1840, 9 vols. to date. Lisbon, 1962–.

Domesday Book, Liber censualis vocatus Domesday-Book, 2 vols. London, 1783.

The Earliest Lincolnshire Assize Rolls, A.D. 1202–1209, ed. Doris M. Stenton. Lincoln, 1926.

The Earliest Northamptonshire Assize Rolls, A.D. 1202 and 1203, ed. Doris Mary Stenton. London and Lincoln, 1930.

English Historical Documents, 1042–1189, ed. David C. Douglas and George W. Greenaway, 13 vols. New York, 1981.

España Sagrada. Teatro Geographico-Historico de la Iglesia de España: Origen, Divisiones, y Terminos de Todas Sus Provincias Antigüedades Traslaciónes y Estado en Todos los Dominios de España y Portugal, ed. Enrique Florez de Setien y Huidobro et al. 41 vols. Madrid, 1754–1879.

Fleta, ed. and trans. H. G. Richardson and G. O. Sayles, 2 vols. Selden Society, vols. 72, 79. London, 1955, 1972.

Florence of Worcester, *Florentii Wigorniensis Monachi Chronicon ex Chronicis*, ed. Benjamin Thorpe, 2 vols. London, 1848–49.

Fori Antiqui Valentiae, ed. Manuel Dualde Serrano. Madrid-Valencia, 1950–67.

El Fuero de Cuenca, ed. Rafael de Ureña y Smenjaud. Madrid, 1935.

El Fuero de Jaca, ed. Mauricio Mohlo. Zaragoza, 1964.

El Fuero de Sepúlveda, ed. Feliciano Callejas. Madrid, 1857.

El Fuero Latino de Teruel, ed. Jaime Caruana Gómez de Barreda. Teruel, 1974.

Los Fueros de Sepúlveda, ed. Emilio Saez. Segovia, 1953.

Gesta Comitum Barchinonensium. Textos Llatí i Català, ed. Louis Barrau-Dihigo and Jaume Massó Torrents. Crònique catalanes, 2. Barcelona, 1925.

Gracia Boix, Rafael. *Autos de fe y Causas de la Inquisición de Córdoba*. Cordoba, 1983.

Hemmingi Chartularium Ecclesiae Wigoriensis, ed. Thomas Hearne. Oxford, 1723.

Henry of Huntingdon, *Henrici Huntendunensis Historia Anglorum*, ed. Thomas Arnold, Rolls Series, 74. London, 1879.
The History of Feudalism, ed. David Herlihy. New York, 1970.
John of Salisbury, *Policraticus: The Statesman's Book*, trans. Murray E. Markland. New York, 1977.
The Laws of the Kings of England from Edmund to Henry I, ed. and trans. A. J. Robertson. 2 vols. Cambridge, 1968.
Liber de Antiquiis Legibus, seu Chronica Maiorum et Vicecomitum Londoniarum, ed. T. Stapleton. London, 1846.
Liber Feudorum Maior, ed. Francisco Miguel Rosell, 2 vols. Barcelona, 1945–47.
Libro de los Fueros de Castilla, ed. Galo Sánchez. Barcelona, 1981.
Llibre dels Quatre Senyals del General de Catalunya Continent Diverses Capitols de Corts, Ordinations, Declarations, Privilegis y Cartas Reales Fahents per lo dit General. Barcelona, 1634.
López de Ayala, Pedro. *Cronica del Rey Don Pedro Primero*, In *CRC*, 1, *BAE*, 66. 393–614.
Pedro López de Ayala, *Cronica del Rey Don Enrique Segundo de Castilla*, *CRC*, 2, *BAE*, 68. 1–64.
Marca Hispanica sive Limes Hispanicus, Hoc Est, Geographica et Historica Cataloniae, Ruscinonis, et Circumiacentium Populorum, comp. by Pierre de Marca; ed. Etienne Baluze F. Maguet. 1688. Repr. Barcelona, 1972.
Martorell, Joanot and Marti Joan de Galba. *Tirant lo Blanc*, trans. David H. Rosenthal. New York, 1984.
Medieval Legal Records Edited in Memory of C. A. F. Meekings, ed. R. F. Hunnisett and J. B. Post. London, 1978.
The Mirror of Justices, ed. and trans. Andrew Horne. 1642. Repr. Washington, DC, 1903.
Monumenta Missionaria Africana: Africa Occidental, ed. António Brásio, 15 vols. Lisbon, 1952–1988.
The 1235 Surrey Eyre, ed. C. A. F. Meekings. Castle Arch, Guildford, 1979.
Orderic Vitalis, *The Ecclesiastical History*, ed. and trans. Marjorie Chibnall, 6 vols. Oxford, 1969–80.
Placita Corone or La Corone Pledee Devant Justices, ed. and trans. J. M. Kaye. Selden Society Supplementary Series, 4. London, 1966.
Placitorum in Domo Capitulari Westmonasteriensi Asservatorum Abbreviatio Temporibus Regum Ricardi, Johannis, Henrici III, Edwardi I, Edwardi II. London, 1831.
Perez de Guzman, Fernan. *Generaciones y Semblanzas*. Buenos Aires, 1947.
Pleas of the Crown for the County of Gloucestershire . . . 1221, ed. F. W. Maitland. London, 1884.
Pleas before the King and his Justices, ed. and trans. Doris Mary Stenton. 4 vols. Selden Society, 67, 68, 83, 84. London, 1953–54, 1967.
The Political Songs of England: From the Reign of John to that of Edward II, ed. Thomas Wright. London, 1849.
Pulgar, Hernando del. *Claros Varones de Castilla*. Madrid, 1954.
Regesta Regum Anglo-Normannorum, 1100–1135, ed. Charles Johnson and H. A. Cronne, 4 vols. Oxford, 1956.
Register of Walter Bronescombe, 1257–80, Episcopal Registers of Exeter:

Bronescombe, Quivil, Bytton (1257–1307), ed. F. C. Hingeston-Randolph. London, 1889.

Rodulfi Glabri Historiarum Libri Quinque, ed. and trans. John France. Oxford, 1989.

The Roll and Writ File of the Berkshire Eyre of 1248, ed. M. T. Clanchy. Selden Society, 90. London, 1973.

The Roll of the Shropshire Eyre of 1256, ed. and trans. Alan Harding. Selden Society, 96. London, 1981.

Rolls of the Justices in Eyre . . . for Gloucestershire, Warwickshire, and Staffordshire, 1221, 1222, ed. Doris Mary Stenton. Selden Society, 53. London, 1940.

Rolls of the Justices in Eyre . . . for Yorkshire in 3 Henry III (1218–19), ed. Doris Mary Stenton. Selden Society, 56. London, 1934.

Rotuli Curiae Regis: Rolls and Records of the Court Held before the King's Justiciars or Justices, ed. Sir Francis Palgrave. 2 vols. Great Britain, 1835.

Rotuli Roberti Grosseteste, Episcopi Lincolniensis (1235–1253), ed. F. N. Davis. Horncastle, 1914.

Scriptores Rerum Gestarum Willelmi Conquestoris, ed. John A. Giles. London, 1845.

Select Pleas of the Crown, A.D. 1200–1225, ed. Frederick William Maitland. Selden Society, 1. 1888. Repr. London, 1955.

Simeon of Durham, *Symeonis Monachi Opera Omnia*, ed. Thomas Arnold, 2 vols. Rolls Series, 75. London, 1882–85.

Socarraris, Joannis de. *In Tractatum Petri Alberti Canonici Barchinonensis De Consuetudinibus Cataloniae inter Dominos & Vassalos*. Barcelona, 1551.

Statutes of the Realm, ed. A. Luders et al. 12 vols. London, 1810–28.

The Treatise on the Laws and Customs of England Commonly Called Glanvill, ed. and trans. G. D. G. Hall. 1965. Repr. Oxford, 1993.

Usatges de Barcelona. El Codí a Mitjan Segle XII, ed. Joan Bastardas. Barcelona, 1984.

Los Usatges de Barcelona i Commeracions de Pere Albert, ed. Josep Rovira i Ermengol Barcelona, 1933.

The Usatges of Barcelona. The Fundamental Law of Catalonia, trans. Donald J. Kagay Philadelphia, 1994.

The Visigothic Code, trans. Samuel Parsons Scott. Boston, 1910.

William of Malmesbury, *Willelmi Malmesbiriensis Monachi de Gestis Regum Anglorum*, ed. William Stubbs, 2 vols. Rolls Series, 90–91. London, 1887–89.

Secondary Sources

Abels, Richard P. *Lordship and Military Obligation in Anglo-Saxon England*. Berkeley, 1988.

Albuquerque, Luís de. *Astronomical Navigation*. Lisbon, 1988.

Appleby, John T. *The Troubled Reign of King Stephen*. New York, 1970.

Aylward, Edward T. *Martorell's Tirant lo Blanch: A Program for Military and Social Reform for Military and Social Reform in Fiftienth Century Christendom*, North Carolina Studies in the Romance Languages and Literatures, vol. 225. Chapel Hill NC, 1985.

Bachrach, Bernard. *Fulk Nerra, the Neo-Roman Consul, 987–1040*. Berkeley, 1993.

Balaguer, Victor. *Historia de Cataluña y de la Corona de Aragon, Escrita para Dar la a Conocer al Pueblo, Recordandole los Grandes Hechos de Sus Ascendientes en Virtud, Patriotismo y Armas y para Difundir entre Todas las Classes el Amor al Pais y la Memoria de Sus Glorias Pasadas*, 5 vols. Barcelona, 1861.

Bamford, Paul. *Fighting Ships and Prisons: The Mediterranean Galleys of Louis XIV* Minneapolis, 1973.

Bannassar, Bartolomé. *The Spanish Character. Attitudes and Mentalities from the Sixteenth to the Nineteenth Century*, trans. Benjamin Keen. Berkeley, 1979.

Barata, Oscar. *Cabo Verde, Guiné, São Tomé e Príncipe*. Lisbon, 1965.

Barber, Richard. *The Knight and Chivalry*. New York, 1970.

Beattie, J. M. "The Criminality of Women in Eighteenth-Century England." *Journal of Social History* 8(1974–75): 80–116.

———. *Crime and the Courts in England 1660–1800*. Princeton, 1986.

Bellaçois, François. *The Duel, Its Rise and Fall in Early Modern France*, ed. and trans. Trista Selous. New Haven CT, 1990.

Bellamy, J. G. *Crime and Public Order in England in the Later Middle Ages*. London, 1973.

Bentley-Duncan, T. *Atlantic Islands; Madeira, the Azores and the Cape Verdes in Seventeenth Century Commerce and Navigation*. Chicago, 1972.

Benton, John F., ed. *Self and Society in Medieval France: The Memoirs of Abbot Guibert of Nogent*. New York, 1970.

Binué, Eulalia Rodón. *El lenguaje técnico del feudalismo en el siglo XI en Cataluña*. Barcelona, 1957.

Birrell, Jean. "Common Rights in Medieval Forests." *Past and Present* 117(1987): 22–49.

Bisson, Thomas N. "Feudalism in Twelfth-Century Catalonia." In *Structures féodales et féodalisme dans l'occident et mediterranéen (Xe–XIIIe siècles)*, Colloque International Organisé par le Centre de la Recherche Scientifique et l'École Française de Rome, October 1978. Paris, 1983. 172–92.

Blake, John W. *West Africa: Quest for God and Gold, 1454–1578*. London, 1977.

Bloch, Marc. *Feudal Society*, trans. L. A. Manyon, 2 vols. 1961. Repr. Chicago, 1964.

Boase, Roger. *The Troubadour Revival: A Study of Social Change and Traditionalism in Late Medieval Spain*. London, 1978.

Bois, Guy. *The Transformation of the Year One Thousand*, trans. Jean Birrell. New York, 1992.

Bonnassie, Pierre. *La catalogue du milieu du Xe siècle à la fin du XIe siècle: croissance et mutations d'une société*. Toulouse, 1975.

———. *From Slavery to Feudalism in South-Western Europe*, trans. Jean Birrell. Cambridge, 1991.

Boxer, Charles R. *The Portuguese Seaborne Empire, 1415–1825*. London, 1977.

Brackett, John K. *Criminal Justice and Crime in Late Renaissance Florence, 1537–1609*. New York, 1992.

Brown, Bertram Wyatt. *Southern Honor: Ethics and Behavior in the Old South*. Oxford, 1982.

Brown, Peter. *The Cult of the Saints: Its Rise and Function in Latin Christianity.* Chicago, 1981.

Brucker, Gene. *Giovanni and Lusanna: Love and Marriage in Renaissance Florence.* Berkeley, 1986.

Bryson, Frederick R. *The Point of Honor in Sixteenth-Century Italy: An Aspect of the Life of the Gentleman.* New York, 1935.

———. *The Sixteenth-Century Italian Duel.* Chicago, 1938.

Bull, Marcus. *Knightly Piety and the Lay Response to the First Crusade in the Limousin and Gascony, c.970–c.1130.* Oxford, 1993.

Burke, Peter. *The Historical Anthropology of Early Modern Italy.* Cambridge, 1987.

——— with Roy Porter. *The Social History of Language.* Cambridge, 1982.

——— with Roy Porter. *Language, Self and Society: A Social History of Language.* Cambridge, 1991.

Burkhardt, Jacob. *The Civilization of the Renaissance in Italy.* 1929. Repr. New York, 1958.

Caetano Perreira e Sousa, Joaquim José. *Primeiras Linhas sobre o Processo Criminal.* Lisbon, 1827.

Callahan, Daniel. "Ademar of Chabannes and the Peace Council of Limoges of 1031." *Revue Benedictine* 101(1991): 32–49.

Cameron, Alan. *Circus Factions: Blues and Greens at Rome and Byzantium.* Oxford, 1976.

Caro Baroja, Julio. "Honour and Shame: A Historical Account of Several Conflicts," trans. R. Johnson. In *Honour and Shame: The Values of a Mediterranean Society,* ed. J. G. Peristiany. 1966. Repr. Chicago, 1974. 1–137.

Carreras i Candi, Francesch and Siegfried Bosch. "Desafiaments a Catalunya en el Segle XVI." *BRABLB* 16(1933–6): 39–64.

Carreter, Fernando Lázaro. *"Lazarillo de Tormes" en la Picaresca.* Barcelona, 1972.

Chardin, Sir John. *Voyages.* Amsterdam, 1711.

Chibnall, Marjorie. "Ecclesiastical Patronage and the Growth of Feudal Estates at the Time of the Norman Conquest." *Annales de Normandie* 8(1958): 103–118.

———. *The Empress Matilda: Queen Consort, Queen Mother and Lady of the English.* Oxford, 1992.

Cockburn, J. S., and T. A. Green, eds. *Twelve Good Men and True: The Criminal Trial Jury in England, 1200–1800.* Princeton, 1988.

Coronel, Diego Gutierrez. *Historia Genealogica de la Casa de Mendoza,* ed, Angel Gonzalez Palencia. Cuenca, 1946.

Cortesão, Armando. *History of Portuguese Cartography.* Lisbon, 1969.

Cowdrey, H. E. J. "The Peace and Truce of God in the Eleventh Century." *Past and Present* 46(1970): 42–67.

Cronne, H. A. *The Reign of Stephen, 1135–54: Anarchy in England.* London, 1970.

Crouch, David. *The Beaumont Twins: The Roots and Branches of Power in the Twelfth Century.* Cambridge, 1986.

David, C. W. *Robert Curthose, Duke of Normandy.* Cambridge MA, 1920.

Davie, Maurice R. *The Evolution of War: A Study of its Role in Early Societies.* New Haven CT, 1929.

Davis, Natalie Zemon. *Fiction in the Archives: Pardon Tales and their Tellers in Sixteenth Century France*. Stanford, 1987.

Davis, R. H. C. *King Stephen, 1135–1154*. New York, 1990.

Davis, Robert C. *The War of the Fists: Popular Culture and Public Violence in Late Renaissance Venice*. New York, 1994.

Defourneaux, Marcelin. *Daily Life in Spain in the Golden Age*, trans. Newton Branch. Stanford CA, 1970.

Devailly, Guy. *Le Berry du Xe au milieu du XIIIe siècle: étude politique, religieuse, sociale et economique*. Paris, 1973.

Deyermond, A. D. *Lazarillo de Tormes*. Madrid, 1909.

Diffie, Bailey W., and George D. Winius. *Foundations of the Portuguese Empire, 1415–1580*. Minneapolis, 1977.

Dillard, Heath. *Daughters of the Reconquest: Women in Castilian Town Society, 1100–1300*. Cambridge, 1984.

Duby, Georges. *The Chivalrous Society*, trans. Cynthia Postan. Berkeley, 1977.

——. *La Société aux XIe et XIIe siècles dans la région maçonnaise*. 1953. Repr. Paris, 1971.

——. *The Three Orders: Feudal Society Imagined*, trans. Arthur Goldhammer. Chicago, 1978.

Dugdale, William. *Monasticon Anglicanum*, ed. John Caley et al., 6 vols. in 8 pts. London, 1817–30.

Eibesfeldt, Irnaus Eibl. *The Biology of Peace and War: Men, Animals, and Aggression*, trans. Eric Mosbacher. New York, 1979.

Elkiss, T. H. "On Service to the Crown-Portuguese Overseas Expansion: A Neglected Aspect." *Journal of the American Portuguese Society*, 10:1(1976): 44–53.

Elliott, J. H. *The Revolt of the Catalans: A Study in the Decline of Spain (1598–1640)*. Cambridge, 1963.

Erdmann, Carl. *The Origin of the Idea of Crusade*, trans. Marshall W. Baldwin and Walter Goffart. Princeton, 1977.

Estanislau de Barros, Eugénio. *As Galés Portuguesas do Século XVI*. Lisbon, 1930.

Estow, Clara. *Pedro the Cruel of Castile, 1350–1369*. Leiden, 1995.

Farrer, William. *An Outline Itinerary of Henry I*. Oxford, 1920.

Ferguson, Arthur B. *The Chivalric Tradition in Renaissance England*. Washington, 1986.

——. *The Indian Summer of English Chivalry: Studies in the Decline and Transformation of Chivalric Idealism*. Durham NC, 1960.

Fichtenau, Heinrich. *Feudalism*, trans. Philip Grierson. 1961. Repr. New York, 1964.

——. *Living in the Tenth Century: Mentalities and Social Orders*, trans. Patrick J. Geary. Chicago, 1991.

Figueiredo, José Anastasio de. *Memorias de Litteratura Portugueza*, 8 vols. Lisbon, 1792.

Fishman, Joshua A. *The Sociology of Language: An Interdisciplinary Social Science Approach to Language in Society*. Rowley MA, 1972.

Fleming, Robin. "Monastic Lands and England's Defence in the Viking Age." *EHR* 100(1985): 249–65.

Floor, Willem M. "Guilds and Futuvvat in Iran." *Zeitschrift der deutschen morgenländischen Gesellschaft* 134(1984): 106–14

——. "The *Lutis*, a Social Phenomenon in Qajar Persia: A Reappraisal." *Die Welt des Islams* 13(1971): 103–20.

Frassetto, Michael. "The Art of Forgery: The Sermons of Ademar of Chabannes and the Cult of St. Martial of Limoges." *Comitatus* 26(1995): 11–26.

Freire de Oliveira, Eduardo. *Elementos para a História do Município de Lisboa*, 17 vols. Lisbon, 1882–1911.

Gama Barros, Henrique de. *História da Administração Pública em Portugal nos Séculos XII a XV*, 5 vols. Lisbon, 1947–54.

Ganshof, François Louis. *Frankish Institutions under Charlemagne*, trans. Bryce Lyon. Providence RI, 1968.

Garcia, Carlos Alberto. "A Ilha de S. Tomé como Centro Experimental do Comportamento do Luso nos Trópicos." *Studia* 19(1966): 209–21.

Garcia de Valdeavellano y Arcimus, Luis. *Curso de Historia de los Instituciones Españoles de los Origenes al Final de la Edad Media*. Madrid, 1968.

Garfield, Robert. *A History of São Tomé Island, 1470–1655: The Key to Guinea*. San Francisco, 1992.

Geary, Patrick. *Furta Sacra: Thefts of Relics in the Central Middle Ages*. Princeton, 1990.

Gilchrist, James P. *A Brief Display or the Origins and History of Ordeals, Trials by Battle and Chivalry or Honour and the Decision of Private Quarrels by Single Combat*. London, 1821.

Given, James Buchanan. *Society and Homicide in Thirteenth-Century England*. Stanford, 1977.

Grassotti, Hilda. "La ira regia en León y Castilla." In *Miscellanea de Estudios sobre Instituciones Castellano-Leonesas*. Bilbao, 1978. 3–132.

Green, Judith A. *The Government of England under Henry I*. Cambridge, 1986.

Green, Otis H. *Spain and the Western Tradition: The Castilian Mind in Literature from "El Cid" to Calderón*. 4 vols. Madison, 1968.

Green, T. A. "Societal Concepts of Criminal Liability for Homicide in Medieval England." *Speculum* 47(1972): 669–74.

——. *Verdict According to Conscience*. Chicago, 1985.

Hanawalt, Barbara A. *Crime and Conflict in English Communities: 1300–1348*. Cambridge MA, 1979.

——. "The Female Felon in Fourteenth-Century England." *Viator* 5(1974): 253–68.

Harnack, Adolf. *Militia Christi: The Christian Religion and the Military in the First Three Centuries*, trans. David McInnes Gracie. Philadelphia, 1981.

Head, Thomas. *Hagiography and the Cult of the Saints*. Cambridge, 1990.

—— with Richard Landes, eds. *The Peace of God: Social Violence and Religious Response in France around the Year 1000*. Ithaca NY, 1992.

Hein, Jeanne. "Early Portuguese Communication with Africans on the Sea Route to India." *Terrae Incognitae* 25(1993): 41–52.

Hicks, Sandy Burton. "The Impact of William Clito upon the Continental Policies of Henry I of England." *Viator* 10(1979): 1–21.

Hill, David. *An Atlas of Anglo-Saxon England*. Toronto, 1981.

Hilton, R. H. "The Origins of Robin Hood." *Past and Present* 17(1959): 22–49.

Hollister, C. Warren. "The Anglo-Norman Succession Debate of 1126: Prelude to Stephen's Anarchy." *Journal of Medieval History* 1(1975): 19–41.

Holt, J. C. "The Origins and Audience of the Ballads of Robin Hood." *Past and Present* 18(1960): 89–107.

Jacob, E. F. *Studies in the Period of Baronial Reform and Rebellion: 1258–1267.* Vol. 7 of *Oxford Studies in Social and Legal History,* ed. P. Vinogradoff, 7 vols. Oxford, 1925.

Jolliffe, J. E. A. *The Constitutional History of Medieval England: From the English Settlement to 1485.* New York, 1961.

Johnson, Charles. "Notes on Thirteenth-Century Judicial Procedure." *EHR* 67(1947): 508–11.

Jones, C. A. "Honour in Golden Age Drama: Its Relation to Real Life and to Morals." *Bulletin of Hispanic Studies* 35–36(1958–59): 199–210.

Kaempfer, Engelbert. *Am Hofe des persischen Grosskönigs,* ed. W. Hinz. Leipzig, 1940.

Kamen, Henry. *Spain, 1468–1714.* London, 1991.

Keen, Maurice. *Chivalry.* New Haven CT, 1989.

———. "Robin Hood: Peasant or Gentleman?" *Past and Present* 19(1961): 7–15.

Kennelly, Karen. "Catalan Peace and Truce Assemblies." *Studies in Culture* 5(1975): 41–52.

Kermode J., and G. Walker, eds. *Women, Crime and the Courts in Early Modern England.* Chapel Hill NC, 1994.

Keynes, Simon, and Michael Lapidge, trans. *Alfred the Great: Asser's Life of King Alfred and Other Contemporary Sources.* London, 1983.

Keyvani, Mehdi. *Artisans and Guild Life in the Later Safavid Period.* Berlin, 1982.

Kiernan, Victor. *The Duel.* Oxford, 1986.

King, Edmund. "King Stephen and the Anglo-Norman Aristocracy." *History* 59(1974): 180–94.

King, P. D. *Law and Society in the Visigothic Kingdom.* Cambridge, 1972.

Knowles, David. *The Monastic Order in England.* Cambridge, 1963.

——— with R. Neville Hadcock, eds. *Medieval Religious Houses: England and Wales.* London, 1972.

——— and R. Neville Hadcock. *Medieval Religious Houses in England and Wales.* London, 1953.

Koziol, Geoffrey. *Begging Pardon and Favor: Ritual and Political Order in Early Medieval France.* Ithaca NY, 1992.

Krusinski, Tadeusz Judasz. *The History of the Late Revolutions of Persia,* 2 vols. London, 1750.

Kuehn, Thomas. "Reading Microhistory: The Example of Giovanni and Lusanna." *Journal of Modern History* 61(1989): 512–34.

Larner, John. *The Lords of Romagna. Romagnol Society and the Origins of the Signorie.* New York, 1965.

———. "Order and Disorder in Romagna, 1450–1500." In *Violence and Civil Disorder in Italian Cities,* ed. Lauro Martines. Berkeley, 1972. 39–71.

Lea, Henry Charles. *Superstition and Force.* Philadelphia, 1866. Pts. 1–2. Reprinted as *The Duel and the Oath,* ed. Edward Peters. Philadelphia, 1974.

Leblond, Bernard. *Naufragés sous Barfleur.* Coutances, 1969.

Le Patourel, John. "Le gouvernement de Henri II Plantagenêt et la mer de la

Manche." In *Recueil d'études offert en hommage au doyen Michel de Boüard*, 2 vols. Caen, 1982. 2:323–33.

———. *The Norman Empire*. Oxford, 1976.

Leyser, Karl. "The Anglo-Norman Succession, 1120–1125." *Anglo-Norman Studies* 13(1990): 225–41.

Lomax, Derek W. *La Orden de Santiago (1179–1275)*. Madrid, 1965.

MacKinney, Loren C. "The People and Public Opinion in the Eleventh-Century Peace Movement." *Speculum* 5(1930): 181–206.

Magalhães Godinho, Vitorino. *A Economia dos Descobrimentos Henriquinos*. Lisbon, 1962.

———. *História Económica e Social da Expansão Portuguesa*. Lisbon, 1947.

Magnou-Nortier, Elizabeth. *La société laïque et l'église dans la province écclésiastique de Narbonne de la fin du VIIIe siècle à la fin du XIIe siècle*. Toulouse, 1974.

Malcolm, Sir John. *A History of Persia*. 2 vols. London, 1829.

Martindale, Jane. "Succession and Politics in the Romance-speaking World, c.1000–1140." In *England and her Neighbors, 1066–1453: Essays in Honour of Pierre Chaplais*, ed. Michael Jones and Malcolm Vale. London, 1989. 19–41.

Mascarenhas, Jeronimo de. *História de la Cuidad de Ceuta*. Lisbon, 1915.

Mason, Emma. "The King, the Chamberlain and Southwick Priory." *BIHR* 53(1980): 1–10.

———. "The Mauduits and their Chamberlainship of the Exchequer." *BIHR* 49(1976): 1–23.

Meintel, Deirdre. *Race, Culture, and Portuguese Colonialism in Cabo Verde*. Syracuse NY, 1984.

Manescal, Honofre. *Sermo Vulgarament Anomenat del Serenissim Senyor Don Jaume Segon*. Barcelona, 1603.

Miller, E. *War in the North: The Anglo-Scottish Wars of the Middle Ages*. Hull, 1960.

Moorman, J. R. H. *Church Life in England in the Thirteenth-Century*. Cambridge, 1955.

Muir, Edward. *Mad Blood Stirring. Vendetta and Faction in Friuli during the Renaissance*. Baltimore, 1993.

Muñido, Francisco-Filipe Olesa. *La Organización Naval de los Estados Mediterráneos y en Especial España durante los Siglos XVI y XVII*. 2 vols. Madrid, 1968.

Musset, Lucien. "Les ports en Normandie du XIe au XIIIe siècle: esquisse d'histoire institionnelle." In *Autour du pouvoir sucal normand, Xe–XIIe siècles*, ed. Lucien Musset, Jean-Marie Bouvris, and Jean-Marie Maillefer. Cahiers des Annales de Normandie, 17. Caen, 1985. 113–28.

Nader, Helen. *The Mendoza in the Spanish Renaissance*. Rutgers NJ, 1979.

Nelson, George. *Trial by Combat*. New York, 1891.

Neville, C. J. "The Law of Treason in the English Border Counties in the Later Middle Ages," *Law and History Review* 9(1991): 1–30.

Newman, Charlotte A. *The Anglo-Norman Nobility: The Second Generation*. Philadelphia, 1988.

Noel, Eugenio. *Escritos Antitaurinos*, ed. Eugenio Muñoz Mesonero. Temas de España, 59. Madrid, 1967.

Oliveira Marques, A. H. de. *História de Portugal*, 2 vols. Lisbon, 1978.

————. *Introdução à História da Agricultura em Portugal: A Questão Cerealífera durante a Idade Média*. Lisbon, 1978.

Ong, Walter. *Orality and Literacy: The Technologizing of the Word*. London, 1982.

Painter, Sidney. *Feudalism and Liberty*, ed. Fred A. Cazel Jr. Baltimore, 1961.

Peres, Damião. *História dos Descobrimentos Portugueses*. 1959. Repr. Oporto, 1982.

Perroy, Eduard. *The Hundred Years War*, trans. W. B. Wells. New York, 1965.

Pollock, Frederick, and Frederic William Maitland. *The History of English Law before the Time of Edward I*. 2 vols. Cambridge, 1968.

Poly, Jean Pierre, and Eric Bournazel. *The Feudal Transformation, 900–1200*, trans. Caroline Higgitt. New York, 1991.

Powell, Edward. "Social Research and the Use of Medieval Criminal Records." *Michigan Law Review* 79(1981): 967–78.

Powicke, Maurice. *King Henry III and the Lord Edward*, 2 vols. Oxford, 1947.

————. *The Thirteenth Century*. Oxford, 1962.

Pugh, R. B. "The Duration of Criminal Trials in Medieval England." In *Law, Litigants and the Legal Profession*, ed. E. W. Ives and A. H. Manchester. London, 1983. 104–10.

————. *Imprisonment in Medieval England*. Cambridge, 1968.

Reilly, Bernard F. *The Kingdom of León-Castilla under King Alfonso VI, 1065–1109*. Princeton, 1988.

————. *The Kingdom of León-Castilla under Queen Urraca, 1109–1126*. Princeton, 1982.

Reynolds, Susan. *Fiefs and Vassals: The Medieval Evidence Reinterpreted*. Oxford, 1994.

Ribeiro, Orlando. *Aspectos e Problems da Expansão Portuguesa*. Lisbon, 1962.

Rivera Garretas, Milagros. *La encomienda, el priorato y la villa de Uclés en la Edad Media: Formación de un señorio de la Orden de Santiago*. Madrid, 1985.

Rohrkasten, Jens. *Die englischen Krazeugen, 1130–1330*. Berliner historishe Studien, 16. Berlin, 1990.

Round, J. H. "Bernard the King's Scribe." *EHR* 14(1899): 417–30.

———— *Geoffrey de Mandeville*. London, 1892.

Ruggiero, Guido. *Violence in Early Renaissance Venice*. New Brunswick NJ, 1980.

Russell, P. E. "Galés Portugueses ao Serviço de Ricardo II de Inglaterra (1385–89)." *Revista de Letras* 2nd ser. 28(1953): 61–73.

Salazar y Castro, Luis. *Historia Genealogica de la Casa de Lara*, 4 vols. Madrid, 1694–97.

Saunders, A. C. de C. M. *A Social History of Black Slaves and Freedmen in Portugal*. Cambridge, 1982.

Seitz, Don C. *Famous American Duels*. New York, 1929.

Sieber, Henry. *Language and Society in "La Vida de Lazarillo de Tormes."* Baltimore, 1978.

Silva Telles, Francisco Xavier de. *A Transportação Penal e a Colonização*. Lisbon, 1903.

Spierenburg, Pieter. *The Prison Experience: Disciplinary Institutions and their Inmates in Early Modern Europe*. New Brunswick NJ, 1991.

Sutherland, Donald W. "Mesne Process upon Personal Actions in the Early Common Law." *Law Quarterly Review* 82(1966): 482–90.

Stenton, Frank M. *Anglo-Saxon England*. Oxford, 1971.

Stubbs, William. *The Constitutional History of England and its Origin and Development*. 3 vols. Oxford, 1874.

Symonds, J. A. *A Short History of the Renaissance in Italy*, ed. A. Pearson. New York, 1926.

Tavernier, Jean Baptiste. *Les six voyages*. Paris, 1677.

Teixeira da Mota, A. *Mar Além Mar: Estudos e Ensaios de História e Geografia*. Lisbon, 1972.

————. *Some Aspects of Portuguese Colonization and Sea Trade in West Africa in the Fifteenth and Sixteenth Centuries*. Bloomington IN, 1978.

Thimmes, Pamela Lee. *Studies in the Biblical Sea-Storm-Type Scene: Convention and Invention*. San Francisco, 1992.

Tout, T. F. *Chapters in the Administrative History of Medieval England*. 6 vols. 1920. Repr. Manchester, 1967.

Treharne, R. F. *The Baronial Plan of Reform, 1258–1263*. Manchester, 1932.

————. "The Personal Role of Simon de Montfort in the Period of Baronial Reform and Rebellion, 1258–1265." *Proceedings of the British Academy* 40(1955): 75–102.

————. "The Significance of the Baronial Reform Movement." *TRHS* 4th ser. 25(1943): 35–72.

————. *Simon de Montfort and Baronial Reform*. Rio Grande OH, 1986.

Tuck, J. A. "War and Society in the Medieval North." *Northern History* 21(1985): 33–52.

Turner, Ralph V. "The Children of Anglo-Norman Royalty and their Upbringing." *Medieval Prosopography* 11(1990): 17–52.

Ullmann, Walter. *The Individual and Society in the Middle Ages*. Baltimore, 1966.

Vaigts, Alfred. *A History of Militarism*. 1937. Repr. New York, 1959.

Valle, Pietro della. *Voyages dans la Turquie, l'Egypte, la Palestine, la Perse, les Indes Orientales et autres lieux*, 6 vols. Rouen, 1712–1745.

Van Dam, Raymond. *Saints and their Miracles in Late Antique Gaul*. Princeton, 1993.

van Dülmen, Richard. *Theatre of Horror: Crime and Punishment in Early Modern Germany*, trans. Elisabeth Neu. Cambridge, 1990.

Vaughn, Sally N. *Anselm of Bec and Robert of Meulan: The Innocence of the Dove and the Wisdom of the Serpent*. Berkeley, 1987.

Verlinden, Charles. *The Beginnings of Modern Colonization*, trans. Yvonne Freccero. Ithaca NY, 1970.

Vitoria, Francisco. *De Indis e de Jure Belli Relectiones*, trans. John Pawley Bate. The Classics of International Law, 7. Washington, 1971.

Wallace-Hadrill, J. M. *The Frankish Church*. Oxford, 1983.

Watson, Robert Grant. *A History of Persia from the Beginnings of the Seventeenth Century*. London, 1866.

GLOSSARY

Affidamentum Establishment of feudal ties.

Amercement A money penalty assessed for some infringement of court procedure. In theory the offender was "in the king's mercy" and could have all his or her goods seized. In practice, an amercement was usually a routine payment of a moderate amount, often a half mark. To be **amerced**: to be assessed such a penalty.

Appeal Criminal charges brought to the court by a private individual concerning a crime done to him or her, or in the case of homicide, brought by someone bound to the victim by a very near relationship, a close relative, lord, or vassal. **Appellor**: person who brought an appeal (accuser) **Appellee**: the appealed person (accused).

Battle (Batallia, Torna) A form of proof consisting of a regulated and supervised battle between the appellor and appellee: also called the judicial duel.

Concord An agreement worked out between the parties to a lawsuit or appeal by which the dispute was settled.

Convenientia A feudal pact specifying the duties and rights of lord and vassal.

Consilium The offense of acting as an accessory to a crime by advising or encouraging the perpetrator or planning or directing the crime.

County court A royal court nominally presided over by the sheriff and held on a regular basis, often every four to six weeks.

Denization Admittance of a person or thing to the full protection of the law.

Diffidamentum A formal rupture of feudal ties between vassal and lord.

Duellum A judicial duel similar to the battle.

Ecclesiastical jurisdiction Matters of persons within the competence of church courts, such as clergy who were accused of crimes.

Exception A reason given by a defendant why a civil action or criminal appeal should not proceed; an example would be the assertion that an accusation was based, not on an actual offense, but because of hatred and malice (*odio et atia*). Once the objection was raised a jury was consulted on its veracity; if the exception was upheld the appeal was quashed.

Eyre An itinerant division of the royal courts of justice. Royal justices commissioned to travel through the kingdom on a more or less regular basis and hold court sessions, usually pre-empting the meeting and personnel of the county court, about matters concerning the king or legal causes that fell within his jurisdiction.

Frankpledge The system by which every freeborn male twelve or over, with certain exceptions (see **mainpast**, below), was to be in a group called a **tithing**, which was obligated to produce that individual when needed, for example to answer to an accusation.

Fryd A general English host of all the male population called out during times of great crisis.

Heriot A payment made to a lord by a vassal's family on the demise of the vassal.

Hide An English measure of land (60 to 120 acres) which would support a free household.

Jury A group of knights or other lawful men of the neighborhood in which an offense was committed (or in which the object of a civil suit existed) who stated their knowledge or suspicions, usually on oath, about the matter at hand. The thirteenth-century jury did not hear evidence and reach a decision; it reported its understanding of the events of the case to the court.

Levari Facias Writ of execution by which a sheriff was enabled to confiscate goods of a debtor to pay off debt.

Mainpast The household and retainers of a freeholder. He was obligated to produce any of them when required for purposes of the court, as in the **frank-pledge** system, above.

Make fine To make a payment ("pecuniary mulct," Maitland) to be discharged from or to avoid imprisonment for some matter arising in court; from *finem facere*, to make an end (to a matter).

Manucaptors (Same as **Mainpernors**) A surety for the appearance of a person under arrest, who was delivered out of custody into the hands of his bail.

Mark A monetary unit representing about two-thirds of a pound, a little over thirteen shillings, the amount needed to buy two cows.

Mayorazgo Right of secession ordinarily bestowed on the first-born son of a family; an entail.

Ordeal A means of proof – a test by means of immersion in water or carrying a hot iron, for example – the result of which would be held to determine guilt or innocence. The ordeal officially was ended when the Fourth Lateran Council in 1215, banned clergy participation, thus removing its supernatural basis.

Outlawry The placing of a male offender "outside the law," usually for flight to avoid trial on a criminal charge. The outlaw's movable goods were confiscated and he was considered to be outside the protection of the law. In the thirteenth century, in remote areas, he could be killed with impunity.

Plaint An all-purpose suit that could be brought without writ under certain circumstances, and did not have the rigid restrictions of an appeal.

Plea Rolls Records of cases heard in the royal courts of justice, written on parchment membranes and at some time sewn together to make rolls, now housed in the Public Record Office (PRO).

Precipue (var. **Pracipue**) Writ of covenant; a writ applied for by the party to whom lands were to be conveyed, based upon a supposed agreement of covenant which bound one party to convey land to the other.

Presentment The written notice taken by a grand jury of any offense which they personally knew of or had seen without any bill of indictment having been laid before them by the government. A **presentment jury**, composed of twelve knights or, if knights were not available, "good and lawful men" of the hundred and from the four nearest townships, had the duty of stating on oath if any of certain serious crimes had been committed in their neighborhood and who was suspected of having committed them.

Put oneself on the country, the jury To ask for a jury verdict on some point arising during a trial, usually by raising an **objection**.

Reptamentum A public accusation.

Seisin Possession of a piece of land or some movable good, not necessarily congruent with a firm right to the land or object.

Tithing The group, usually of ten (as the name suggest) or a dozen men, responsible for producing its members as required by the court, and subject to an amercement if it failed to do so.

Tourn In Old English law, a court of record which had criminal jurisdiction and was held twice a year in each county before the sheriff.

Waif A female who had undergone a process analogous to **outlawry**; she was considered to be waived, to be removed from the normal legal protection of any male guardian.